CHASING IMMORTALITY
IN WORLD RELIGIONS

ALSO BY DEBORAH M. COULTER-HARRIS

The Queen of Sheba:
Legend, Literature and Lore (McFarland, 2013)

CHASING IMMORTALITY IN WORLD RELIGIONS

Deborah M. Coulter-Harris

McFarland & Company, Inc., Publishers
Jefferson, North Carolina

LIBRARY OF CONGRESS CATALOGUING-IN-PUBLICATION DATA

Names: Coulter-Harris, Deborah M., author.
Title: Chasing immortality in world religions / Deborah M.
　Coulter-Harris.
Description: Jefferson, North Carolina : Mcfarland & Company,
　Inc., Publishers, 2016. | Includes bibliographical references
　and index.
Identifiers: LCCN 2016028718 | ISBN 9780786497928
　(softcover : acid free paper) ∞
Subjects: LCSH: Immortality. | Future life. | Religions.
Classification: LCC BL530 .C68 2016 | DDC 202/.3—dc23
LC record available at https://lccn.loc.gov/2016028718

BRITISH LIBRARY CATALOGUING DATA ARE AVAILABLE

ISBN (print) 978-0-7864-9792-8
ISBN (ebook) 978-1-4766-2524-9

Front cover: illustration of Adam and Eve cast out of Paradise
© 2016 duncan1890/iStock

Printed in the United States of America

McFarland & Company, Inc., Publishers
　Box 611, Jefferson, North Carolina 28640
　www.mcfarlandpub.com

To my sweet husband,
Anthony Val Harris,
my steadfast confidant and protector for 35 years.

Table of Contents

Preface

I am terrified of death, and I assume most of my readers are not that enamored of the prospect of their eventual journey to the unknown. As I grow older, the potential for my demise has cultivated an inordinate interest in the possibility of achieving immortality after death, based upon my Roman Catholic cultural heritage, religious beliefs, and a lifetime exploring world religions. While I was tempted to rush headlong into appealing ideologies that aroused intellectual curiosity and, at times, beckoned insights that demanded I renounce all that I previously understood to be eternal truths, I confess that I cannot overcome my Abrahamic legacy and adopt a new set of religious doctrines. This book has been a difficult journey that has profoundly changed me in inexplicable ways, but has not shaken my faith or belief in the slightest, even though the process of research and discovery at times has often caused me great psychic pain.

My passage into the supernatural includes visiting concepts of immortality, the afterlife, the substance of the human soul, and theories of rewards and punishments from ancient Sumer to Islam. Beginning with ancient Sumer and traversing ideas in ancient Egypt, Greece, India, and in the Abrahamic religions of Judaism, Christianity, and Islam, I attempted to discover how earlier, regional, religious models influenced subsequent theories, and if this multitudinous array of thinking developed simply as a reaction to historical events or to an assimilation of cultural values.

Chapter 1 begins my journey in a search for meaning in the *Epic of Gilgamesh*, as the story provides a wealth of information about human life in Mesopotamia circa 3000 to 2000 BCE. The text suggests people revered a king called Gilgamesh and were polytheistic, afraid of nature and the natural world, literate, lived within a social, hierarchal structure of gods, demigods, kings, and citizens, and had a hard time facing human mortality. This epic continues its allegorical relevance to human life today because humans continue to struggle with the aging process and death's specter. *The Epic of Gilgamesh* is the original foundation of the Jungian idea that recurring patterns of situations, characters, and symbols exist universally within the collective human unconsciousness; archetypes like Gilgamesh are stored in the human mind, the psychological legacy of humankind, and stories within these epics, such as the Great Flood, have repeated themselves in religious literature over millennia.

The next part of my excursion took to me to ancient Egypt, during which Chapter 2 investigates the Egyptian obsession with the afterlife. Egyptian immortality replicated life on earth more favorably than the Sumerians or Babylonians, but this existence was retributively karmic, and subject to the power and directives of a higher authority. Foreshadowing concepts of heaven and hell, Egyptian judgment came in the form of rewards and punishments, and souls experienced reversals of fortune according to their deeds on earth; a divine or mystical power transported souls either to a realm of happiness or to a region of torment. One Egyptian belief was the tripartite soul, an entity organized into three distinct units—*Ka, Ba,* and *Akh.* Each unit had its own distinctive purpose, but for these to operate harmoniously, the body had to survive intact. I found clear connections regarding the afterlife between the ancient Egyptian religion and Judaism and Christianity. The Jews under Abraham traveled into Egypt during a great famine and lived there for nearly 400 years, and Moses who later led the Hebrews out of Egypt was knowledgeable in Egyptian theology. Without question, Egyptian religious and philosophical ideas were amalgamated into the Hebrew faith, which later shaped Christian views of salvation after death.

The next section of the adventure, in Chapter 3, proceeds to ancient Greece where there was a period in literary mythology and religious history when "Immortal Gods" walked with humans. This is not so startling if readers familiar with Abrahamic religious texts consider the Book of Genesis report that God walked in the Garden of Eden and spoke with Adam and Eve. The Greeks believed their pantheon of immortal gods controlled all aspects of nature, and their human lives were totally at the mercy of the will of the gods. Interactions between people and gods were generally considered friendly, but the gods could dispense harsh punishment to mortals who were conceited, arrogant, overly ambitious, or wealthy. Many mortals tried to trick or challenge the gods, and all were punished, some of them for all eternity.

Classical Greek literature reflected that culture's views on the human condition and its place in the hierarchy of gods. The immortal Greek gods are depicted as unpredictable, flippant, and often immoral; their unique characteristic is not goodness but power. While much of Greek literature involves the gods, these writings also explore the nature or texture of the human soul, the nature of the intellect, the source of consciousness, and resurrection concepts. The classical Greeks thinkers and authors also argued their developing theories of the human soul that later influenced Judaism, Christianity, and Islam. Ancient India was the following stop on my sojourn, where Chapter 4 presents the ancient Hindu religion, which ignores any notion or possibility that physical materiality, while a person is alive, could transform into any type of bodily immortal existence. In Hinduism grew the idea of a special substance in all living organisms that is eternal, but materiality cannot coexist with this type of eternal, as the substance, or Atman, is supra-material, and is beyond any identifiable or known element. Hindus embrace the idea of successive karmic rebirths into other life forms that are shaped by a person's actions in a previous life; ancient Hindus developed the theory that reincarnations incorporated lower spectrums of life, and all reawakened varieties of life depended on the moral character and actions of the person. Nirvana, the end of incarnating in material forms, is the Hindu goal for eternal existence when the individual becomes part of the god-essence.

This theory is in antithesis to the glorious heavens of the Abrahamic religions that painted scenes of breathtaking beauty and wellness, and the promise of a transfigured material body into an immortal, glorified body in the presence of God. In many religions and philosophical discussions, the soul is defined as an immaterial essence that is immortal and connects to the divine while retaining the personality or particular characteristics of the person. Alternatively, Hinduism believes that these personality traits are temporary, and do not transfigure into the eternal Atman, the authentic spirit. Like other religions, Hinduism promotes the idea that our actions have consequences in this life and future lives; there are universal laws that dictate the reciprocity of behavior in this life, and there are universally held beliefs in the effects of behaviors in the next. Hindus believe that the concept of an eternal heaven or hell is illogical and runs in antithesis to the natural laws of the universe because an eternal result cannot be the product of a finite, transient action.

After an exhaustive trip into the intricacies of Hinduism, Chapter 5 studies the complexity and evolution of immortality, the afterlife, the human soul, and corporeal resurrection in Judaism; these issues evolved during varied historical eras and were further complicated with philosophical and supplemental teachings at later intervals. The concept of an immortal soul distinct from the corporeal body did not exist in Judaism before the Babylonian Exile (598–596 BCE), but later developed as a result of interaction with other philosophies and religious influences, particularly those from Egypt and Greece. Jewish adherents generally embraced the idea that condemned souls would be annihilated but that there was no such event as eternal punishment in a place like hell, which was earlier conceptualized by the Egyptians and the Greeks. Changes in Jewish belief in an afterlife were a result of the miseries inflicted on the Hebrews during the Babylonian invasion in the early part of the sixth century BCE, the destruction of the Temple of Solomon, the exile in Babylon, and their subsequent homecoming to Israel. These events dramatically altered earthly karmic concepts of rewards, punishments, and justice, and influenced the idea that justice would only be rendered by God after death within the framework of an afterlife.

Judaism has traditionally supported faith in an afterlife, but the characteristics that this belief has adopted, and the ways in which this faith has been expressed, have fluctuated from era to era. The chapter delineates immortality concepts that are articulated in the Hebrew Bible, in the eschatological literature of the Sadducees, Pharisees, and Essenes (530 BCE to 70 CE), in the Talmud (200 to 500 CE), in the *Midrash* of the Post-Temple era (400 to 1500 CE), in Kabalistic literature (1200–1300 CE), and in current Jewish theology. Strikingly similar to Hindu theology, Kabbalistic eschatology conceives of a soul separated into parts, whose origin is divine emanation, and whose incarnation is designed to accomplish a specific mission—returning a part of the divinity back to the all-embracing Divine.

Turning to my own religious heritage, Chapter 6 analyzes how Christianity inherited Judaism's apocalyptic beliefs, as early Christian believers were Jews with deep spiritual roots in the mother religion. As centuries progressed non–Jewish Christians could not deny the contribution that Judaism had on their faith, and the Jewish apocalyptic tradition became a vital part of the new offshoot religion. The early Christian hope for bodily resurrection is clearly Jewish in origin; the Hebrew Pharisee and later Christian evangelist Paul of Tarsus clearly believed in the Jewish doctrine of resurrection that was strengthened by the reported resurrection of Jesus. The doctrine that espouses that the souls of the dead separate from the body at death and carry on living in heaven or hell because the soul is supposedly immortal is not a Christian innovation. Clearly presaging concepts of heaven and hell, Egyptian judgment came in the form of rewards and punishments where some souls experienced reversals of fortune according to their deeds on earth; a divine or mystical power transports souls either to a realm of happiness or to a region of torment.

There has been endless speculation that the story of Jesus might parallel the myth of the Egyptian Isis, Osiris, and Horus. There are claims that the Jesus story is simply a reincarnation of the earlier Egyptian myth contained in the 5000 year old *Egyptian Book of the Dead,* which has led to many comparisons. Biblical writers had to be aware of the Horus myth and might have simply transferred the attributes of the old god to the new because their ideas were rooted in Egyptian religious literature, or because Osiris and Horus became precursor archetypes of Jesus Christ. When Christianity proliferated, Greek influence on the faith created an amalgamated view of the afterlife, one which embraced the dualistic, platonic Greek view that the spirit or soul was independent of the physical body; the soul's immortality was one of the basic principles of Platonism that was in some measure embraced by the Christian church. Christianity upended the prime importance of immortality of the human soul in favor of corporeal resurrection from the dead; at the end of history, souls would reunite with bodies that would be transformed into an indestructible state and then transported to a new heaven and a new earth. As Christianity progressed throughout the Mediterranean region, apologists and theologians who accepted immortality at resurrection modified their teaching on immortality to blend with Greek and Jewish philosophies.

It is in Chapter 7 that a discussion of the associations among the Abrahamic religions is offered: how Islam presented righteous people with immortality in exchange for submission, just as Christianity had offered immortality in exchange for belief in Jesus Christ as the Messiah, and just as some sects of Judaism had conferred immortality in exchange for adherence to the law. There are numerous connections among Islam, Judaism, and Christianity regarding belief in resurrection from the dead, final judgment, concepts of heaven and hell, and in magical beings like angels. As in Islam, the Jewish, Roman Catholic, and other Christian teachings describe angels as closest to the material world and human beings; there has been a preponderance of stories in all religions of unusual visitors who bring revelatory messages, announcements, warnings, and comfort to humans, and Islam is no different. Greek philosophers have also played a small part in shaping concepts of the soul in Islam. Plato's theory regarding the existence of the human soul before creation of the material body was accepted among many Muslim mystics and philosophers; even so, the theory that the incorporeal soul is eternally severed from a material body is unacceptable to them. Just as in Christianity, the return of the soul without any material body at the Resurrection is not accepted by Islam. Muslims believe that death brings about a type of metaphysical division of a human being that becomes unified again only at Resurrection when the authentic individual returns after a long physical and supernatural separation.

Humans throughout millennia have wondered and worried about what happens after death. Many modern religions teach that we will live again, and archaeologists tell us that even ancient Neanderthals buried their loved ones with grave goods for the afterlife. Today most of the religious world believes in an immortal soul that lives on in some form; this is a shared teaching of

Hinduism, Judaism, Buddhism, Christianity, and Islam, as well as of tribal religions throughout Africa, the Americas, and elsewhere. Some say that the soul will live forever in either a heaven or a hell. Others suppose that after death the soul will reanimate as other life forms in an endless cycle of reincarnation. Most nonbelievers, of course, dispute the idea of a soul, convinced that after death there is only nothingness.

But from where have these ideas come? Alan F. Segal, late professor of Jewish studies, wrote that each religion's views of the rewards and punishments of the afterlife reflect the particular values and aspirations or "goals and interests" of that culture (16, 17); this indicates that ideas of immortality are purely a mortal paradigm mirroring self-interest. Interpretations of life after death reproduce the human experience and social values, so anthropologists deduced that humans designed religion and religious beliefs to explain life's experiences and to provide comfort and consolation during hard times (16, 17). At the end of my own arduous voyage, I question whether this is a correct analysis.

The book's final chapter reviews, summarizes, and analyzes all of the doctrines previously discussed and considers the present human condition in light of these religious theories and philosophies. There have been endless debates and speculation all over the globe through the millennia regarding the origin of the idea of God, and more conjecture over the soul's shape, substance, origin, and ability to transmigrate, whether the soul dies with the body, whether it is immortal from conception and birth or is a natural and immortal emanation of God's spirit become flesh. In addition, there have been persistent discussions and teachings on the ability of God to resurrect the dead, the time when bodies are reunited with their souls. The chapter also considers the theoretical possibility of immortality, but realistically concludes that no scientifically proven explanation for aging and death is forthcoming, and that faith in what is unseen is all that humans are able to possess, and on which they must rely.

I would like to thank my readers, Sabrina Peters-Whitehead, Sara J. Yaklin, Alexandra L. DeRosa, and Suzanne E. Smith, for help with the final manuscript, and special thanks go also to Chafic Elkhechen and Abdullah Aklharboush.

1

Gilgamesh:
So Human a Demigod

Now then, Gilgamesh, who, will assemble the gods for your sake?
Who will convince them to grant you the eternal life that you seek?

The most disconcerting aspects of human life are death and the afterlife; to unravel the variety and complexity of religious attitudes towards these unknowns requires an analytic look at the influence *The Epic of Gilgamesh* might have had on the formation of later religious attitudes towards these mysteries. The epic confirms that, from the most ancient eras, human beings have wanted to leave a legacy and deny mortality; the human quest to remain perpetually young or live eternally like the ancient "gods" is futile, as every human being dies, a lesson the demigod Gilgamesh eventually understands. There are famous religious, literary stories from every culture and age regarding the search for immortality. The very oldest tales in religious literature that speak of immortals and demigods, the changeling offspring of a god and a human, need to be interpreted and demystified, as these stories provide deeper insight into the origins of religion and god worship, and trace humankind's fear of death and concepts of the afterlife to the very beginning of history. *The Epic of Gilgamesh* is an allegory of human frailty and vulnerability and the impossible quest for eternal youth, fame, and immortality. It is an archetypal tale of adventure, morality, a search for knowledge, and an escape from the ordinary life of a human; Gilgamesh is the first story of a tragic hero in literature.

The tale also provides a wealth of information about human life in Mesopotamia circa 3000 to 2000 BCE. The very existence of the text suggests people revered a king called Gilgamesh, and were polytheistic, afraid of nature and the natural world, literate, lived within a social, hierarchal structure of gods, demigods, kings, and citizens, and had a hard time facing human mortality.

This epic continues its allegorical relevance to human life today because humans continue to struggle with the aging process and death's specter; the supreme human fear is an unproven, unsubstantiated life or consciousness beyond living reality. Religions relieve this psychological angst by teaching a greater life after death: some religions promise humans eternal life, but these adherents have to die first and supernaturally resurrect later; other religions, primarily from the East, espouse the theory of reincarnation, of endless cycles of life and death through transmigration of souls. Meanwhile, in the midst of a selection of beliefs, people try to find meaning through setting goals, creating tasks and chores, and keeping a healthy self-interest in surviving to old age.

While the human quest to remain forever young or live eternally like the gods appears unsuccessful, there are biblical stories suggesting that Enoch and the prophet Elijah never tasted death, but were "taken up." So, is there a possibility that a human could become physically immortal in this life and never experience death? This is the possibility that the writer of Gilgamesh wanted to explore and capture in his story about self-indulgence, sexual depravity, violence, tyranny,[1] friendships, death, and a failed attempt to achieve immortality and eternal youth; the author wanted to show the transition that people go through in their lifetimes through Gilgamesh's story. The Epic also is an allegory about the spiritual, moral, and intellectual growth of a king whose reign begins in abuse and terror, and ends in glory. Although the gods have granted Gilgamesh intelligence, strength, height, beauty, power and riches, he wants more—he does not want to die like a mortal. The Epic concludes with Gilgamesh's mature spiritual growth; he becomes socially responsible, and returns to the religion of his ancestors. Gilgamesh reconciles himself in self-knowledge that demigods all perish with few exceptions, and even though he is a demigod, he is also human and must experience death. The Epic celebrates what it is to be human, contends with the relationships between mortals and gods, explores how life experiences tame expectations, and instructs kings in their duties to their people and to their gods.

Sumerian Ideas of Death, Afterlife and the Gods

The Gilgamesh story clearly shows that humans have been preoccupied with the fear of death, or *thanatophobia,* and have sought a way to achieve immortality since the beginning of recorded history (Christmas 297). The ancient Sumerians believed in a multitude of gods and goddesses, although the earliest cuneiform tablets identified specific gods, such as: Enlil, ruler of the sky; Barbar, the sun god; Enki, the Earth God; and An or Anu, the father/

creator god; by the end of the Sumerian Epoch, they had thousands of gods in their pantheon (Uttal 93), and some of these "gods" ruled the underworld. A large number of gods inhabited the netherworld, and were assigned there for a specific purpose; other gods were condemned to go there from the heavens for aiding humans, or for making theological speculations. These judgmental, mortuary gods were confined in the Netherworld with humans, and were unable to travel to earth or to the heavens and associate with other gods (Holland 153). Human souls could find contentment and happiness there if they offered gods the right gifts, and a person's family could help by offering funeral prayers (Forrest 7).

The gods, particularly the queen Ereshkigal, Ishtar's sister, and her consort Nergal, ruled the Netherworld. The Annun'aki gods helped administer the Netherworld, which was constructed like a city with seven walls and seven gates, but before passing through these gates, the deceased had to cross the demon-infested steppe lands and the river Huber (Walton 318). These iconic "seven gates" would later manifest in other world religious imagery, such as in Islam's seven gates of heaven and seven gates of hell.

Death and the search for immortality played a central role in ancient Sumerian religious epics; "after death a god would travel to the 'Land without Return' across the 'Waters of Death' and be magically reborn" (Uttal 93), so death and resurrection of the gods were basic tenets of Sumerian cosmology, and had a metaphorical connection with the solar calendar. These most ancient of beliefs may have influenced Egypt's later stories of a resurrected Osiris and Christianity's belief in a resurrected God; both are resonant with Sumerian influence. Gilgamesh travels across the "Waters of Death" to meet Utnapishtim who holds the secret to immortality; it is there in the "Land of the Living" that Gilgamesh accepts his mortality and becomes spiritually reborn.

Mesopotamian religious beliefs included an afterlife of suffering, but this original idea was a type of hell that included more sorrow than punishment (Adams 52; Thompson 61). The supernatural land, or "Land without Return," was a transitory stopover not only for gods but for humans as well; somewhat like the Roman Catholic idea of purgatory[2] developed millennia later, this supernatural destination was not regarded either as heaven or a hell but "...a place where gods would judge humans and decide how long they would remain" (Uttal 94). Sumerian cosmology viewed the universe as a tripartite structure: heaven for the gods, earth for humans, and the netherworld for deceased humans and mortuary gods (Wright 29).

The Sumerian religion also believed in a type of heaven: their conception of paradise was that of an Edenic region and time that existed before the Flood, a golden age, a pure and bright place called Dilmun.[3] Although Dilmun was a land of abundance, ordinary humans could never enter this paradise because it was reserved only for gods, demigods, and super humans (Dickson 5); Dilmun is the residence of Gilgamesh's grandfather, Utnapishtim, in the epic, and Gilgamesh will travel there to ask for immortality (Wright 30). Dilmun's exact geographical location has changed and been the object of controversy; Bahrain and the adjacent Eastern Province of Saudi Arabia are reported to be the heart of Dilmun. "A predecessor of the celebrated Dilmun polity that flourished on Bahrain has long been recognized in the potential third-millennium center on Tarut Island, Saudi Arabia" (Laursen 156).

Sumerian concepts of whether a person was destined to a heaven or a hell had nothing to do with leading a virtuous life. Sumerian religious beliefs proposed the possibility of an immortal Paradise, but this was not a reward for being moral in this life (Najovits 4). The moral state of people's souls had nothing to do with their afterlife circumstances; their social and economic status in this life translated to the next world, as Sumerian burials signified. As a person was in life, so would she be in death. All souls depended on the living to attain a type of prophetic or divine status (Holland 152); the living could freely practice necromancy and solicit the dead's assistance in the here and now (Hays 55), a custom condemned by later Abrahamic religions.

The ultimate failure of Gilgamesh's quest is a recurring theme not only in the epic but also in most Mesopotamian myths. The Sumerians, Akkadians, and even the ancient Greeks did not believe in a reward after death. The body returned to clay and a duplicate phantom or shadow entered a sad netherworld where one led a gloomy existence forever (Ryan and Pitman 245). Death was expected, and the grave was the final destination for all humans, as the Annun'aki gods had decreed. A later version of the Gilgamesh Epic states, "The Annun'aki, the great Gods ... were assembled. They established life and death. Death they fixed to have no ending" (qtd. in Hays 31). Utnapishtim reinforces the gods' control over human destiny, and admonishes Gilgamesh for his foolish quest:

> You have worn yourself out through ceaseless striving,
> you have filled your muscles with pain and anguish.
> And what have you achieved but to bring yourself
> one day nearer to the end of your days?
> ... the gods of heaven stay awake and watch us,
> unsleeping, undying. This is the way
> the world is established, from ancient times [Mitchell 157].

SUMERIAN INFLUENCE ON GREEK RELIGIOUS THEORIES

The Sumerian belief in gods controlling the inescapable fates of humans can later be found in ancient Greek religious beliefs—the gods predestined peoples' fates. Ancient Greek dramas provide evidence of these tenets in plays such as *Oedipus Rex* and *Medea*. Sophocles portrays the gods as all-knowing and all-powerful beings who were never wrong, and who possess a superior morality and sense of truth. The gods made sure to control Oedipus' journey and fulfill every detail the oracle had predicted, just as the gods in the epic control Gilgamesh. If the gods had not interfered, Oedipus might have been able to escape his fate and live happily. Euripedes' *Medea* provides a rather different Greek view of the gods; as the main character Medea is a demigod and the granddaughter of Helios, the play portrays the gods as jealous and capable of inexplicable evil. This play suggests that gods rule through superior physical power and frighteningly turbulent emotions, rather than through a sense of moral superiority over humans. Moral and immoral, just and unjust, the gods remain integral to the ancient stories still read and studied today, but understanding the relationships between gods and mortals begins with the story of Gilgamesh.

DEATH AND SOCIAL IMMORTALITY

According to ancient Sumerian beliefs, the Gods punished humans for evil deeds in this life as a type of karmic retribution, but some good people were punished unjustly; the next life was simply a place where the spirit descended into a dark and gloomy place (Hays 29). According to *The Epic of Gilgamesh*, the overall Mesopotamian perception of the underworld was negative—a land of darkness, where the dead ate dust and clay. In the Epic, Enkidu reports his dream of the afterlife to Gilgamesh, and he describes the underworld as dark and dusty, where its inhabitants suffer if their descendants do not give grave offerings (Hays 50).

> Enkidu said ... the creature touched me
> And suddenly feathers covered my arms,
> he bound them behind me and forced me down
> to the underworld, the house of darkness,
> the home of the dead, where all who enter
> never return to the sweet earth again.
> Those who dwell there squat in the darkness,
> dirt is their food, their drink is clay,
> they are dressed in feather garments like birds,
> they never see the light... [Mitchell 131].

Despite the eventuality of death and nothingness, people could attain a social immortality in ancient Sumerian culture, if they achieved great and noble deeds. In the Epic, Gilgamesh assures Enkidu that dying in combat guarantees the fighter a type of immortality; he will either succumb in battle and win an immortal name or he will escape death and live to see another battle. When Gilgamesh and Enkidu face combat with Humbaba, Gilgamesh further encourages his friend by telling him that death is inevitable for everyone, but an honorable death will bring them immortality, as people will remember their courage and noble birth.[4] Gilgamesh declares:

> Courage, dear brother,
> this is no time to give in to fear.
> We have come so far, across so many mountains,
> and our journey is about to reach its goal.
> ...
> Shout out your battle cry, let your voice pound
> like a kettle drum. Let your heart inspire you
> to be joyous in battle, to forget about death.
> If we help each other and fight side by side,
> we will make a lasting name for ourselves,
> we will stamp our fame on men's minds forever [Mitchell 114].

Clearly, one of the basic flaws in Gilgamesh's early behavior is his total disregard for the gods and their control over his life and fortunes, which makes his journey all the more difficult. He perceives that his physical strength and sheer will power will make him successful, and, as the story progresses, it is clear the gods will teach him lessons in humility, an obvious, Sumerian concept of virtue that has been passed down through endless generations in an array of religious teachings.

The Epic's Historical Background: Importance of the Flood Story

Gilgamesh might actually have been a real ruler in the late Early Second Dynastic period; according to the Sumerian King List, King Gilgamesh was the fifth king ruling after the flood. Ryan and Pitman explain: "According to the Sumerian King List, Gilgamesh was the fifth king of the First Dynasty of Uruk (biblical Erech), a city-state on the banks of the Euphrates River during the Second Early Dynastic Period of Sumer (2700 BCE). Within two hundred years, Gilgamesh was widely revered as a god in Sumer" (225; Lawler 28). The Epic began as a collection of Sumerian legends and poems in cuneiform script dating back to the early third or late second millennium BCE, and later combined into a longer Akkadian poem; the most complete version existing today, preserved on twelve clay tablets, dates from the twelfth to 10th century BCE. The earliest Sumerian versions of *The Epic of Gilgamesh* date from as early as the Third Dynasty of Ur (2150–2000 BCE), and the earliest Akkadian[5] renditions date to the early second millennium. Alan Segal verifies that "The basic story of Gilgamesh was gradually augmented over the millennia in

Akkadian—specifically in the Babylonian and Assyrian dialects of Akkadian, as these two empires asserted influence over the area" (83).[6] *The Epic of Gilgamesh* is regarded as the most important literary work to come out of Mesopotamia; the text has been written and rewritten over a two thousand year period. There have been many different versions in a variety of languages, such as Sumerian, Semitic, and Indo-European. The very fact that the epic endured throughout generations is evidence that Gilgamesh attained premier status among all literary masterpieces originating from Mesopotamia (Ryan and Pitman 48).

The Babylonian scribe Sin-liqe-unninni wrote the "standard" Akkadian version between 1300 and 1000 BCE in standard Babylonian, a dialect of Akkadian used to write literature; this version consisted of the twelve clay tablets that were discovered in 1849 in the library of the seventh century BCE Assyrian king Ashurbanipal, in Nineveh, the capital of the ancient Assyrian empire.[7] Fragments of other accounts of the Gilgamesh story have been found as far away as Syria and Turkey. There are five shorter poems in the Sumerian language that are more than one thousand years older than the Nineveh tablets: "Gilgamesh and Huwawa," "Gilgamesh and the Bull of Heaven," "Gilgamesh and Agga of Kish," "Gilgamesh, Enkidu and the Netherworld," and "Death of Gilgamesh" (Lemming 56). The Akkadian standard edition is the basis of most modern translations, with the older Sumerian versions used to supplement it and fill in the gaps or lacunae ("Other Ancient Civilizations").

There are three ancient surviving Babylonian deluge epics with Noah types: Ziusudra in *Eridu Genesis* (2150 BCE) in the kingdom of Shuruppak, the Akkadian Atrahasis in the *Epic of Atrahasis* (1700 BCE) in the city kingdom of Kish, and Utnapishtim in varied versions of *The Epic of Gilgamesh* (1200–1000 BCE) in the city kingdom of Uruk. *The Epic of Gilgamesh* contains a Flood story that provides insight into ancient conceptions of immortals and their interactions with humans and demigods. *The Epic of Gilgamesh* refers to the Noah character as Utnapishtim, who became an "immortal" for surviving the flood[8]; in earlier Sumerian he is called Ziusudra, king and priest of Shuruppak,[9] or the last king of Sumer before the Flood (Mitchell 6, 276). Shuruppak was one of the first five cities established by the Annun'aki in Sumer. The Sumerian King List recension records Ziusudra as having reigned 3,600 years; according to the Hebrew Bible, Noah lived 950 years (Langdon 251–259). The Ziusudra story is the earliest recorded account of the Great Flood story, and is found on one fragmentary tablet excavated in Nippur, sometimes called the *Eridu Genesis*; it is datable by its script to 2150 BCE during the first Babylonian dynasty, when Sumerian was still the predominant language of writing (Davila 202–203).

The Epic of Gilgamesh contains an abbreviated story of the Flood, but provides no particular reasons for what caused the discord between the gods and humans, except that Enlil wanted all humanity dead because they were noisy and violent; Enlil was upset with Ea for forewarning Utnapishtim about the deluge. The earlier *Atrahasis* epic was an ancient Babylonian account of the Great Deluge, when the Eden of the Bible became "…a brackish desolate plain. As the epic states, there was mass starvation, disease became rampant, and the survivors had to resort to cannibalism." The gods of ancient Sumer, who found the human numbers and noise disturbing, imposed this condition. In the Sumerian *Epic of Gilgamesh*, the ancient gods in counsel decided the deluge (Boulay 97, 99).

The *Epic of Gilgamesh* includes a great flood tale that is also very similar to the biblical story of Noah in Genesis.[10] There are details from the Gilgamesh flood myth that are closely duplicated in the story of Noah's ark in the Bible and the Qur'an, such as: the construction of a special boat to save lives, a boat that eventually rests on a mountain top, and a dove sent out to find dry land. Although the biblical account appears to be based upon these earlier epics, there is a clear distinction regarding the concept of the Hebrew God and the Sumerian pantheon of gods. In the Bible, Yahweh directly warns Noah; there is no mention of other gods intervening in Noah's destiny, and there is no mention of Noah being an immortal, although living to a phenomenal age.

In the epic, Utnapishim recounts to his grandson Gilgamesh how the god Enlil sent a great flood to destroy humankind because they were too violent and noisy, but Enlil's brother Ea (Enki) alerted Utnapishtim, and instructed him to build a ship to save his possessions, his family, and the seeds of all life. After the flood receded, Utnapishim's boat landed on the mountain of Nisir,[11] where he sent a dove, then a swallow, and then a raven to check for dry land. Enlil was outraged that humans had survived his flood, but, with Ea's encouragement, eventually blessed Utnapishtim and his wife, granted them immortality, and moved them to the land of the gods on the island of Dilmun.[12]

One of the important aspects of the flood story in the *Epic of Gilgamesh* is the characterization of the immortal Utnapishtim, whose behavior further clarifies Sumerian concepts of the divide between humans and the "others." Not as generous as Enlil was to him, immortal Utnapishtim grudgingly gives Gilgamesh a shot at immortality by insisting on a test: Gilgamesh must stay awake for six days and seven nights, an impossibility for any human. Weak with human frailty, Gilgamesh falls asleep immediately, awakens after seven days of sleep, endures Utnapishtim's derision, and then prepares to return to Uruk. It is a woman who has compassion for the hero. As Gilgamesh and the ferryman Ushanabi leave, Utnapishtim's wife convinces her husband to tell Gilgamesh about a plant that grows at the bottom of the ocean that will make him forever young. Gilgamesh ties stones to his feet, so he can walk on the bottom of the sea, and he finds the special plant, but he later places the plant on the shore of a lake while he bathes; a snake steals the plant, loses its skin, and is reborn. Utnapishtim teaches Gilgamesh important specifics about human weakness in the face of unrealistic human quests.

The loss of the plant of life in the story becomes an allegory of a renewed life attitude. While our hero may have the final notion that a plant may be a panacea to his aging and death prospects, he is reckless and does not foresee unexpected circumstances that would have required better security, for the serpent steals the plant and becomes immortal. As the serpent often is associated with wisdom,[13] this story could be interpreted as a definitive foreshadowing of the religious concept of eternal life, of shedding off the old life for the eternally new. In the Pallas myth, "Athena slew and skinned a human giant called Pallas, clothing herself in his skin." In this version, she is like "the snake that emerges from the dead skin of the old form" (Baring and Cashford 344). The hero must face reality, shed off the skin of his old life and ways, and be prepared to age and die. Gilgamesh cries because he failed both chances to obtain immortality; he then returns home to Uruk. At the end of his journey, Gilgamesh restores the ancient religious rites and temples that the flood had destroyed. While everlasting life is not his destiny, Gilgamesh will leave behind him a name that endures to this day.

The Story of Gilgamesh: So Human a Demigod

Gilgamesh is a violent and handsome giant of a man who is reportedly one-third human and two-thirds divine; he used this celestial bloodline to intimidate and oppress the people he ruled. Gilgamesh was not only considered a semi-divine king, but his ultimate destiny was that of an actual god of the netherworld. "In many later texts, it is clear that Gilgamesh was identified as a major deity, especially as king and judge of the netherworld.[14] At least in the case of Gilgamesh, his descent to the netherworld, retention of royal status, and even exaltation as a deity are clear" (Shipp 96). Gilgamesh is the son of Lugalbanda, who became a god, and the goddess Ninsun (Mitchell 274; Dickin 77). Henrietta McCall further confirms Gilgamesh's divine origins: "The Sumerian King List[15] tells us his father was a 'high priest of Kullab' … this made Gilgamesh semi-divine" (38). In another tradition Lugalbanda was Uruk's guardian deity (Mitchell 273, 274). Lugalbanda emerges in Sumerian literary sources as early as the third millennium, as evidenced in a legendary work from Abu Salabikh, an excavated archaeological site in Iraq that depicts a romantic relationship between Lugalbanda and Ninsun (Jacobsen 3). In the Old Babylonian period, King Sin-kashid of Uruk (1803–1777 BCE) is known to have built a temple called É-KI.KAL dedicated to Lugalbanda and Ninsun, and to have assigned his daughter Nisi-ini-su as the *eresh-dingir*[16] priestess of Lugalbanda (Duncan 215–221). Nisi-ini-su would have been considered a demigoddess, as her mother was a full-blooded Annun'aki princess.

Despite his wealth and social position, Gilgamesh murders his own people, rapes women, and uses his position as king to rape every virgin bride in his kingdom. The epic records the relationship between gods and ordinary humans, for his citizens pray to Anu,[17] the father god, to save them from their king. Anu answers their prayers by ordering the goddess Aruru[18] to create a double or alter ego, as the king's friend and companion, for Gilgamesh to bring peace to Uruk. Aruru creates the wild man, Enkidu, who is tamed in the wilderness through sexual relations nonstop for seven days and nights. Enkidu eventually is made presentable, and travels to Eridu where he challenges Gilgamesh to a wrestling match that ends in a tie; the two become fast friends.

Gilgamesh is ambitious and self-serving, and wants to achieve an immortal name; he enlists Enkidu's support on a venture to kill the infamous Humbaba, the guardian of the Cedar Forest where the gods live; it was Enlil, Anu's son, who assigned Humbaba as a terror to human beings. Gilgamesh defies the gods and he boasts: "I will cut down the tree, I will kill Humbaba. I will make a lasting name for myself; I will stamp my fame on men's minds forever" (Mitchell 95). An immortal name is easier for him to achieve than an immortal life, as he will learn. He and Enkidu kill the God of the forest, Humbaba, but this angers the Gods, so they kill Enkidu as recompense. Gilgamesh's companion eventually teaches Gilgamesh what it means to be human; he teaches him the meaning of love and compassion, the meaning of loss, of growing older, the meaning of mortality. Gilgamesh cannot accept Enkidu's death, even after his burial and memorial statue is erected. The passage where Gilgamesh mourns his friend is one of the most moving in ancient literature:

> My friend, my brother, whom I loved so dearly
> who accompanied me through every danger—
> the fate of mankind has overwhelmed him.
> For six days I would not let him be buried,
> thinking, "If my grief is violent enough,
> perhaps he will come back to life again."
> For six days and seven nights I mourned him,
> until a maggot fell out of his nose.
> Then I was terrified by death,
> and I set out to roam the wilderness....
> My beloved friend has turned into clay—
> my beloved Enkidu has turned into clay
> And won't I too lie down in the dirt
> like him, and never rise again? [Mitchell 149, 150].

Physical and spiritual transformations occur throughout the story. Death's power and control over the psychological condition of the human mind cause Gilgamesh to undergo a physical change that duplicates Enkidu's original, savage appearance (see figure 1). Regressing to a savage state, Gilgamesh rends his garments, replacing them with grubby animal skins. Psychologically, he

Figure 1 Gilgamesh and Enkidu Slay Humbaba. When Gilgamesh and Enkidu face combat with Humbaba, Gilgamesh further encourages his friend by telling him that death is inevitable for everyone, but an honorable death will bring them both a type of immortality, as people will remember their courage and noble birth ("Gilgamesh and Enkidu"). Two heroes pin down a bearded foe, while grabbing at his pronged headdress. The context may be related to the Gilgamesh epic, and display Gilgamesh and Enkidu in their fight with Humbaba (Relief with Two Heroes: 10th century BCE Neo-Hittite/Hurritic courtesy of Walters Art Museum).

wishes to resurrect his friend Enkidu by becoming him; refusing to accept mortality, Gilgamesh refuses to accept the death of his shadow, so he continues his journey to seek immortality. When he arrives at Mashu and enters the mountain, he suffers a consuming and unbearable darkness; like all human beings, the terrifying experience or vision of death's void tests him. However, Gilgamesh is reborn when he enters a luxurious garden filled with brightly colored fruit and flowers; he has entered a place where no mortal man has gone, and is symbolically born again. He has sought salvation and thinks that immortality is the answer to his problems, but he will find that salvation and immortality take on varied forms.

Gilgamesh becomes Everyman whose quest for eternal life and immortality are futile. The king who triumphed over humans and monsters could not prevent his friend from dying, and he must now face the inevitability of his own death. Gilgamesh abandons Uruk and begins a search for Utnapishtim, his grandfather, the man who survived the Great Flood and was granted immortality by the gods; if he can learn the secret of Utnapishtim's favor with the gods, he too might live forever (Freeman 36). Gilgamesh becomes preoccupied with death and finding immortality; he wants to separate himself from the inevitable human condition, and considers his royal birth and his noble deeds as nothing in the face of death. He fails in both attempts to achieve immortality, and eventually listens to and embraces the tavern keeper Shiduri's carpe diem guidance:

> You will never find the eternal life
> that you seek. When the gods created mankind,
> they also created death, and they held back
> eternal life for themselves alone.
> Humans are born, they live, then they die,
> this is the order that the gods have decreed.
> But until the end comes, enjoy your life,
> spend it in happiness, not despair.
> Savor your food, make each of your days
> a delight, bathe and anoint yourself,
> wear bright clothes that are sparkling clean,
> let music and dancing fill your house....
> That is the best way for a man to live [Mitchell 150–151].

Gilgamesh is reconciled to his ultimate fate, and returns to Uruk (Holland 154), which indicates that the prevailing philosophy towards life and death in Mesopotamia is acquiescence to the predestined lot of all human kind (Segal 83). Life leads to eternal physical extinction; only the gods live forever. In spite of this universal resignation to mortality, the writer of the Gilgamesh epic provides hope in the character of Utnapishtim, a typology of Noah who has been rewarded with the gift of immortality for saving the lives of his family and animals. He has avoided going to the underworld as an *etemmu*[19] because he obeyed the gods' commands, and achieved a superhuman feat.

Gilgamesh as Original Archetype and Allegory

Jung proposes that archetypal patterns, which recur throughout the history of literature, are so deeply embedded in the human consciousness that they manifest in the psychological apparatus of contemporary human thought. According to Jung, "The concept of the archetype is derived from the repeated observation that, for instance, the myths and fairy-tales of world literature contain definite motifs, which crop up everywhere. We meet these same motifs in the fantasies, dreams, deliria, and delusions of individuals living today" (382).

From the ancient Sumerians to spiritual people today, everyone wants to live eternally in some type of afterlife abode; this is the fundamental core of most religions. *The Epic of Gilgamesh* is the original foundation of the Jungian idea that recurring patterns of situations, characters, and symbols exist universally within the collective human unconsciousness; archetypes are stored in the human mind, the psychological legacy of humankind. Gilgamesh is on the archetypal hero's journey, or what Joseph Campbell called the "monomyth."[20] This journey is about a person who leaves home to achieve grand feats on behalf of his people or his culture, and contains life changes that include a character's evolution from immaturity and pride to a world of consciousness beyond self. *The Epic of Gilgamesh* follows the stock hero's journey from a life in the everyday mundane world to the appeal for mysterious exploits; the hero faces misfortunes and hardships when he confronts death, faces his deepest fears, achieves and loses a reward, and returns home to initiate social and self-transformation (Campbell 11–15).

The Epic follows Campbell's patterns, for according to Stephen N. Dunning, "The story of this adventure varies slightly from culture to culture, but all expressions conform to what Campbell calls the monomyth, which is a pattern of ... withdrawal from family and society to pursue one's own heroic destiny, initiation into the mystery that is the truth of human life, and return with that knowledge to family and society" (61, 62). According to Alan Dickin, "Gilgamesh was the archetypal hero in ancient mythology and probably inspired many of the heroic characters of later cultures, including those of Assyria, Persia, Greece and Rome (77). The *Epic of Gilgamesh* also uses archetypal situations that represent the origins of storytelling: these include an epic expedition, a confrontation with a monster, the search for immortality, the death of a hero, some type of tragedy, a loss of innocence, and the beginning of psychological and social transformation. Other obvious archetypes in the epic are the flood story and the mysterious and devious serpent. Just as the serpent steals eternal life from Gilgamesh, the writer of the ensuing Genesis story transformed the serpent into the archetypal icon of evil based on the Gilgamesh source material.

Readers comprehend the eternal and the spiritual through a series of signs and symbols in concrete language or metaphors; allegories represent abstract ideas or ideologies through characters or events in narrative, dramatic, or metaphorical structure. An allegory "...conceals meaning from the uninitiated while making it visible to those 'with eyes to see and ears to hear'" (Finke 52). The story of Gilgamesh is a metaphoric allegory of the soul's transformation from immaturity and irresponsibility to maturity and wisdom, from prideful thinking that human potential is unlimited and our physicality impregnable to recognizing that there are limits to the materiality and sustainability of the body. The story provides a universal and timeless reality check that death hovers above all humans' heads like the Sword of Damocles, and that God or the gods are in control.

The end of *The Epic of Gilgamesh* brings readers back where the hero started: mortality. Gilgamesh is only half-god, and arrives back in Uruk as a mortal. He has achieved a fame that will lead to a kind of immortality, but he will still die like the rest of us. He has no choice but to accept it. Earlier in his quest, the tavern-keeper Siduri tries to make this point:

> Savour your food, make each of your days a delight … let music and dancing fill your house, love the child who holds you by the hand, and give your wife pleasure in your embrace. That is the best way for a man to live [Mitchell 150–151].

The story also imparts an allegory about the character of kings and rulers, about the survival of a nation, its relationship with its gods, and its relationship with the spiritual world (Petrolle 143). The citizens had earlier beseeched the gods to deliver them from their king, and the gods speedily answered their request. In the end, King Gilgamesh faces his limited human nature, is humbled before the gods, and recognizes that even the greatest leaders or kings must die; this self-awareness transforms him from tyrant to a socially responsible, loving ruler who acts in the best interests of his citizens. He achieves an immortal name not for physical feats or adventures but for his wisdom and kindness.

As my readers venture into the mystery that is immortality, and the possibility that there have been people granted seemingly immortal lives, ones who have not tasted death, it is important to meditate on the lesson of Utnapishtim. According to the ancient Sumerian story, the gods granted him immortality because he became their vessel for saving the lives of his family and the world's guiltless animals; he achieved a successful, herculean feat that was beyond his own desires and ambitions. He had not asked for immortality or a reward of any kind, and placed himself in grave danger because Enlil originally wanted him as dead as the rest of humanity; lucky for Utnapishtim that Enlil relented of his anger and awarded him immortality and paradise. On the other hand, Gilgamesh's plans and deeds were egotistical and self-serving; he taunted the gods with his disobedience, and flaunted his power and control over others. Just when he thought he had been successful at winning immortality, the gods in the form of a serpent, stole the magic plant and reasserted their supremacy. Gilgamesh had finally achieved real wisdom.

This is humanity's oldest recorded story, and is the foundational template for all other similar stories. The significant issues that Gilgamesh ponders are the same issues every human is anxious about: having meaningful relationships, making life significant, living as long as possible, but accepting that physical life is not forever. Like Gilgamesh, the young feel invincible, and are unconcerned with death until some event brings death to their doorstep. Despite Gilgamesh's sadistic and brutal past and his failure to achieve immortality, he is spiritually reborn on his journey home. He becomes a benevolent ruler, who shares the wisdom of his blockbuster journeys with his people. He finally listens to Utnapishtim's advice and accepts his preordained fate:

> *You were made from the flesh of both gods and humans ...*
> *from your birth they assigned you a throne*
> *and told you "Rule over men!"* [156].

It is apparent, according to ancient texts, that the earliest humans created doctrines which proposed immortality based upon the human soul's ability to survive after death in some type of existence. So, the question arises whether these early humans indeed knew something about the afterlife from some type of teaching or mysterious means, or they simply invented a type of fantasy to appease their fears about dying. The invention of heaven and hell could have been a means of controlling early human behavior, as there is no greater motivator to good behavior than fear of punishment. These first, civilized humans devised and believed in a pantheon of gods and in a hierarchy of immortal gods, demigods, and humans, who all interacted in a natural order; there was also a strong belief that a demigod might have the chance to become an immortal. The old Babylonian religion held a demoralizing vision of the afterlife, where souls entered a shadowy world without hope, and where the conditions of existence in the other world depended on the livings' generosity and remembrance. Babylonian beliefs, however, were nowhere as complex as the Egyptian's faith in an immortal spirit or tripartite soul that disconnected from the body at death.

2

Ancient Egypt:
Democratic and
Magical Views of Immortality

*Do You not know, Asclepius, that Egypt is an image of heaven, or,
to speak more exactly, in Egypt all the operations of the powers which rule and
work in heaven have been transferred to Earth below?* (Asclepius III, 24b)

The idea of an immortal soul existed in the Sumerian, Akkadian, and Babylonian originators long before the founding of Hinduism, Judaism, Buddhism, Christianity, or Islam, and all religions focus on the greatest enigmas of human life—aging and death. Since earliest recorded civilizations, humans like Gilgamesh have tried to evade the laws of nature that fated them to decay and die, so people looked for ways to stay young, created ritual structures that became religions, and dreamt of what it would be like to live forever as the immortal gods. The earliest humans created doctrines that proposed eternal life based upon the universal, antediluvian doctrine of the survivability of the human soul after death. The old Babylonian religion held a depressing view of the afterlife or *lower world*; individual souls entered a dark world without hope or direction, and the quality of existence in the other world depended on the livings' generosity and remembrance.

Babylonian beliefs, however, were nowhere as complex as the Egyptian's faith in an immortal spirit or soul that disconnected from the body at death, but maintained the individuality or persona of the person, gave the spirit a home in the sky with the gods, and provided a home in its burial chamber. This belief lasted until the sixth century CE, and clearly influenced Judaic and Christian faith in an afterlife and in burial rituals (Reisner 2, 3); Christian beliefs, particularly those of the Roman Catholic Church, have continued the respectful Egyptian tradition of honoring the dead through strict funerary practices and burials, and hold a conviction in the soul's ascending to heaven where all troubles, trials, tribulations, and sicknesses end. The Egyptians, however, believed the soul or spirit, containing the personality of the individual after death, experienced the same human pressures and concerns of earthly life. Egyptians reasoned that a human was naturally made of visible and invisible parts: the observable physical body, and the invisible two souls that lived on after the body's death, which they named the *Ka* and *Ba* souls. The ancient Greek historian Herodotus (fifth century BCE) tells us in his *History* that the ancient Egyptians were the first to teach that the soul of man is separable from the body, immortal, transmigratory, and cyclic (Rawlinson 197), a key connection to later Hindu theories of reincarnation.

Egyptians were obsessed with the afterlife, and humans today are left with visible monuments to the ancient Egyptian dead and an inherited belief in some type of afterlife. Archeologists have unearthed numerous tombs along the Nile that offer visible evidence of Egyptian confidence in an eternal or divine characteristic of life that extended beyond physical existence. Egyptian immortality replicated life on earth more favorably than the Babylonians, but this existence was retributively karmic, and subject to the power and directives of a higher authority. Clearly presaging concepts of heaven and hell, Egyptian judgment came in the form of rewards and punishments, and souls experienced reversals of fortune according to their deeds on earth; a divine or mystical power transported souls either to a realm of happiness or to a region of torment.

Egyptian civilization's earliest beliefs in the immortality of the soul persisted for more than 3000 years, and contributed to the kingdom's political and religious stability. In the Old Kingdom (2649–2150 BCE), which lasted for more than 500 years, only the pharaoh lived beyond death. Egypt's immortality rites celebrated an early belief that the pharaoh was god incarnate: after all, humans regarded pharaohs as immortal, based upon the belief that they were reincarnations of the popular gods of Egypt at the time (Tomasino 96). The idea that the pharaoh was divine, a living god on earth, who would return to the celestial stars after dying, ensured a caste system that manipulated the masses into believing any insult against the king was an insult to the gods; this forced the masses into an existentialist reality. A millennium after the Old Kingdom fell, immortality democratically included ordinary people in what historians label "the democratization" of the afterlife; the common person in Egypt embraced belief in immortality, and state religion taught that everyone became Osiris in death (David 140; Wilson 87). The New Kingdom's (1550–1070 BCE) democratization of death, resurrection, and immortality was a brilliant strategy that also ensured loyalty to the pharaoh as a divine god incarnate who could influence a person's destiny in this life and in the life to come. This idea clearly referenced inspiration from Sumerian, Akkadian, and Babylonian earlier canons that incorporated a celestial hierarchy of gods, demigods, and immortals. The good news for Egyptian royals was that common people could never become gods, but their souls or spirits could become immortal after dying based upon a tripartite soul structure: the Ka, the Ba, and the Akh.

The Tripartite Soul

The Egyptians saw the immortal afterlife as another of life's natural dimensions where great dangers existed just as they did during earthly existence. The *Book of the Dead* provided tips for avoiding these dangers to ensure that a soul would not have to suffer a second death. The concept of the second death carried "…the connotation of a final and irrevocable death, from which no salvation is possible" (Willems 190; Gardiner, "Exhibition Journey" 56). Sigfried Morenz writes: "What men fear and seek to avoid on this plane is the second death mentioned in the titles of so many spells in the *Coffin Texts* and the *Books of the Dead*, e.g.: 'Spell of Not Dying a Second Time in the Realm of the Dead'" (207). The Egyptians were the first to concoct a second death experience that clearly reverberated later in the Christian Book of Revelation: "He who conquers shall not be hurt by the second death" (2:11); and, "This is the second death, the lake of fire; and if anyone's name was not found written in the book of life, he was thrown into the lake of fire" (20:14–15).

This second death, mentioned several times in the *Book of the Dead*, was such a terrifying prospect to the ancient Egyptians that three chapters in the books were devoted to the theme of not dying a second time; these chapters were seen as a warning, as Egyptians believed that only the utterly worthless suffered a second death. The Roman Catholic Church and later Christian sects continued the dogma of the second death as a perceptions management tool that terrified people into dogmatic beliefs of a tortured afterlife (Massey 190); their doctrine of the first death was a temporary sleeping until resurrection and judgment, but the second death was eternal damnation.

One Egyptian belief that did not make it into Christian or Catholic dogma was the tripartite soul, an entity organized into three distinct units— *Ka, Ba,* and *Akh*—and each unit had its own distinctive purpose, but for these to operate harmoniously, the body had to survive intact. The living had an obligation to build and maintain tombs for current and future corpses, as tombs became the intersection between earthly time and eternity; this belief in a home for the dead body naturally included the preservation of the deceased's body, as it was only in death that a human could reach full potential (Murray 86–96). The promise of an impending burial, physical conservancy, and a type of other-dimensional perfection or enlightenment were ideas that entered later religious tenets, where they continued to placate human fears of the unknown.

The Ka

Egyptians associated the *Ka* as the life force within the material, corporal human body that could depart during astral travel while a person slept or was in a coma; it was a shadow or negative silhouette of a person (Von Dassow 152). After death, the *Ka* returned home at night to the mummified body; the *Ka* required food, water, a safe place to sleep, and other necessities to sustain it. Hieroglyphic threats and images of the deceased were painted on tomb walls to warn grave robbers of the *Ka*'s revenge, but these drawings were often destroyed (Mafouz 78).

Egyptians believed that the goddess Heket or Meshkenet bestowed the *Ka* to humans at birth by breathing energy into them. Meshkenet was invoked to thwart evils affecting human existence, particularly by mothers concerned with infant mortality (Budge 193); Meshkenet was a goddess of childbirth who decided the destiny of the child; in the afterlife she weighed the scales of the heart (Wilkinson 153). She was also summoned as an intercessor for the dead with the other underworld gods, in order that the dead might be born into the afterlife with success. Meshkenet was the chief goddess of the *Ka*. Heket was the very important goddess of childbirth and the afterlife; she was the frog goddess who was first mentioned in the *Pyramid Texts* around 2345 BCE, when she and Meshkenet assisted in childbirth at the last stages of labor. Heket was also invoked as a traveling companion who escorted deceased kings to the afterlife (Wasilewska 131). Heket was later mentioned in a Middle Kingdom papyrus (2055–1650 BCE) when she acted as midwife for the birth of a new king, son of the high priest of Re (Remier 79). She was one of the most popular Egyptian goddesses, as women commonly wore amulets and scarabs with Heket's likeness during pregnancy and labor for good luck (79). Women wore amulets of Heket to help them carry their babies to term and for a safe delivery. Households often possessed an ivory knife bearing an image of Heket as a magical protection to keep everyone safe. As the divine midwife, she helped all midwives in their work (Remier 79; Rosen 309).

At death, this *Ka* or life force became an invisible double of the deceased, and the probable reason for the elaborate and detailed preparations of human

bodies for eternity. Just as in life the *Ka* had to have a home, after death the deceased's survivors provided tombs to house bread, beer, and livestock, as well as servants, weapons, jewelry, clothes, and mummified pets, in their tombs—anything that would help them in the afterlife. The tombs included the trendy *shabti* statues, carved representations of servants who would assist the Ka in the tomb-home by performing menial household duties (Mills, "Something Old, Something New" 20) (see **figure 2.1**). Egyptologists believe that common Egyptians imagined a more fertile Nile Valley with limitless beer and easy labor after death; the more shabti figures people were buried with, the less work would be required of them (Taylor 116; Stewart 8; Thomas 87–88). As a visual representation of servants of the dead, these shabti statuettes represented freedom from social class structure in Egypt; now everyone could have servants in the afterlife, even if they were only carved stones or molded figurines.

Figure 2.1 Shabti Figure. Not everyone could have servants during their lifetime, but at death these shabti figures were symbolic servants who performed menial household duties on behalf of the dead (courtesy of Harrogate Museums and Arts, Mercer Art Gallery, Harrogate Borough Council).

In the pharaohs' minds, they would always be superior to the commoners; they reveled in the best food and drink, communed with Egyptian gods such as Re, and battled evil forces to ensure Egypt's continued existence. Pharaohs looked forward to the trip of their *Ka* and *Ba* to heaven, but this destination could only be reached through the services of an intercessor, a ferryman (Cooney, "Gender Transformation in Death" 235); this echoes the character of Urshanabi, the ferryman, who worked for Utnapishtim in the

Epic of Gilgamesh, whom Gilgamesh sought for his journey to Dilmun. The Egyptian ferryman is also an archetype that later influenced the creation of the Greek's old gentleman Charon, who exclusively transported pure, moral, and just people to paradise (Pinch 122).

Chapters 98 to 104 in the *Book of the Dead* present a "Formula for Bringing the Ferryman in the Sky to Oneself and Voyaging with Ra," which is a dialogue among the deceased and the ferryman called Mahaf and his guardian Aqen (Schumann-Antelme and Rossini 64). Of course, there was always the possibility that Osiris would question the dead, weighing each candidate's heart in the scale against a feather to test for truthfulness. Those who failed this final examination would be "condemned to lie forever in their tombs, hungering and thirsting, fed upon by hideous crocodiles, and never coming forth to see the sun" (Durant 202). Here again we have the concept of a binary division of locations for dead souls that particularly influenced the hells of later religions where souls suffered in pain and anguish, condemned to eternal darkness, and tormented by demonic creatures.

The Ba

The *Ba* was not a separate being, but a powerful aspect or expression of the same person that was within the person even before birth. As the *Ba* was not usually associated with the living, it was believed to become manifest at the time just at the point of death, before the resurrection of the soul, and is endowed with "physical vitality" (Zabkar 97). The *Ba* immediately departed the person at death, and contained varied aspects of the individual's temperament and personality, similar to the Christian view of the soul (Resner 30–31; Zabkar 162–163; Schumann-Antelme and Rossini 4). Similar to the Ka, the Ba needed food for energy and survival in the afterlife. The *Ba* was depicted as a human-headed bird hovering over the dead body or flying from the tomb etched on hieroglyphics; the *Ba* was given the attribute of flight, so that the soul could voyage between the worlds of the living and the dead (see **figure 2.2**). During the Old Kingdom, only the king had a *Ba*, but this tenet was amended in later periods of Egyptian history when every person had a *Ba*.

There are images from *Ramesside Books of the Dead* that show the *Ba* perched on the arm of the deceased, or clasped to its body, like a pet parrot. The small pyramids built over the tomb chapels at Deir el Medina contained a little niche near the top where the Ba could roost to watch the sunrise, and observe the goings-on in the village where it had lived (Dunand and Lichtenberg 104; Taylor 124). Equating the *Ba*-bird with the soul of the deceased,

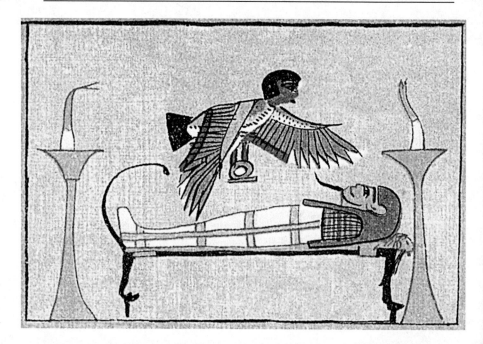

Figure 2.2 Image of the Ba. The *Ba* is represented as a human-headed bird that leaves the body when a person dies. The face of *Ba* was the exact likeness of the deceased person. Prior to the New Kingdom, no representations of the *Ba* are certain, though some funerary statues created during the Old Kingdom are thought to show the *Ba* in fully human form. Only in the *Book of the Dead* do we find illustrations that are clearly of the *Ba*, in the form of a bird with a human head or other human attributes (Budge, Facsimile of *Ba* Figure from 1300 BCE).

however, would be misleading. According to L. V. Zabkar, the term *Ba* itself has no exact equivalent in any modern, classical, or Semitic language; it may be that the word "animated" or "manifestation" is closest, so that "spirit" might better express its meaning (73–74). In other words, the *Ba*, as explained by Henri Frankfort, was the deceased's "animated manifestation" as well as its "animation," which had the power to move in and out of the tomb, the eternal house, and even to shape-shift into whatever form it wished (96–100). So, the *Ba* gives movement to the soul, allowing it to travel and return to its tomb home as it desires.

The Akh

Since the beginning of literary records, every religious persuasion stakes claim to be chosen, select, or special. The Egyptians created strong, post-mortem, final judgment scenarios that determined whether a person had earned a blissful eternity or a second death; the future happiness of the soul was based upon good deeds and a moral life. Echoes of these ideas are clearly heard in later religious philosophies and afterlife canons. The *Ka* and *Ba* were spiritual entities that everyone possessed, but the *Akh* was an entity reserved for only the select few who were deserving of *maatkheru*. Maat, the Goddess of Truth, Justice, and Balance,[1] took the form of an ostrich feather; the final trial of the deceased would have its heart weighed against Maat and judged by Osiris (Hood, "The Decalogue" 54).[2] If the person had led a good and decent life, his or her heart would be in balance and pass into the afterlife, but if the weight of the heart did not balance with Maat, a monster named by the *Book of Gates* as the Devourer consumed his heart, and this led to the second death (Hornung, "Black Holes" 136–137). Here we have the first real evidence of a belief in a terrifying, demonic or satanic entity whose name is repeated in the minor prophet Malachi:

> I will rebuke the *devourer* for you, so that it will not destroy the fruits of your soil; and your vine in the field shall not fail to bear, says the Lord of hosts [3:11].

Although Malachi may be referring to natural forces of nature that ruined crops, unexplained natural destructions became personified as monsters who were at the ready to harm humans in Egyptian and in later Hebrew and Greek thought. Christianity evidently inherited its other worldly beasts and monsters from its forebears in Egypt, Israel, and Greece.

Egyptologists refer to the *Akh* as "the blessed dead" or "radiant one"; when travelling to the solar realm, the *Akh* becomes a star in the sky (Remier 5; Wilkinson 342; Von Dassow 152). The *Akh* was the transformed human essence of good people who outlived death through Osiris' *maatkheru* justification, and who were able to associate with the gods after being judged. The *Akh* was an absent soul-feature of Egypt's condemned criminals; they could never have an *Akh*, and had no possibility of surviving in the afterlife, so they never could become a stellar or solar being. Dr. Ogden Goelet writes: "As an Akh the deceased was transfigured in an incorporeal state, having become a stellar or solar being. Unlike the Ka and the Ba, the Akh does not have much to do with the earthly realm" (152). Before the *Ba* combined with the *Ka* to form the *Akh*, a funerary practice had to be observed; the mouth of the dead person had to be opened to allow the *Ba* to leave the body (Teeter 24–28). The Egyptians believed that this reunification could go wrong if funeral rites were not carefully respected. The *Akh* also became the transfigured immortal form that could torment the living for not providing offerings to the dead (Najovits 52); thus, participation in burial rituals and care of tombs became a cultural tradition.

The *Coffin Texts* and the *Book of the Dead* were Egyptian literary texts that provided funerary, offertory, and reunification guidelines into the after-life; the texts suggest that the tripartite soul of an individual is immortal. In one version of the *Book of the Dead*, dating from the 15th century BCE, the *Ba* of a deceased person asks one of the Egyptian gods, "How long have I to live?" To which the god replied: "Thou shalt exist for millions of millions of years, a period of millions of years" (Benjamin 183). The completed journey of the righteous who attained *Akh* became eternal fixtures in the sky, as the *Akhu*, the plural form of *Akh*, were believed to be stars in the night sky that represented the reunification of the *Ba* and the *Ka*; originally, the imagery of the star was reserved only for royalty, but later became democratized, so that anyone could attain the *Akh* status in the afterlife (Benjamin 183). This star imagery harkened back to Sumer, as the star or *dingir* symbol always repre-sented God's name in cuneiform, and the Sumerian word for god always sig-nified the name *An* (*Anu*) and heaven; this symbol later became part of the Akkadian Semitic language and meant god (Boulay 67; Selin 244).

The soul in an *Akh* condition provided a way for Egyptian people to achieve divine status. Earle de Motte writes: "...the Egyptian conceived (or perceived) a visionary mystical state, in which a person or his 'soul' could experience his or her being as a divine, luminous intelligence; this was the Akh. They encountered or became such a being when they crossed the threshold to the super physical world, either in an altered state of consciousness or after death" (81). This *Akh* luminosity imagery reverberates in the prophet Daniel and St. Paul who both write about the resurrection from the dead when the righteous would become immortal: "Those who are wise will shine like the brightness of the heavens, and those who lead many to righteousness, like the stars forever and ever" (Daniel 12:3). Several hundred years later St. Paul would write that after the resurrection the saved would shine like stars, but their luminosity or spiritual body would have varied levels (1 Cor. 15: 40–44):

> There are celestial bodies and there are terrestrial bodies; but the glory of the celestial is one, and the glory of the terrestrial is another. There is one glory of the sun, and another glory of the moon, and another glory of the stars; for star differs from star in glory. So is it with the resurrection of the dead. What is sown is perishable, what is raised is imperishable. It is sown in dishonor, it is raised in glory. It is sown in weakness, it is raised in power. It is sown a physical body, it is raised a spiritual body.

There are clear connections regarding the afterlife between the ancient Egyptian religion and Judaism and Christianity. The Jews under Abraham traveled into Egypt during a great famine, and lived there for nearly 400 years, and Moses who later led the Hebrews out of Egypt was knowledgeable in Egyptian theology. Without question, Egyptian religious and philosophical ideas were amalgamated into the Hebrew faith, which later shaped Christian views of salvation after death.

Passing Through the Twelve Gates

The *Book of Gates*[3] is a solar funerary text dating from the New Kingdom (18th and 19th Dynasties, 1500–1200 BCE) that describes the journey of a recently deceased soul into the world of the afterlife; this voyage duplicates the passage of the sun through the abode of the dead during the hours of the night (Murdock 272; Hornung 55). As such, the text was a pharaoh's main guide to navigate his way with the sun god to a place where his soul would be resurrected. Budge asserts that the text was written "in spite of the pretentions of the priests of Amen-Ra," to prove that "Osiris was Lord of the underworld and that his kingdom was everlasting" (85). Just as in later religious texts that describe a tiered journey into the afterlife, the *Book of Gates* teaches that human souls must pass through twelve gates staffed with twelve gatekeeping goddesses whom the deceased must identify. The goddesses listed in *The Book of Gates* are daughters of the sun god Ra, or frequently called "The Hours"; they control the fates and years of humans' lives, have varied designations, wear varied colored robes, and have a five-pointed star crown on their heads (Hart 76). These goddesses do not appear anywhere else in Egyptian lore, so it has been proposed that the *Book of Gates* may have started as a method for governing the hours of the night with each goddess as a symbol of the visible main star during a particular hour.

The *Book of Gates* indicates that some souls will pass through safely and unscathed, but that others will anguish in *a lake of fire* in the realm of the dead in a place called *Tuat* (Budge 158), another clear derivation that influenced the Christian conception of hell and the Lake of Fire in Revelation 20:14–15: "And death and Hades were cast into the lake of fire. This is the second death, even *the lake of fire*. And if any was not found written in the book of life, he was cast into the lake of fire." About the Egyptian concept of hell, Budge writes:

> …the Tuat possessed the characteristics of all these names [Hell, Sheol, Hades], for it was an unseen place, and it contained abysmal depths of darkness, and there were pits of ire in it where the damned, i.e., the enemies of Osiris and Ra were consumed, and certain parts of it were the homes of monsters in various shapes and forms which lived upon the unfortunate creatures whom they were able to destroy [88].

Imagery in the *Book of Gates* clearly echoed Sumerian and Babylonian beliefs and influenced later imagery in Greek and Jewish thinking, and profoundly influenced descriptions of torment and eschatological events in the Christian Book of Revelation. The *Book of Gates* depicts a dried-up riverbed and a giant serpent accompanied by demonic enemies of the sun god. This scene is consistent with the one in Revelation 16 that describes the drying up of a river and a dragon from which emerge evil entities to gather for the final battle against the forces of "God the Almighty" at Armageddon: "The sixth angel poured out his bowl on the great river Euphrates, and its water was dried up to prepare the way for the kings from the East" (16:12).

The *Book of Gates* is an invaluable source for cultural excavation because early humans imagined the fate of the damned and an afterlife location, and these ideas of hell and a type of apocalypse have influenced the outlook on death and the "great beyond" until today. Wilkinson notes that the Egyptian concept of the Lake of Fire contained the bodies of the damned who would suffer eternally: "According to the *Coffin Texts* and other works, the underworld contained fiery rivers and lakes as well as fire demons (identified by fire signs on their heads), which threatened the wicked…. In a similar manner, in a scene from the funerary Book of Gates, the damned are subjected to the fiery breath of a huge serpent…" (161). The *Book of Gates* describes the horrors and torments of the condemned including burning and dismemberment that extinguishes any hope of resurrection or attainment of Akh.

The most complete copy of the *Book of Gates* known to us is found inscribed on the alabaster sarcophagus of Seti I, king of Egypt about BCE 1375, and consists of two parts, a series of texts and pictures which depict the sun god's boat moving towards the kingdom of Osiris, the Judgment of the Dead, and the punishment of the wicked enemies of the sun god; there is also a depiction of magical ceremonies performed in ancient times to reanimate or resurrect the body of the Sun to make it rise each day (86). This Egyptian resurrection imagery was reinforced with texts about Osiris and later influenced Jewish, Christian, and Islamic beliefs in resurrection from the dead. Beginning with the Sumerian civilization, ancient ideas evidenced in literary and visual texts still influence contemporary human rituals and thinking about immortality and the afterlife. These texts are closely woven into the fabric of a human consciousness that has not dramatically changed its conceptions of death, heaven, or hell in 6000 years. These beliefs may also be vestiges of chromosomal memories from antecedents, or might simply have originated as a way of fantasizing about immortality, death, and the afterlife in order to cope with mortality. Or, the ancients were more advanced in knowledge than given credit.

The Osirian Connection

The Egyptian concept of life after death was based on one of their myths that involved Osiris.[4] This story offered a democratized idea of immortality after death, so anyone could hope to join Osiris in heaven. Every night the sun descended into the underworld and met with Osiris, and having mutually energized each other, they both arose again the next day. The Egyptians believed that each person followed a similar cycle. The mummy was a representative of Osiris, which made preservation of the body important. The tomb where the mummy was kept was a personal Tuat; the *Ba* would descend into the tomb each night much like the sun, and would return to the physical body. Each morning it would depart once again to join with the *Ka*. Deceased persons all faced a "Judgment Day" in the Underworld before Osiris and a panel of other gods. The heart of the deceased was weighed on a Balance against the "feather of truth," and Thoth reported the result to Osiris. If the heart was "wracked with wrongs committed against society and against the divine order," it could not enter heaven with Osiris and was thrown to a monster; the deceased could never enter into the company of the gods (qtd. in Hare 33).

Pharaohs claimed divinity on earth and beyond death, so the Osiris myth of the Earth-god of the living who had died and returned as god of the dead, was a strong controlling factor in their politics. Later Egyptian beliefs about immortality included the possibility that everyone could reach heaven and live with Osiris, who was trapped in a coffin, and later torn into pieces by his brother Set, a metaphor for death. After Isis resurrected Osiris, he became lord of the underworld and judge of the dead; his story not only associates with mummification in preparation for the afterlife, but also affected later resurrection metaphors in the Abrahamic religions. In his monumental work *The Golden Bough,* James G. Frazer noted that Egyptian commoners copied the ritual ceremonies Isis had followed as "a representation of the divine mystery" that would bequeath to them life after death. A virtuous life, worshipping the gods, and a proper funeral were the only requirements for a happy afterlife (367). The mummy of the dead person was said to be a place of return for the wandering spirit, so it was ritually and magically preserved and protected. From that point in Egyptian history everyone could achieve eternal life.

These Osirian stories and burial customs spread among the common people who swathed dead relatives, but real mummification was only for the rich. The cagey priests of the Osiris-Isis religion made money on the Osirian religion by offering immortality by initiation; of course, their teachings would cost and not everyone could afford to pay (Donadoni 145–146). The priests instructed people in the proper rites and prayers to secure eternal life among the great gods, and they offered to reveal the answers to questions for an additional fee. The priests would bless the tomb for money, and advised people to fit out the tomb with food, drink, and servants to nourish and help the dead; a full set of the famous board game *senet* was also included as part of the grave goods that accompanied the dead on their voyage (Delgado,

"Rhampsinitus" 98). They filled the tomb with talismans pleasing to the gods, particularly the scarab, which, because it reproduced itself with fertilization, typified the resurrected soul (Braunstein, "The Meaning of Egyptian-Style Objects" 2011). If a priest properly blessed the tomb, people believed this would frighten away every tomb robber and annihilate every evil. According to Sir John Garner Wilkinson, the priests offered sacrifices to Osiris, a prayer was read in the midst of incense and libation, mourning relatives were present at the rite, and priests continued to pray as long as the people paid them for their services (383–384). These burial customs particularly influenced Christian funeral rites, whose rituals continue to this very day.

Ancient Egyptian civilization was the greatest cult of death that humanity has ever known, and influenced concepts of the afterlife in many later religions. Egyptians believed the physical body was important for an afterlife, and there is no evidence to suggest that ancient Egyptians practiced cremation. The desert climate effectively preserved the body and reduced decay of hair and skin; when early Egyptians saw well-preserved corpses they likely assumed some part of the person was still there. The elaborate Egyptian mummification and burial rituals were designed to sustain and strengthen the *Ka*, so it could undertake the arduous journey to reunite with the *Ba* and become an *Akh*. If the heart of the deceased was not heavy with sin on Judgment Day, the *Akh* could pass into a land of eternal youth in the company of family and loved ones and live among gods.

Myth and Legends of Thoth: Egyptian Magic and Immortality

Thoth was the god of secret wisdom and secret knowledge who invented language and writing; he was deputy of the sun god Ra, the divine physician, the god without a mother, a self-creating deity, the navigator of the boat of the sun god, and symbolized by an Ibis and a Baboon (Pinch 209–210; Remier 190; Von Dassow 144). He civilized humans by teaching them writing, medicine, music; he was the master magician (Ellis 46). Thoth, the record keeper of the gods, along with the librarian Seshat,[5] knew the past and the future, and wrote the fate of humans on the birth beds of their mother. He was a judge and an enforcer of law, and advocated for the slain Osiris before the Divine Tribunal, and he was in charge of funerary spells. Thoth played a critical role in the afterlife: "In the Pyramid Texts the dead kings fly up on the wings of Thoth. In the middle kingdom *Book of Two Ways*, the Mansion of Thoth provides a safe haven for spirits who can use his magic to get past the demons of the underworld. Some of the royal Underworld Books of the New

Kingdom name Thoth as presiding over the mystical union of Ra and Osiris that allowed the dead to reawaken each night" (Pinch 210).

Just as Gilgamesh attempted to secure and ingest a plant that would ensure immortality, in legends of Thoth, there are references to Thoth and Seshat drinking "white drops," also referred to as "liquid gold," which provided them with immortality. This sacred liquid, or potion of immortal life, has been an encouragement to people throughout the ages and in many religions to pierce the barrier of death and allay the fear of mortality. David A. Leeming writes:

> The elixir is found in Arabic texts where it is referred to as the *elixir of immortality* or *Dancing Water*. The elixir is sometimes equated with the alchemist's philosopher's stone. As well, it can be found in the myths of Enoch, Thoth, and of course Hermes Trismegistus (Thrice-blessed Hermes). In all the myths the hero has drunk the "white drops" (liquid gold) and thus achieved immortality. We can even find reference in the Quran (Sura 18; the Khidr) and it is mentioned as well in one of the Nag Hammadi texts [427].

Thoth was the Divine Alchemist and used the Milk of the Gods, which are referred to through history as white drops, white powder, manna, or the Fruit of the Tree of Life, Star Fire Gold of the Gods, and eventually the Philosopher's Stone. The ancients believed this substance would facilitate extraordinary life spans, and cure many diseases; they were the key to immortality. Just as varied nomenclatures over the ages referred to the white drops, so also the name of Thoth changed in later civilizations and traditions. Robert D. Tonelli writes: "In David Hudson's research on monatomic elements, he states, 'There is some material from ancient Egypt, it is called the Egyptian *Book of the Dead*, found about 3500 B.C. ... and all of it goes back to a man the Hebrews called Enoch, the Egyptians called Thoth, the Aztecs called Quetzalcoatl, in Greece they call him Hermes Trimesgritus; this is the same man. It is claimed he ascended by partaking of the white drops, the man who never died ... he ascended because he was so perfect" (qtd. in 89).

Known to the Egyptians as Thoth, the "Lord of Magic and Time," and to the Greeks as Hermes, "messenger of the gods," he is even remembered in the Celtic tradition as the enigmatic wizard Merlin, who disappears up an apple tree to mythic Avalon, seeking the secret of immortality and vowing to return (Emerys 24; Matthews 267; Penczak 246). As one who attained immortality, the secret of how we might become as gods, Thoth/Enoch promises to return at the end of time with the keys to the gates of the sacred land. This concept of an immortal returning during the last days clearly impacted stories of a later messiah or savior who would return to rescue humans and transport them to a new sacred earth or heaven.

According to ancient tradition, The *Book of Thoth* was the legendary repository of the Egyptian mysteries; as such, it is forever connected with occult knowledge, mystery schools, and the esoteric secrets and magical systems that these schools taught, and these mystery systems of thought made their way into later mainstream religious beliefs. Manly P. Hall writes that

Nothing definite is known about the Book of Thoth other than its pages were covered with strange hieroglyphic figures and symbols, which gave to those acquainted with their use unlimited power over the spirits of the air and the subterranean divinities. When certain areas of the brain are stimulated by the secret processes of the Mysteries, the consciousness of man is extended and he is permitted to behold the Immortals and enter into the presence of the superior gods. The Book of Thoth described the method whereby this stimulation was accomplished. In truth, therefore, it was the "Key to Immortality" [XXXVIII].

THOTH AS A MULTIPLE FUNCTIONARY

Thoth, scribe of the Egyptian gods, is usually illustrated as an ibis-headed man with a pen-and-ink holder. He became known as the god of the foundation of the law, mystical wisdom, magic, learning, hieroglyphic writing, arithmetic, and astrology. Thus, he was called "The Lord of the Divine Books" and "Scribe of the Company of Gods." According to classical belief, it was Thoth who brought the idea of creation into existence by uttering the thoughts of the creator; Ptah then put those spoken words into reality. Thoth was the principal deity of the city of Hermopolis (the City of Hermes) or Khemnu as the Egyptians called it (Ellis 45). According to Egyptian legend, the temple of Hermopolis housed fragments of the cosmic egg from which Thoth, as the divine Ibis, had been hatched on the Island of Creation, from the egg from which the first sun had risen (David 192; Ellis 46). Thoth's association with the creation myth also extended to the divine birth of the pharaohs themselves.

Thoth was not only associated with the creation of the physical world and revered as the inventor of the written word in the form of hieroglyphs, he is also credited with the authorship of *The Book of the Dead* (*The Book of Am Tuat*), a book of spells, prayers, and rituals that would assist the dead on their journey to the afterlife. According to Egyptian understanding, the deceased person would be judged by a panel of 42 assessors of the dead, which corresponded with the 42 administrative areas into which Egypt was divided. From this originates the legend of the 42 *Books of Thoth*, which describe instructions for achieving immortality (Gyurme 27; Pankhurst 139). One of Thoth's numerous roles was to record the outcome for the deceased person who had entered the Hall of Judgment (Guiley 134; Hayes 299). Anubis would check the weight of the dead person's heart on the scales against the weight of the feather of Maat[6] to see if they balanced each other (Hayes 299; "Anubis Speaks!" 180). And it was Thoth who declared the deceased to be "true of voice" or vindicated, if the feather balanced.

As the god of magic, Thoth taught Isis the craft of magic, enabling her to bring Osiris back to life and save the life of Horus when a scorpion had stung him and he faced imminent death (Remier 190; Strong 62). According to legend, Thoth, both a healer and magician, also restored the Eye of Horus that was torn to bits when the latter fought his uncle Seth (Set) to revenge the death of his father Osiris (Reisner 36; Wegner, "Gateway" 50). The eye of Horus, also known as the *udjat* eye, became the funerary amulet and magical, all-seeing eye (Potts 17), which later became a well known image in Masonry. Thoth was the patron god of the occultists of ancient Egypt, and was petitioned in many of the spells contained in the Egyptian *Book of the Dead*, such as the opening-of-the-mouth spell to reanimate a corpse, which was recited over a mummy by a high priest (Pinch 209–211; Teeter 24–28). According to legend, Thoth/Hermes gave to his successors the *Book of Thoth*, or the "Key to Immortality," which contained the secret processes for the regeneration of humanity and the expansion of consciousness that would enable mankind to behold the gods. There are stories, or theories, concerning the *Book of Thoth*, that some say at first was kept in a temple in a sealed golden box, and used in the ancient Mysteries (Wall 79). When the practice of these Mysteries declined, it was carried to another unknown land, where legend reports it exists after being safely preserved, and it still leads disciples to the presence of the Immortals. Others believe that the *Book of Thoth* is simply represented in the Tarot deck (Gurley 13).

Final Thoughts on Egyptian Concepts of Immortality

Most humans have always wondered and worried about what happens after death. Many modern religions teach that we will live again, but archaeologists tell us that even ancient Neanderthals buried their loved ones with flowers and grave goods for the afterlife (Spivey 270–274). Today most of the religious world believes in an immortal soul that lives on in some form. It is a shared teaching of Hinduism, Judaism, Buddhism, Christianity, Islam and Bahá'í, as well as of native and tribal religions throughout Africa, the Americas and elsewhere. Some say that the soul will live forever in either a heaven or a hell. Others, such as Hinduism, suppose that after death the soul will reanimate other life forms in an endless cycle of reincarnation. Most nonbelievers, of course, dispute the idea of a soul, being convinced that after death there is only nothingness. But from where have these ideas come? In the well-known book, *Life After Death: A History of the Afterlife in Western Religion,* Alan F. Segal, late professor of Jewish studies, wrote that every religion's views of recompense after death directly mirror the moral codes and desires of the culture within which the particular religion exists, making visions of immortality a human invention (16–17). It is because perceptions of the afterlife respond to the human condition and cultural values that anthropologists have often theorized that humans invented religion and devised religious beliefs to offer solace from the inevitable death experience.

In later Egyptian history, the effects of Egyptian religious thought and conceptions of immortality through Egyptian marriage alliances with the Greeks are clearly evident in later Greek and Roman thinking. The pharaoh controlled all territory as far north to Syria, west to Libya, all of southern Egypt and the Sudan. George A. Reisner writes that during the Ptolemaic period this belief became the most characteristic feature of the Egyptian conception of life after death (46).[7] After the death of Alexander the Great in 323 BCE, Ptolemy I Soter founded the Ptolemaic dynasty after declaring himself pharaoh. This Hellenistic dynasty, stretching from Syria to Cyrene to Nubia, ended with the death of Cleopatra VII and the Roman conquest of Egypt in 30 BCE. The Greek conquerors adapted to Egyptian culture by marrying their siblings and practicing Egyptian religion. There are clear connections between Egyptian religious thought and rituals and later Greek and Roman religious tenets and ceremonial rites associated with death, burial, resurrection, and immortality.[8]

Ancient Egyptians, like other early humans, observed the continuous cycles of nature: in the firmament, the sun was reborn or resurrected every morning, and then died and disappeared every night. The spring season brought a rebirth of vegetation, and was always associated with the idea of youth; like a well-structured story or play, in autumn all life reached its denouement of completeness, and then began to decline, enter into decay, and face the end. Naturally in winter all plants withered into death, and the strength of the sun faded, and the light of day was shortened, but afterwards the cycle of spring began anew and provided hope. The idea of immortality was born from nature's endless rebirths. Egyptians interpreted these models of birth, death, and renewed life and applied them to human existence. There are strong associations between these Egyptian models and later Greek religious tenets and ceremonial rites associated with death, burial, resurrection, and immortality.

3

Ancient Greece:
Defining Immortality
in an Age of Gods and Mortals

All of the Muses in their sweet responsion
Sing of the gods' eternal gifts, the hardships
Of humans at the hands of the Immortals,
Our mindless, hapless lives that never find
A cure for death, a guard against old age.
—Hymn to Apollo 3.188–192 (qtd. in Ruden 25)

Many religions based their rituals upon earth's natural cycle, studying the growth and death of flora, fauna, and humanity in their search to seek the answer to why we must die, and if there is anything humans could do to become immortal. Gilgamesh was reportedly a demigod in search of immortality, for immortality was not likely even for a demigod and king, and ordinary Sumerian humans could never achieve a corporeal eternity. There developed a history of immortal god-kings and their families who ruled the ancient cities of Mesopotamia during Sumerian, Akkadian, and Babylonian civilizations, and many of their customs, including designating people and places, continue today in parts of the Middle East, and particularly on the Arabian Peninsula. The Egyptians developed an elaborate system of death and resurrection rituals that would continue in the Abrahamic religions, and they also had a pantheon of immortal gods who offered kindness and hope. It is the characteristics, traits, personalities, behaviors, and anthropomorphic temperaments of the Greek gods that is crucial to studying later religious writings and stories. The custom of depicting god(s) with human features even appears in Judaism when Moses and the 70 elders of Israel "...saw the God of Israel. Under his feet was something like a pavement made of lapis lazuli, as bright blue as the sky. And he did not lay his hand on the chief

39

men of the people of Israel; they beheld God, and ate and drank" (Gen. 24: 10, 11).

There was a period in Greek literary mythology and religious history when "immortal gods" walked with humans. This is not so startling to readers familiar with Abrahamic religious texts who consider the Book of Genesis report that God walked in the Garden of Eden and spoke with Adam and Eve: "And they heard the sound of the Lord God walking in the garden in the cool of the day, and the man and his wife hid themselves from the presence of the Lord God among the trees of the garden. But the Lord God called to the man, and said to him, 'Where are you?' And he said, 'I heard the sound of thee in the garden, and I was afraid, because I was naked; and I hid myself'" (3: 8–10). These stories could simply have been the product of human imagination struggling to make sense of natural forces and the brutal facts of living and dying; or, they could have been a hyperbolic embellishment of famous men's feats in an historical timeline. Perhaps there could have been long-lived personages, the "mighty men" of old; the Sumerian King's List recension records Ziusudra as having reigned 3600 years, and according to the Hebrew Bible, Noah lived 950 years (Langdon 251–259; Genesis 9:29). The earliest Sumerian, Akkadian, and Babylonian religious texts all record humans interacting with "gods," and the ancient Egyptians believed that the pharaoh was the descendant of a god, so there has always been a common belief since the beginning of recorded civilizations that humans encountered gods and immortal beings who walked the earth; the belief in the possibility of demigods and humans becoming immortal has appeared in many religions.

Greeks believed there was a familial pantheon of immortal gods, but only a demigod could become an immortal and only with the consent and will of a god; this belief is not so far removed from Gilgamesh's epic struggle to gain favor, find a cure for aging and death, and achieve immortality. The gods never changed common mortals into immortals, so the ancient Greeks did not offer immortality on a democratic basis. Greek religion believed in a celestial and selective ruling class whose entrance within was determined by strict genealogy and an ancient belief in bloodlines, a clear continuation of convictions rooted in Mesopotamia. This bloodline belief originated in ancient Sumer, and later plodded into Egyptian doctrines, which is why all pharaohs were related to the gods figuratively or literally, as was the belief. The ancient Sumerian gods, demigods, and their descendants married within the family to keep genetic bloodlines pure, and this tradition continued with the pharaohs.[1]

The Greeks believed that their immortal gods controlled all aspects of nature, and their human lives were totally at the mercy of the will of the gods.

In Greek literary texts, interactions between people and gods were generally considered friendly, but the gods could dispense harsh punishment to mortals who were conceited, arrogant, overly ambitious, or wealthy. Many mortals tried to trick or challenge the gods, and all were punished, some of them for all eternity. For example, King Ixion, son of the god Ares or of Phlegyas, king of the Lapiths in Thessaly[2] who was in trouble for murdering his father-in-law, went to Zeus for forgiveness. While on Mt. Olympus, he made the mistake of trying to rape Hera. Zeus found out and tricked Ixion with a cloud in the shape of the goddess. He was punished by being bound to a burning solar wheel for all eternity (Fiore 209; Kierkegaard 324).

It is clear that part of the unnatural breeding of humans and animals was strictly reserved for the gods, as evidenced in the *Odes of Pindar* when Ixion's son Centaurus mated with Magnesian mares and produced a race of centaurs. Of course, this could have been literary symbolism influenced by tales of the Ibis-headed gods of Egypt (Grant 82; March 116). Or perhaps these are tales of obscene, advanced genetic manipulations, which is not so fanciful in light of current gene splicing experiments that have mixed human DNA with pigs.

The classical Greek thinkers and authors also argued their developing theories of the human soul that later influenced Christianity and Islam. Plato developed the theory that the human soul is an incorporeal entity that pre-exists before attaching itself to a body; materiality is simply the carrier for immateriality. In Plato's *Phaedo*, his teacher Socrates asserts the soul to be immortal, cognizant, and resurrection-able; the soul was also in constant conflict with the needs of the body (34; Ahrensdorf 156; Shields 131–132). Homer's epic poems and odes see the soul as something lost when dying in battle, or something that leaves a person's body and travels to the underworld, where it lives as a shadow (Snell 19). According to Aristotle, the form of the soul exists within the form of the body.

The Family of Primary Greek Immortal Gods

Greek religious mythology likely stemmed from the original religions in Crete, where the country's original civilization appeared around 3000 BCE. George F. Moore writes, "Hesiod's story of the birth of Zeus is derived from Cretan myths; his mother Rhea is the Cretan goddess" (434). Sparta and Crete claimed divine origins: Apollo for Sparta and Zeus for Crete (Mikalson 210). The Greeks believed that the gods, particularly Zeus, chose Mount Olympus in Thessaly as their home, where they shaped a hierarchical society of power and influence. Zeus ruled from a palace atop Olympus with his divine family of ten gods and goddesses; this familial structure was a clear echo of the original Annun'aki gods of Sumer who were in control of natural forces and humans. As Nicholas de Vere writes, "As we know the positions of the gods in the various pantheons and their attributes and relationships to each other, we can re-identify who they really are. Surprisingly we find that the separate pantheons of the Sumerians, Egyptians, and Greeks … and so on, all appear to be derived from a very ancient family genealogy of 'gods.' These gods furthermore seem to stem from the early Sumerian pantheon" (199) (see chart). According to ancient literature, gods could travel at will within the sky or heaven, the sea, and earth. "In Greek mythology, the sun god crossed the sky in a chariot and, in the Bible, Elijah was taken by in a fiery chariot of his own" (Bostock 220). These ascension stories clearly recall the ancient flying Annun'aki gods, and strengthen the theory that god and goddess archetypes rematerialize in different eras and cultures, but are all rooted directly or indirectly in the worship of the ancient Dragon or Annun'aki gods. The recognition of these ancient narratives that connect to an equally ancient religion enhances understanding of this planet's history and clarifies these mysteries, which are not mysteries but histories that were not exactly hidden, but have not been promoted by religious academics and clerics.

Zeus commanded the gods, and was the spiritual father of all gods and humans; his very temperamental and jealous wife, Hera, was queen of heaven

Comparative Chart of Greek Gods and Sumerian Gods			
Greek	*Attributes*	*Sumer*	*Attributes*
Zeus	Sky god with thunderbolt, rules other gods, punishes evil humans	Anu Enlil	Sky god Punitive storm god
Poseidon	Lord of the sea, wields trident, causes earthquakes and sea storms, protects Greeks	EA (Enki)	Lord of all waters; devoted to humans' well-being
Hades and Persephone	Lord of the dead Queen of the dead	Ereshkigal Ninhursag	Queen of the dead Great Mother Goddess
Hera	Queen of the gods, goddess of marriage	Ninhursag	Goddess of childbirth Queen of the mountains
Aphrodite	Daughter of Zeus	Ishtar or Inanna	Goddess of fertility and warfare
Apollo	Son of Zeus, god of the sun, patron of arts, god of healing	Shamash	God of light, truth, and justice

and guardian of marriage. Other gods associated with heaven were Hephaestus, god of fire and metalworkers; Athena, goddess of wisdom and war; Apollo, god of light, poetry, and music. Poseidon ruled the sea with his wife Amphitrite, and commanded less important sea gods, such as the *Nereids* and *Tritons* (Impelluso 238; Muller 535). Demeter, the goddess of agriculture, was associated with the earth. Hades, an important god but not an Olympian, ruled the underworld, where he lived with his wife Persephone. Dionysus, as the god of wine and pleasure, became almost as important and popular as Zeus, and was accompanied by a host of genetically altered, incubus type creatures, such as satyrs, centaurs, and nymphs (see genealogy).

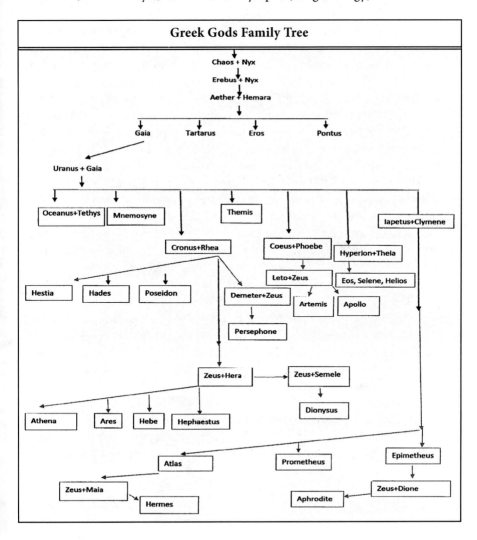

Characteristic Behaviors of the Immortal Gods

Greek civilization developed around 2000 BCE, and included a mythology whose beliefs and ritual observances consisted of a body of diverse stories and legends about a pantheon of immortal gods. Greek mythology had become fully developed by about 800 to 700 BCE, as evidenced in the classic myths of Hesiod's *Theogony* and in Homer's *Iliad* and *Odyssey*. In these myths, the Greek gods appeared as humans and exhibited human behaviors. In his *Sacred History*, Euhemerus, a mythographer from the third century BCE, chronicled the common conviction that these myths were actual historical distortions of glorified heroes and kings who had been deified (Eliade 490), and a bit earlier in the fourth century BCE, Herodotus considered that Greek religious traditions were inherited from the Egyptians. Yaachov Shavit writes, "The early Greeks, he [Herodotus] noted, borrowed from the Egyptians most of their gods and religious rituals, as well as the annual calendar" (67). However, unlike former ancient religions, Greek mythology had no formal structure, such as a church government, and no written code, such as a sacred book.

Classical Greek literature reflected its culture's views on the human condition and its place in the hierarchy of gods, who are depicted as unpredictable, flippant, and often immoral; their unique characteristic is not goodness but power: "The distinguishing quality of the [Greek] gods is, above everything, power" (Bowra 58). Power defines a god: "A [Greek] god is a power that represents a type of action, a kind of force" (Vernant 273). Thus Aphrodite is the force of love and lust; Zeus is the power of the thunderbolt and of kingship; Ares is the power of battle, and so on. Some mythical full Greek goddesses are self-assured, such as Hera, Athena, and Aphrodite, and to all are ascribed supernatural powers.

The Greek conception of the immortal gods could be understood as a longing to escape mundane mortality, a wishful thinking that would grant humans power in the face of a hostile environment. The Greek Immortals lived forever; they could be wounded, but they could not be killed. They lived in palaces, and traveled in golden chariots drawn by magnificent creatures. They had fabulous weapons such as the thunderbolts hurled by Zeus. They could control the weather. They had the magical power of shape-shifting, transforming themselves into animals or inanimate objects, and also had the power to transform others into terrible monsters or objects such as trees. Their blood was a bright unearthly fluid called Ichor that had the power of eternal life.

The Immortal gods resembled mortals, but they were superior in every way: more beautiful, taller, stronger, and with superior intellects and abilities. The Immortal gods married and sired families; needed food, drink and sleep to nourish their bodies; wore the same styles of clothes as mortals but fashioned from more luxurious materials; and used similar styles of weapons as humans. The Immortal gods had the same emotions as mortals, and displayed feelings of love, gratitude, jealousy, hate, and revenge. These gods became the idealized version of humans, as the gods overcome every mortal's weakness and desire for revenge; there are no moral, sexual, or social rules for the Immortals that are imposed on humans to control their behavior.

Zeus and Hera: Sex Without Limits

The god Zeus was worshipped as far back as 7000 BCE as a sky god by Greek-speaking tribes in the Russian Steppes and south of the Caucasus; in 1680 BCE, Zeus worshippers invaded mainland Greece and began the Mycenaean civilization, which later invaded Crete in 1480 BCE and dominated all of Greece. At this time, Zeus is brought into anthropomorphic form, and establishes rule on Mount Olympus. Zeus was an all-powerful, lightning-throwing god who was prone to punish other gods and demigods, and often diverted the course of history. In Homer's *Iliad*, Zeus directs the destinies of heroes and controls the dynamics of other gods (Lopez-Ruiz 4). Randy Cerveny writes that, as lightning was the exclusive property of the gods, any attempt to imitate that power was considered sacrilegious. "Salmoneus, king of Elis, found out the hard way. The king sought the divine worship of his subjects, so he made thunder by riding his chariot over a bronze bridge and produced 'lightning' by hurling torches from the chariot." Zeus burned the false deity to a crisp for his blasphemy (56; Poling, "Salmoneus" 126). When the god Prometheus steals fire from the Immortals, Zeus punishes him by chaining him to a rock and having his liver eaten by an eagle until Heracles saves him (Dowden 5).

Zeus is the ultimate god who controls all things on earth. He is married to Hera, but has many children with human women, and produces a race of demigods. Hera was the daughter of the Titans Kronos and Rhea, sister-wife of Zeus, and she inherited the title of "Great Mother of All" (Leeming and Page 98). Most of Hera's stories from Greek mythology concern acts of vengeance against Zeus' endless infidelities, his mistresses, and their offspring.

Stories of Zeus' inability to contain his sexual urges were likely lessons taught to warn humans that such behavior was only reserved for the gods, and any attempt to emulate those types of taboo activities would end in disaster. Also, these stories instructed ancient Greek women to accept men as innately polyamorous and polygamous with uncontrollable sexual instincts and impulses; after all, if a god could not contain his sexual desires what human man could? Zeus wanted to have sex with his sister Hera, but she refused, so he disguised himself as the cuckoo bird that Hera loved; Zeus shape-shifts into his real form and rapes a humiliated Hera who marries him and becomes his seventh wife (Morford 73; Jordan 121; Daly 67). Of course, Zeus also raped his own mother, Rhea (Conway 53); enraged that his mother forbade him to marry, he threatens to rape her, but she transforms into a fanged serpent. Zeus in turn transforms into a serpent, coils around his mother and rapes her, and later rapes the daughter this union produced (Edmonds 179).

Sex emerges as a weapon rather than a divine union, such as Osiris had with Isis, and at this time a patriarchal ascendancy arises—a masculine sexual force sublimates the ancient feminine principle (Leeming and Page 99, 133). If a masculine god had full control over a goddess, human women would be taught to sit on a lower seat, transferring feminine, innate power to enrich the strength of male control.

Stories of powerful women often feature a female with an air of supernatural mystery who mates with another powerful ruler, and is a mother to her nation. Some mythical, powerful women are actually goddesses who are self-assured in their wisdom, like the powerful women of Greek myth such as Hera, Athena, and Aphrodite, who all have supernatural powers. According to Baring and Cashford, "Hera may reach back to the Neolithic Snake Goddess who ruled the heavenly waters, and Homer and Plato both connected her name with the air. In the *Iliad* she is called the 'Queen of Heaven' and 'Hera of the Goddess Throne.'" She was also Goddess of Earth, and was personified in ancient times as a cow, recalling legends of the Sumerian Ninhursag and the Egyptian Hathor (311); Hera was the Greek's Great Mother Goddess.

Apparently, there has always been a Queen of Heaven since prehistory, and Blessed Mary later assumed this throne in the West's Christianity, when the rule of a masculine god appeared. Mary has been proclaimed as the Queen of Heaven and Queen of Angels, a distinct reference back to the original Sumerian goddesses who were given the same or similar designations. It is startling to note that the Roman Catholic doctrines of Mary's Immaculate Conception and Assumption only became dogma in 1854 and 1950 CE respectively, and the tradition of offering cakes to the goddess, so vigorously condemned as idolatry in the Bible, survived in many folk traditions honoring Mary during the Easter season with hot-cross buns (Leeming and Page 162). The very word "Easter" is derived from Ishtar or Astarte, the "Queen of Heaven," who was vilified as pagan.

ATHENA: A MASCULINIZED VIRGIN

Athena continues the tradition of serpent or dragon gods and snake symbolism; as she was a virgin, the association of snakes with the phallus or sexual potency is misplaced. Her snake emblems may specifically recall the winged serpents that earlier represented the holiness or inviolability of the pharaohs or ancient gods and goddesses. The warrior goddess Athena was perceived as the rock upon which the Acropolis was built, and thus reminiscent of the Great Mother goddess, Cybele, who had been left exposed on an Anatolian mountain. Athena's standard representation as a serpent goddess clearly connects to the Annun'aki gods of ancient Sumer; she is depicted as winged with snakes protruding from the edges of her robe, and "There is an older image of a wild and awesome Goddess, wreathed in snakes, where snakes wind round her head as hair and crown" (Baring and Cashford 332, 334). Athena has often been associated with Medusa because she is frequently portrayed with serpent iconography. As A.S. Yauhuda observed, "We must take it as a fact that serpent worship and serpent symbolism belong to the oldest and most primitive manifestations of human thought" (qtd. in Joines vi).

Ancient Israelite culture used the serpent to signify the sovereignty of its divine king, and to communicate the sexual or productive power of Yahweh; the serpent symbol was widely used in Solomon's temple (Joines 100, 101). In the very earliest civilization in Mesopotamia, the divine right of kings was in the blood and carried through the line of females, so ascension to the throne was only through matriarchal blood inheritance: "The rule of kingly descent through the senior female line appears to have been established from the outset when a dispute over entitlement arose between the brothers Enki and Enlil" (Ploeg 41).

In a long line of celibate queens, Athena was worshipped as a virgin and represents a sublimation of the feminine, which was a distinct and reported choice of lifestyle for female leaders. Recalling the acts of the original Sumerian and Mesopotamian goddesses, Athena became renowned as the patroness of art, a teacher of agriculture, and a home-economics goddess who taught mortals how to weave and sew. There are also lewd stories that the misshapen god Hephaistos, who was her brother, had semen rubbed onto her thigh, but she was mostly known as the goddess of wisdom and daughter of Metis.[3] The most popular myth was that she was the daughter of Zeus with Metis, a product of rape and born of man, emerging from Zeus' head after he swallowed Metis to avoid having a boy who could depose him. Hephaistos cracked open Zeus' skull, and Athena popped out of his head (see **figure 3.1**). Zeus willed a daughter who would not challenge him, so Athena is born of the creative mind that cannot be constrained; she is the feminine archetype for logic and autonomy, a self-realized entity. Yet, Athena is a masculinized woman, and her birth-giving powers are taken over by male supremacy, as Homer calls her "the daughter of the powerful father" (Wilde 93–94). She is also the motherless child who becomes a symbol

Figure 3.1 The Birth of Athena. Athena was the daughter of Zeus with Metis, a product of rape and born of a man: Hephaistos cracked open Zeus' skull, and Athena popped out of his head (from a vase painting, ca. 19 C.E. German book).

of the new patriarchal order that ensures a male-dominated political succession.

APHRODITE: NYMPHO-MANIACAL VIRGIN

Among the host of all the queens of heaven since the beginning of religion in Mesopotamia, Aphrodite was the later Greek queen of heaven, and was identified as the daughter of Zeus and Dione in the *Iliad*, but in Hesiod's *Theogony*, she is created from the sperm of the gods in the ocean when Cronus castrated his father Uranus, and threw his penis into the sea; she was not born of a mother, just like Athena (Sacks and Murray 24). Stories of these motherless, non–vaginally born goddesses align with the biblical Eden's Eve who was created from the rib of a man, according to Genesis 2: 21–23. These stories imply that goddesses and Great Mothers are created through a type of creative, supernatural medical science that does not require a female carrier; these legends also may have suggested to ancient Greek interpreters that it is the Patriarch who creates, so therefore He rules.

Aphrodite, a nymphomaniac and goddess of sexual passion and fertility, is often called Urania; she is the earth goddess most closely associated with Ishtar and Isis. Aphrodite recalls Inanna-Ishtar as the brightest star in heaven, the morning or evening star; she is a direct descendant of the Sumerian Inanna-Ishtar, and later Astarte in Phoenicia, Ashteroth by the Hebrews (Budin, "A Reconsideration" 95). She was married to Hera's son, the misshapen god, but she took the drunken god of war, Ares, as a lover; many gods vied to marry her, including Poseidon, Apollo and Hermes (Baring and Cashford 140–141).

Often called the Goddess of the Sea, Aphrodite continually renewed her virginity by bathing and swimming in the sea; this oddly recalls a type of baptism that washes a person's soul from all past sin and guilt, erases all history of vice, and asserts power over evil. Her bathing is also a symbol of her regenerative powers with water being central to her needs. Even earlier Sumerian legends say the ancient Annun'aki god Enki rescued Innana by sprinkling the water of life on her, so that she could assume a human form (Wilde 134). These stories clearly reveal a typology of baptism: Aphrodite's story is a surrendering to renewing waters that cleansed the goddess, so that she became a virgin; water baptism is both an act and a motif that originated in ancient Sumer and Mesopotamia and has been preserved up to the present day in all Christian churches and in the living waters of the Jewish Mikvah as a means of salvation that ensures the possibility of entrance into an eternal heaven.

There is no restraint from physical pleasure in stories of Aphrodite, but, as a result of Uranus' castration, her very birth associates with pain and aggression, all a part of the ancient Greek erotic experience (Cyrino 31). Aphrodite challenges the notion associated with Hera that sex is between married partners; she is the archetypal beauty and seductress whose exploits include lies and deceptions, and she has wild sex on the mountains with the handsome mortal Anchises "...on the skins of wild beasts" (Segal 23). Aphrodite breaks social rules and moral codes; she became the patroness of prostitutes because Greek society at the time condemned relations outside of marriage (Brundage 12). Also, from a socio-religious view, a mortal having sex with a goddess was disturbing to the Greeks.

THE JEALOUS IMMORTALS

Ancient Greeks believed their gods were fashioned in the image and likeness of humans, and, as such, they possessed many of their traits, behaviors, and temperaments. They laughed, joked, married, and had affairs. They could be angry, envious, and violent, and did not always get along with each other. Ugly Hephaestus was one of the few gods who was not created physically perfect; he suffered a deformity of his lower limbs (Bonnefoy 85). Suspecting his wife Aphrodite was having an affair with the war-god Ares, he created an invisible net/chain in which to trap them while they slept together in his bed, and then called all the gods out to shame the two lovers (Morford 80; Kreigel 64).[4]

Hera was a vengeful and jealous goddess because of her husband's rampant sexual peccadillos. Hera also had good intelligence on Zeus' affair with Semele, and in an act of deception, she masqueraded as an old woman, and befriended the naive Semele. Hera prodded Semele to obtain a promise from Zeus, and Hera added that Semele should afterwards ask him to reveal himself in his godly glory.[5] Hera knew that this request would end in Semele's death, so the murder of Semele was premeditated. Naturally, Zeus agreed to grant her one promise, and swore to the River Styx to carry out the promise. Semele followed Hera's instructions, Zeus begged Semele to reconsider, but bound by his oath he was forced to comply. So he appeared to Semele in his godly form, a form that no mortal can ever lay eyes upon, and Semele was killed by his thunderbolt (Dixon-Kennedy 182).[6]

Magic Immortal Blood and Food of the Greek Gods

Gods in the Greek Pantheon had a special type of blood, and eschewed eating bread and wine, the very items that Christianity would later adopt: "For they do not eat bread or drink wine, and therefore they are bloodless and called immortal. Iliad V, 341ss" (qtd. in Benardete 79). In Greek mythology *ichor* is the otherworldly, colorless, divine blood of the gods that retains the qualities of ambrosia or nectar, foods that appear in mythological literature as divine sustenance for the immortals of Mount Olympus, making them immune to age or decay (Hard 81). Any human who came into contact with ichor immediately died. Christianity, particularly the Roman Catholic

Church, embraced the concept of the power and magic of the divine blood in the Holy Eucharist; when believers partake of the body and blood of Jesus Christ, the ingestion of the bread and wine is believed to imbue salvation and immortality to humans instead of death.

Although the Greek gods were immortal, they could still be injured or suffer pain. In Book V of Homer's *Iliad*, at the siege of Troy, Diomedes wounds Aeneas, the son of the goddess Aphrodite, and is about to kill him when Aphrodite rushes in to protect her son. Enraged at Aphrodite's interference, Diomedes pursues and wounds her:

> He flew at her and thrust his spear into the flesh of her delicate hand. The point tore through the ambrosial robe which the Graces had woven for her, and pierced the skin between her wrist and the palm of her hand, so that the immortal blood, or ichor, that flows in the veins of the blessed gods, came pouring from the wound; for the gods do not eat bread nor drink wine, hence they have no blood such as ours, and are immortal [Iliad V, 364–382].

While scholars are not entirely certain what the ancient Greeks thought ambrosia actually was, it is believed that these foods were actually honey. Ambrosia in Greek myth was used by the gods and goddesses as a balm to confer grace or even immortality (in the case of mortals) onto the recipient ("Ambrosia"). The Greeks considered immortality in a physical dimension; that is, their gods assumed a human body that did not age or decay. To someone who was physically mortal, ambrosia did not have a long lasting effect. Any attempt to steal the gods' immortal food received swift punishment. After the gods granted Tantalus immortality, he pilfered the gods' nectar and ambrosia, and gave some to his mortal friends (Endsjo 44–45). Unfortunately, they received justice in the form of mortality; Tantalus was condemned to an eternity of hunger and thirst, with water and fruit situated just beyond his grasp.

Forbidden fruit also appears in the Hebrew Bible, when God forbade Adam and Eve to eat the immortal food in the gardens of Eden from the Tree of Life and the Tree of the Knowledge of Good and Evil:

> And out of the ground the Lord God made to grow every tree that is pleasant to the sight and good for food, the tree of life also in the midst of the garden, and the tree of the knowledge of good and evil [Genesis 2:9].

It appears that God was distressed because Adam and Eve's consciousness of good and evil was the first step in their likely attempt to eat the immortal fruit of the Tree of Life. Either through anger at their disobedience or alarm at their impending power, God did not want mankind to become immortal:

> Then the Lord God said, "Behold, the man has become like one of us, knowing good and evil; and now, lest he put forth his hand and take also of the tree of life, and eat, and live forever"—therefore the Lord God sent him forth from the garden of Eden, to till the ground from which he was taken [Genesis 3:22, 23].

Ambrosia was also used for physical preservation, as an ointment that kept the skin from aging and gave the recipient immortality; when the ointment was not applied, the body reverted to its original state of mortality. Ambrosia was used to beautify and perfume Aphrodite; in the *Homeric Hymn to Aphrodite*, the goddess becomes a seductress with the assistance of eau de ambrosia:

> ...there the Graces bathed her and anointed her
> with ambrosian oil such as is rubbed on deathless gods,
> divinely sweet, and made fragrant for her sake [Homer V. 61–63].

In Homer's *Iliad* XIX, 38, the sea-nymph Thetis pours ambrosia and nectar into the nose of the dead warrior Patroclus to preserve his body (Abel 15; Endsjo 45; Crubellier and Laks 28). In the same epic, Zeus calls upon Apollo to anoint the fallen hero Sarpedon with ambrosia, and clothes him in immortalizing vestments (Nagy 141; Iliad XVI 670, 680). Although Athena gave ambrosia to Penelope to beautify her and erase the years to inflame suitors while waiting for Odysseus in the *Odyssey*, Penelope did not become immortal (Abel 15). Nectar bestowed immortality on select mortals, and the theft or misuse of divine ointments was a serious offense.

Demigods: A Physiognomy of Man and God

Most of the early written religious and historical records illustrate gods and demigods who are noble, courageous, holy, and wise; but they also include stories of violence, cowardice, ungodliness, and stupidity. Their stories parallel many of the legends of the original gods and goddesses of Sumer, whose cast of characters has endlessly appeared in religious literature and lore. This same crew with surprisingly new names appears in all the major religions and cultures to this very day; this tradition was uninterrupted in the legends of the Greek Immortals and demigods. In Ancient Greek mythology the Immortal gods and deities visited humans, fell in love, and their children were called *demigods* or "Heroes" who were famous for their courage and great strength. An equivalent type of story is reprised when Genesis 6: 4 records: "The Nephilim were on the earth in those days—and also afterward—when the sons of God went in to the daughters of humans, who bore children to them. These were the heroes that were of old, warriors of renown." The Greek pantheon of gods included mortal heroes and heroines who were promoted to divinity through a process which the Greeks termed *apotheosis*. Some of these humans, like Heracles, received this award for performing good deeds, others received it through marriage to gods, such as Psyche (Neumann 143), and some like Glaucus who, partially echoing the story of Gilgamesh, was brought the herb of immortality by a snake; but while he was well-received by other sea gods, his body was transformed into a fish-like creature (Ovid 8. 917–959; Kristensen 115).

DEMIGOD HERACLES: BIPOLAR AND MURDEROUS APOTHEOTHENAI

In ancient Greek theology, the *Apotheothenai* were demigods who became immortal. The most famous example of an Apotheothenas is Heracles [Herakles or Hercules],[7] who was born a demigod, but was gradually granted immortality and godhood by his father Zeus. According to Thalia Papadopoulou, throughout all of Greek literature Heracles is portrayed in several ways: "On the one hand, he is portrayed as the invincible hero and civilizer of mankind; on the other hand he is presented as the megalomaniac and hubristic conqueror, a representative of excess" (9). There are a multitude of sources for the life of Heracles, mostly from archaic poetry of the eighth century BCE, and he is referred to by other authors a thousand years later. One of the most famous sources is Euripedes' play (Halleran 284).[8]

Heracles was conceived by Alcmene, the human wife of Amphitryon, king of Thebes, while he was absent, but Alcmene was deceived, as Zeus masqueraded as Amphitryon and had sexual relations with her. When Amphitryon unexpectedly returned that same night, Alcmene also had sexual relations with her husband; this resulted in twin boys Heracles, the demigod, and Iphicles, the mortal son. Zeus announced to all the gods that his son Heracles, also a great-grandson of Perseus, would be his successor and become king, but Hera, jealous wife of Zeus, had other plans to delay Heracles's birth. Eurystheus, the cousin of Heracles, was born just before Heracles, and Zeus had to live up to his promise to make the first born of the descendants of Perseus as king (Miselbrook 71; Halleran 284).

According to Greek texts written by Hesiod, Sophocles, Euripides and many others, Heracles was a complicated demigod who strangled Hera's serpents in his infancy, murdered his teacher Linus in self-defense, and was sent away to study archery (Miselbrook 72, 73). He later briefly married Megara, the daughter of the Theban king; Hera made him go mad, so he killed his children and he threatened her father the king. After that string of events, he began his twelve labors in the service of his cousin the king Eurystheus.[9] When Heracles returned home from his famous arduous mission, Eurystheus hid himself in a bronze jar because he was afraid.

After marrying Deianeira in Calydon as a reward for his labors, Heracles accidentally killed one of his father-in-law's pages. As a result of this incident, he had to leave with his wife and son, and when they crossed the River Evenus,

Nessus, the centaur boatman, tried to rape Deianeira, so Heracles killed him. Heracles once again went mad and sold himself as a slave to Omphale, the Queen of Lydia, for three years. During his absence from his wife, he had an affair with Iole, daughter of Eurytus. When Deianeira was apprised of his unfaithfulness, she sent clothing that was saturated with Nessus' blood to Heracles; Nessus had informed Deineira before he died that his blood could be used as a love potion to incite Heracles' affection for her. Heracles donned the poisoned clothing and was overcome with so much pain that he tried to undress, but the clothing could not be removed. Heracles built his own pyre and asked his friends to ignite it. When the flames started to leap into the air, there was a strike of thunder, the chariot of Zeus swirled down from heaven, and Heracles was taken up to heaven; he had just been immortalized (March 235–241; Daly 70). On Olympus, he married Hebe, the goddess of eternal youth and daughter of Hera, and settled his differences with Hera (Colakis and Masello 144). After he killed himself by burning away the mortal parts of his body, Heracles was admitted into the community of the Olympian gods. Heracles does not die "the death of mortals," but he dies "the death which immortalizes" (Bonnefoy 179–180).

Demigod Medea: Vengeful Murderess

Ancient Greek drama is a source of social and cultural norms that relate to rituals and philosophies. Euripides depicted the demigods as violent and vengeful beings with no control over their emotions; they were amoral and incapable of forgiveness. In Euripides' *Medea* (431 BCE), the characteristic nature of a demigod is terrifying: "Medea is extraordinarily skilled at understanding other people so she can manipulate them, and she is exceptionally intelligent at scheming … no one would want her abilities at the cost of having to be like her" (Scodel 12). Creon, the King of Corinth, is deceived and manipulated by Medea into letting her remain in Corinth for another twenty-four hours after he asks her to leave, and she manipulates Jason by telling him exactly what he wants to hear. These manipulations are possible not only because of Medea's intelligence, but also because of Jason and Creon's flaws; she exploits Creon's sense of compassion, which overcomes his sense of survival and reason when he allows Medea to stay for an extra day. She pleads with him, and asks that he take pity on her small children and, because of this, he acts against the prior evidence of her sporadic, vengeful, and dangerous nature, and instead allows her an opportunity with which to exact her retribution. Compassion is one of the greatest virtues a person can have, but in this instance it provided the compassion-devoid Medea with a weapon.

Medea, descendant of the ancient gods, pillaged, plundered, and murdered at will, but escaped in a flying chariot to avoid all retribution because she was a demigod, the granddaughter of Helios [Apollo]. Euripides forever immortalized this Medea, the changeling granddaughter of Helios, the sun god and God of Oaths; Helios was a handsome god crowned with the shining aureole of the sun, who drove a chariot across the sky each day and night. Homer described it as drawn by solar bulls (*Iliad* XVI, 779). As time passed, Helios was increasingly identified with the god of light, Apollo, and also directly corresponds to Ra (Re), the ancient Egyptian sun god.

Medea was an Asian princess of Colchis,[10] who possessed supernatural powers and knowledge; she was able to prophecy the future, and like a sorceress or dragon-god, she flies off in her "Dragon" chariot at the end of the story after murdering her two sons to avenge Jason's infidelity. She indeed acts with the power, authority and prophetic knowledge of a god when she takes the lives of a king and his princess daughter, and commits infanticide; she establishes a festival and ritual in honor of her dead children, reveals her plans for the future, and prophesies the death of Jason, her ex-husband. She murders her conjugal family to avenge her dishonor by Jason, lives outside of the domestic sphere, overthrows the patrilocal system, and becomes a primeval Mother Goddess with power to grant life and death. Violence appears to be a customary characteristic for these demigods.

As there appears to be no remorse for Medea's violence, one quality of a demigod is a lack of guilt, the willingness to take revenge without pity or remorse or sentimentality, and the ability to move in flight. There is a picture of Medea's chariot taken from a Lucanian red-figure calyx krater attributed to the Policoro painter, depicting the final scene of Euripides' Medea when she flies off in her chariot. And there is a well-known image of Helios, God of the Sun, driving a flying chariot from a fifth century BCE Athenian red-figure calyx krater. Both of these chariot depictions were created around 500 BCE, and what is startling about the graphics are the serpent, sun, halo, and wing images that connect to ancient Sumerian iconography (Coulter-Harris 64).

NIOBE: THE ARROGANT DEMIGOD

A delicious story of revenge by gods upon demigods is Niobe's tale. Less than three centuries after Sheba lived, Homer solidified the myth of Niobe, a demigod whose mother was a goddess. Arrogant Niobe crowed about having twelve children, and wanted to be worshipped as a god, so she instigated a feud with another goddess, Leto or Latona, wife of Zeus. Leto was considered the goddess of motherhood and mother of only the twins Apollo and

Figure 3.2 Niobe Vanquished by the Gods. *Apollo and Diana Attacking the Children of Niobe* by Jacques-Louis David, 1772. Oil on canvas. Dallas Museum of Art, Foundation for the Arts Collection, Mrs. John B. O'Hara Fund in honor of Dr. Dorothy Kosinski (courtesy of Dallas Museum of Art).

Artemis. She gave birth to the twins on Delos, the "floating island," because Hera, Zeus' other wife, would not allow her to give birth on land or on an island at sea. Leto's son and daughter later kill Niobe's children, and she is left vanquished and humbled by the gods (see **figure 3.2**).

In Chapter 24 of the *Iliad*, Homer writes:

Even lovely Niobe had to think about eating, though her twelve children—six daughters and six lusty sons—had been all slain in her house. Apollo killed the sons with arrows from his silver bow, to punish Niobe, and Artemis slew the daughters, because Niobe had vaunted herself against Leto; she said Leto had borne two children only, whereas she had herself borne many—whereon the two killed the many. Nine days did they lie weltering, and there was none to bury them, for the son of Saturn turned the people into stone; but on the tenth day the gods in heaven themselves buried them, and Niobe then took food, being worn out with weeping. They say that somewhere among the rocks on the mountain pastures of Sipylus, where the nymphs live that haunt the river Achelous, there, they say, she lives in stone and still nurses the sorrows sent upon her by the hand of heaven.

HELEN: DEMIGOD OF BEAUTY

A further notorious demigod was Helen, whose name meant sun ray or shining light; she was a semi-divine goddess, whose cult was established in the eighth to sixth centuries BCE. Helen was considered a divine figure, and she was worshipped and believed in as a divine power; 19th century scholars surmised that Helen was in fact a metamorphosis of the Ashtaroth, or Astarte, the moon-goddess of the Sidonians, or the "wandering Queen of Heaven," the offspring of the highest god Zeus (Bauer and Zeller 73). Other scholars conclude that Helen was "stunningly solar ... the daughter of the sky god," and thus a solar deity whose aspect is the morning star (Doniger 60, 61). Otto Skutsch has presented linguistic evidence that connects the name of Helen and her stories to a Vedic Indian solar deity whose name was Saranyu, who was the mother of twin horsemen known as the Asvins. In Greece, Helen was the sister of the Dioscouri, twins famous for their horsemanship (188–193). There is inconclusive evidence whether stories about Helen had real roots or were wholly fictional. Her tale led to wars between the Greek states, and her abduction by Paris caused the flames of war to ignite between Troy and Sparta. Scholars like Wendy Doniger analyze Helen as a shallow deceiver; she writes: "The Trojan horse, closely associated with Helen, is, like Pandora's box, an image of the deceptive equine woman, who is hollow inside and full of deceptions" (62).

Homer's *Iliad* and *Odyssey* both report Helen as ravishing, and Homer promoted Helen as a captivating icon in the *Odyssey*, "...whose excessive sexual charisma was a gift from Aphrodite" (Hughes, "Helen the Whore" 38). In the *Iliad*, the story of Helen investigates and focuses on the relationship between gods and mortals. In most sources, including the *Iliad* and the *Odyssey*, Helen is the daughter of Zeus and Leda, the wife of the Spartan king Tyndareus. Euripides' play *Helen*, written in the late fifth century BCE, is the earliest source to report the most familiar account of Helen's birth: that, although her alleged father was Tyndareus, she was actually Zeus' daughter. The Greeks were following the pattern of the pharaoh's claim to have divine origins; this also recaps the legend that the Greek demigod Medea was the granddaughter of Helios, the sun god.

The tale of Helen's birth is mysterious and mystical. In the form of a swan, the king of gods was chased by an eagle, and sought refuge with Leda. The swan gained her affection, and the two mated. Leda then produced an egg, from which Helen emerged. Pseudo-Apollodorus, author of the famous second century BCE *Bibliotheca*,[11] states that Leda had sexual relations with both Zeus and Tyndareus the night she conceived Helen. The oddity of Helen's conception and birth confirms her in myth as a demigod; she also does not die but spends her days in the Elysian Fields[12]; the Elysian Fields and the Isles of the Blessed were two dwelling places for the immortals. Birth and immortality aside, the demigoddess' story was instructional to teach women their proper role within social hierarchal structures, and further instructed them to control their behavioral impulses, a distinct move to suppress the natural feminine.

Immortal Gods Interact with Humans

The Greek gods' behaviors, according to a variety of ancient texts, are patterned on human behaviors, begging the old hypothesis: men create gods in their own image but with superior knowledge and power. The texts tell of gods who are immoral, violent, vengeful, and deceptive, all negative qualities of the human condition. All of this is true, but it is also not the complete picture of the Greek gods. The Greek gods appear in disguise, are offended easily, are licentious, are sometimes thieves, and they engage in trivial disputes. When Greek gods become visible to people and socialize with them, the humans do not know who these beings are; most often they appear to people when they want sexual satisfaction because they are obsessed with beauty. While these gods may have physical and behavioral human attributes, the similarity ends. Humans need food, sleep, and they all grow old and die. The Greek gods never age, never need food except ambrosia and nectar, and never die. The gods may bleed in battle (*Iliad* book 5), but they cannot die of their wounds (Buxton 94). And since the sacrifice when Prometheus tricked Zeus, the gods no longer eat cooked meat, but savor only the smoke from the altars. Though the gods have no need to eat meat to keep their bodies going, they "assemble as guests for the pleasure of it, for the splendor of the celebration and the radiant joy of the banquet" (Vernant 35; qtd. in "Gods and Men in Greek Religion"). The gods are amoral and formidable, and humans must beware of and appease that power; the Greeks admired and feared the Immortals, but did not particularly love them. A pupil of Aristotle wrote: "It would be eccentric for anyone to claim that he loved Zeus" (qtd. in Bowra 71). After all, who could love a god who destined humans to suffer disease, degeneration, and death? This view of human life was not entirely pessimistic, as the Greeks accepted life as fragile and subject to failure, but were still optimistic that their lives could be improved and become fulfilling through dedication and hard work. Success, however, was clearly determined by the gods. "At such times a man realizes his full nature, and if the gods are willing, enjoys an exalted happiness, which is indeed like their own in its celestial completeness" (Bowra 75–76).

Oedipus Rex: No Escape from the Immortals' Plan

There are ancient Greek tales of love and punishment that tell of a time when gods and humans lived together. Tales of love entail incest, or the seduction or rape of a mortal woman by a male god that results in heroic offspring. The stories generally suggest that relationships between gods and mortals are something to avoid; even consenting relationships rarely have happy endings (Mile 38, 39). Sophocles depicted the gods as wise and morally superior to humans. In Sophocles' *Oedipus Rex* (429 BCE), the Greeks' polytheistic religious beliefs and values centered on a predetermined, divine plan for humans who had no control over their fortunes, as gods ruled their fates. In the case of Oedipus, it was clear that no one could escape the god's future plan; humans were predestined from conception. Jean Cocteau's prologue to his *Machine Infernale*, an operatic version of the original Greek play, states: "…Oedipus is at grips with the powers that watch from the other side of death. They have spread for him, since the day of his birth, a trap and you are going to watch it snap shut" (qtd. in Knox 135). Prophecy was one of the great controversies of Sophocles' time: Oedipus "…tried to avoid fulfillment of prophecy … believed he had succeeded … only to find he fulfilled that prophecy years ago" (Knox 137). The play reasserts traditional religious views that man is ignorant, and knowledge belongs only to the gods. This echoes the Garden of Eden story when Adam and Eve were cast out of Eden for daring to eat of the fruit of the knowledge of good and evil.

Anchises: Pillow Talk with a Goddess

In a few cases, a female divinity mates with a mortal man, as in the *Homeric Hymn to Aphrodite*, where the goddess lies with Anchises to produce Aeneas (Faulkner 5, 6; Edgar 73–84). His major claim to fame in Greek mythology is that he was a mortal lover of the goddess Aphrodite (and in Roman mythology, the lover of Venus). One of the earliest mentions of this story is in *The Iliad* (800 BCE): "The strong son of Anchises was leader of the Dardanians, Aeneas, whom Divine Aphrodite bore to Anchises in the folds of Mount Ida, a goddess lying in love with a mortal" (*Iliad* 2.819–821; 5.247–248) (qtd. in Moon 23).

One version is that Aphrodite pretended to be a Phrygian princess and seduced him for nearly two weeks of lovemaking. Anchises learned that his lover was a goddess only nine months later, when she revealed herself and presented him with the infant Aeneas. Aphrodite had warned him that if he boasted of the affair, he would be blasted by the thunderbolt of Zeus. He did and was scorched and/or crippled (Stehle 207, 208).

GANYMEDE, THE CUP BEARER

Many of the gods consorted with humans, though Zeus is perhaps the most infamous for kidnapping innocent humans for sexual gratification. In another one of his best-known conquests, Zeus turned into a swan to impregnate Leda, who laid an egg as a result of the encounter, out of which hatched Helen, Clytemnestra, Castor and Pollux (Littleton 811–813; Apollodorus III. 10, 11, 120, 121). Like many of the gods, Zeus was pansexual, so he also turned into an eagle to abduct Ganymede, a Trojan prince, to serve as Zeus' lover and cupbearer. Ganymede was the blonde son of King Tros of Troy, and the most beautiful boy on earth (Willis 133; White 163; Dowden 49). Although William A. Percy insists that it was the other gods who abducted him, it could be implied that Zeus had commanded them on this mission. "According to the poem [*The Iliad*], Ganymede was "the loveliest born of the race of mortals, and therefore, the gods whisked him away to be Zeus' wine pourer, for the sake of his beauty, so he might be among the immortals (XX, 233–235)" (qtd. in Percy 38). Ken Dowden states that, "This story, in fact, reflects ancient initiation customs known from an instance in Crete. There a person of high status ritually abducts the prime boy of the adolescent age group and gives expensive presents … a drinking cup" (Dowden 49, 50). The myth of Zeus and Ganymede was the archetypal story for acceptance of pederasty and homosexuality in early Greece (Neill 148).

ACTAEON, THE ACCIDENTAL VOYEUR

Only the Greek gods had unrestricted license to kidnap and seduce their choice of humans, but they sometimes annihilated humans who lusted after them. In *Hymn V*, the Hellenistic poet Callimachus wrote: "Whosoever shall behold any of the immortals, when the god himself chooses not, at a heavy price shall he behold" (Maier, trans., v. 93). Actaeon was hunting with his 50 hounds when he beheld Artemis swimming in a lake. Because of this disrespect, she forbade him to speak or else he would be turned into a stag. He resisted her command and summoned his hunting party, so Artemis changed Actaeon into a deer; on the goddess' orders, the dogs trapped, ravaged, and consumed their former owner (Desmond 61; Cartmill 254).

DEMETER, SECRET NANNY OF IMMORTALITY

Another story of gods punishing humans for overstepping their bounds is in the *Homeric Hymn to Demeter* (600 BCE), set during the period when Demeter was in mourning for the rape and kidnapping (Bookidis and Stroud

5) of her daughter Persephone by her uncle Hades with the connivance of Zeus; she lived for some time among the humans, disguising herself as an old woman (Moore 439). She served in the household of King Keleos and Queen Metaneira where she tended to their son Demophon by feeding him the food of the gods:

> Demeter anointed him with ambrosia like one born from a god,
> and breathed sweetly on him, held close to her breast.
> At night, she would bury him like a brand in the fire's might,
> Unknown to his own parents. And great was their wonder
> As he grew miraculously fast; he was like the gods.
> She would have made him ageless and immortal
> If well-girt Metaneira had not in her folly
> kept watch at night in her fragrant chamber
> and spied [verses 237–245].[13]

Queen Metaneira spied on Demeter's activities, and shrieked when she witnessed her son positioned in a fire. This interruption angered Demeter's plan to make Demophon immortal, so the goddess sent a famine to punish Metaneira for her snooping (Dowden 284; Reid 130; Parker 340).

Zeus' and Hermes' Reward: Reincarnation as a Tree

Not all Greek myths end in punishing mortals. In Ovid's moralizing fable, *Metamorphoses* VIII, Zeus and Hermes also disguised themselves as humans during a long journey. They visited a modest old couple, Philemon and Baucis, who considered the gods as honored guests (Ovid v. 611–724). This story is alluded to later in the New Testament, when Paul writes: "Be not forgetful to entertain strangers: for thereby some have entertained angels unawares" (Hebrews 13:2). In return for their kindness and generosity, Zeus and Hermes transformed their home into a temple dedicated to Zeus, with Philemon and Baucis acting as priest and priestess. The couple appealed to the gods to permit them to die at the same time; Zeus and Hermes granted their request and changed the couple into adjoining trees, so they would be near each other even after death (Roman and Roman 102, 103; Court 28).

Resurrection Stories and the Nature of the Greek Soul

While much of Greek literature involves the gods, these writings also explore the nature or texture of the human soul, the nature of the intellect, the source of consciousness, and resurrection concepts. Crivellato and Ribatti write: "Indeed, questions like the source of human thoughts, the mechanism of cognitive activity, and the nature of emotions, perception and voluntary movement, were disputed by Greek scientists since the beginning of Greek civilization" ("Soul, Mind, Brain" 327). Homer (800 BCE), Hesiod (750 BCE), and other ancient texts debated the nature of the soul or *psyche* that corresponded to a human's personal uniqueness or individuality; immortality for ancient Greeks included an immortal union of body and soul, as the soul would live eternally in Hades, but without the body the soul was considered dead.

Although almost everyone had nothing to look forward to but existing as an immaterial dead soul, some men and women reportedly gained physical immortality, and traveled to live forever in either Elysium, the Islands of the Blessed, or heaven, the ocean, or under the ground (Endsjo 417–36). The foremost of these reported immortal men were the heroes of the Trojan and Theban wars: Amphiaraus, Ganymede, Ino, Iphigenia, Menelaus, and Peleus. These heroes reportedly were resurrected from the dead and then achieved physical immortality. Asclepius, killed by Zeus, was also resurrected and transformed into a major deity, the god of medicine (Rice 52–53). In some versions of the Trojan War myth, Achilles, after being killed, was snatched from his funeral pyre by his divine mother Thetis, resurrected, and brought to an immortal existence[14] in either Leuce, the Elysian plains, or the Islands of the Blessed. Achilles wore armor and wielded a spear given by the gods to his father Peleus, a spear that no one else could wield, and he had his magic, immortal horses (Schein 93, 94).

Alcmene, Heracles, and Melicertes were also among the figures sometimes considered to have been resurrected to physical immortality. Alcmene, mother of Heracles, disappeared from her funeral bier, and in place of her body was found a large stone; she was assumed to have been immortalized in heaven (Endjso 56; Hislop 125). Melicertes' mother, Ino, threw the young child into a pot of boiling water, and then into the sea where he came back to life and was immortalized; he became the protector of sailors (Cahill 107; "Ino Leukothea"; Homer 5.333). According to Herodotus, the seventh BCE sage Aristeas of Proconnesus was first found dead, after which his body disappeared from a locked room. Later he was found not only to have been resurrected but to have gained immortality (Endjso 47–104). Generally, traditional Greeks believed that chosen individuals were resurrected from the dead and made physically immortal, while others could only look forward to a disembodied, dead-soul existence.

The Homeric poems use the word "soul" in two distinguishable conditions: something that a human risks in battle and loses in death, or something that at the time of death departs from a person's body and travels to the underworld, where it experiences a less pitiful afterlife as a shadow or copy of the deceased person (Lorenz, "Ancient Theories" 3; Snell 19). The existence of soul delineates a living body from a dead body; however, Homer does not ascribe human activity to the human soul. Usually, when Homer mentions soul, he alludes to death: the soul is referred to only when a person's life is at risk (Furley 4; Lorenz). For example, Achilles states that he is constantly risking his soul (*Iliad* 9.322), and Agenor thinks about the fact that Achilles has just one soul (*Iliad* 11.569) (Lorenz). In the Homeric poems, only human beings are said to have (and to lose) souls.

The ancient Greeks supported strong distinctions between body and soul; the soul was considered pure, holy, and immortal, while the body was evil, earthly, and corruptible (Owen 33). Human life on earth was considered a living death as the soul was trapped within the body; however, the soul was purified when the body died. This belief offered a body-soul duality that emphasized the soul as a nonphysical, divine, and eternal dimension, while the body was judged worthless (Jaeger 135–147). For example, Homer highlights the belief that mortality was not feared but embraced, as Odysseus actually rejects the offer of becoming immortal twice in the *Odyssey* (de Jong 136; Kohen 51). Homer viewed the soul as lost in death and remained in the afterlife as a shadowy form of the dead person (Dylan 74). He defined the soul only as a marker of life; when his characters jeopardized their soul, they risked their life.

By the end of Socrates' life in the fourth century BCE, the soul had acquired "intelligence, emotion, and appetite" (Allen and Springsted 34). In Plato's *Phaedo*, the philosopher has his mentor Socrates declaring the soul as an independent entity, immortal and cognizant, capable of deliberate thought and able to be resurrected; it was the soul that ruled and regulated the body to participate in virtuous actions, and opposed the passions and physical needs of the body (34; Ahrensdorf 156; Shields 131–132). Here is the following assertion from Plato, taken from the *Phaedo*:

> The soul whose inseparable attitude is life will never admit of life's opposite, death. Thus the soul is shown to be immortal, and since immortal, indestructible.... Do we believe there is such a thing as death? To be sure. And is this anything but the separation of the soul and body? And being dead is the attainment of this separation, when the soul exists in herself and separate from the body, and the body is parted from the soul. That is death.... Death is merely the separation of the soul and body [Phaedo 61, 64].

Joseph Owens writes: "The overall tendency of Greek tradition is found to interpret soul in terms of movement, and sensation and knowledge, as though the soul were somehow the source of these activities" (109). Book I of Aristotle's *De Anima* describes the nature of souls possessed by humans, animals or plants; he considered the soul is the essence of all living things (Polansky 37). He embraces the concept that the soul is the *form* or *essence* of any living thing, like a hot wax impression; the soul is not a separate substance from the body (Crivellato and Ribatti, "Soul, Mind, Brain"). Every living organism that requires nourishment and reproduces has a soul; it is the possession of a specialized genre of soul that enlivens any organism. These categories of souls are specific to the type of body the organism possesses. Aristotle (384–322 BCE) opined that the idea of a body without a soul, or of a soul in the wrong classification of body, is completely incomprehensible. He believed that a soul has several parts, and one of those parts is the human intellect, which can exist without the body; other parts of the soul cannot exist without the body (Witt 169). The soul is not independent of the body; the body is the material cause upon which the soul acts. Aristotle defines the soul as the efficient, formal, and final cause of the living being, and its natural body as the material cause (Leunissen 74, 75). Aristotle writes in *De Anima* that "The soul, then, must be substance as the form of a natural body that is potentially alive. Now, the substance is actuality; hence the soul will be the actuality of this specific sort of body" (4121 20–21). The soul is defined by diverse capacities: nutritive and reproductive, appetitive; plants have only the nutritive faculty; all animals have at least touch for sensitivity; humans and all others who might resemble humans have deliberative thinking aptitude and intellect.

The ancient Greek literary and philosophical tradition contributed significant work that inspired later thinking on the concepts of resurrection and the human soul. There are varied literary examples of gods resurrecting humans and demigods from the dead; these stories might have later influenced the Lazarus story and other resurrection accounts from the New Testament. Plato's emphasis on the body as a prison for the soul striving to overcome corporeal desires denigrates the body, which is a beautiful creation in God's likeness. Plato conceived that the soul was immortal, pre-existent, and longing for death's release; the soul had no connection to the body except in its prison state. Aristotle's locus vis-à-vis the soul diverged substantially from Plato, as soul was the form of the body, not a distinct substance that inhabited it. According to Aristotle, the form of the soul exists within the form of the body, and the soul did not exist apart from the body, only differentiating life from nonexistence.

Human Quest to Become an Immortal

Ancient and contemporary cultures, through literature, art, and oral legends, have made "gods" out of humans who demonstrated unnatural or uncommon powers of intellect, unusual beauty, or abnormal strength. Humans want to emulate the gods' powers and beauty, but sometimes, as in the case of Achilles and Helen, "godlike" behavior equals arrogance and pride ("Gods and Men"). There are different rules and protocols for gods and men in ancient Greece, as humans are punished for breaking social rules, but gods are more powerful than humans, and they do not observe legal or moral limits. The gods in Greece are territorial about their position, and hinder attempts for a human to become immortal; they eschew any criticism, but punish those who would mock them. In this hierarchical complex, ordinary humans live tragic lives, and accept the fate given by those above them, which necessitates and demands that humans participate in formal worship. Gods were admired and feared, but not particularly beloved. This view of human life, fate, afterlife, and religion may strike some as pessimistic, but the Greeks did not see it that way. As C. M. Bowra explains:

> [The Greeks] accepted the melancholy fact that much of life is indeed frail and insubstantial and even the greatest endeavors might fail, but they believed that it could suddenly be enhanced and illuminated and made full and wonderful. This could happen only if they exerted their powers to the utmost and set them harmoniously to work. At such times a man realizes his full nature, and if the gods are willing, enjoys an exalted happiness, which is indeed like their own in its celestial completeness [75–76].

The Greek gods often elevated their half-mortal children or grandchildren to the status of heroes, or even to the status of gods. In contrast, their treatment of humans who could boast no divine ancestry was often exploitative or punitive. Only mortals who behaved in a wholly moral, humble manner could hope to be rewarded by the gods, a key connection to other religions.

All men's souls are immortal, but the souls
of the righteous are immortal and divine. (Socrates)

4

Hinduism: An Immortality of Nonexistence

There is neither existence nor is there nonexistence.
Therefore, what source can give rise to death
or immortality? (*Mahabharata,* Volume 4, 290)

The ancient Hindu religion ignores any notion or possibility that physical materiality, while a person is alive, could transform into any type of bodily immortal existence; in Hinduism grew the idea of a special substance in all living organisms that is eternal, but materiality cannot coexist with this type of eternal, as the substance, or *Atman*, is supra-material, and is beyond any identifiable or known element. Hindus embrace the idea of successive karmic rebirths into other life forms that are shaped by a person's actions in a previous life; ancient Hindus developed the theory that reincarnations incorporated lower spectrums of life, and all reawakened varieties of life depended on the moral character and actions of the person. These seemingly torturous, endless cycles continue until the person attains nirvana or enlightenment. Nirvana is a state of spiritual self-actualization, as Hindson and Caner explain: "Nirvana, the fifth key element in Hinduism, is the state of nothingness, which is the Hindu goal for eternal existence. Upon ceasing to exist, the individual becomes part of this god-essence" (264). Therefore, the heaven of Hinduism exists in a vacuum, a void, an abyss, and Hindus are thankful that they will not have to endure incarnating in material form ever again.

This theory is in antithesis to the glorious heavens of the Abrahamic religions that painted scenes of breathtaking beauty, wellness, and the promise of a transfigured material body into an immortal, glorified body in the presence of God. This doctrine of re-enlivened humans, who would eventually be relieved of the anxiety of aging and illness, and become immortal, was a reassuring and hopeful guarantee of a better existence in the future; a person only had to die first, rest in the grave for thousands upon thousands of years, and await the resurrection of the dead. Paul of Tarsus writes about this enigma:

> Behold, I tell you a mystery: We shall not all sleep, but we shall all be changed, in a moment, in the twinkling of an eye, at the last trump: for the trumpet shall sound, and the dead shall be raised incorruptible, and we shall be changed. For this corruptible must put on incorruption, and this mortal must put on immortality [1 Corinthians 15: 50–55].

Most ancient religious texts talk about some type of magic drink or plant that could provide a person with immortality, and Hinduism is no different. The idea that some type of magic drink or plant was reserved only for the gods and for demigods is distinctly referenced in Hinduism. The ancient origins of Hindu's sacred *soma* and *amrita*, immortality potions, clearly influenced Greek and Christian religious beliefs, customs, and rituals associated with salvation, death, and immortality. The ambrosia of the Greeks is a clear echo of the Hindu nectar of immortality. The *Merriam-Webster New Book of World Histories* records: "The Greek and Roman gods were in many ways like mortal men, but they had the distinction of immortality, which came as a result of their eating habits. Ambrosia, the food of the gods, and nectar, their drink, had the property of preventing death" (11). James Davidson revisits Homer's writing about this subject: "Ambrosia and nectar can be used to feed a newborn god, to change a mortal into an immortal, or even to keep a corpse from rotting.... Ambrosia and nectar could thus be said to be a treatment for immortality, substances that give a body the ability to resist time and defy death. On immortal bodies, a regular application of them sustains beauty, brilliance and energy" (241). Polytheistic Hinduism's attitude towards immortality-delivering substances was strictly reserved for their many gods; *amrita,* literally meaning immortality, was their food, and first appeared as an idea in the *Rig Veda*, where it is a synonym of *soma,* the cocktail that gives the "gods" immortality.

Atman: The Soul's Immortal Pre-existence

Atman is the immortal quality of human existence and the very essence of every living thing; it is that divine, invisible substance that unites human immateriality with that of the divine, so there is no distinction between the immortal gods and the immortal soul of humans (Halligan 82). Perhaps this very practical and encouraging theory was referenced in the Psalms of the Hebrew Bible, as it is written: "I said, 'You are gods, and all of you are sons of the Most High. Nevertheless you will die like men, and fall like *any* one of the princes'" (82:6, 7). When accused of blasphemy, Jesus recounted this scripture in His own defense by stating: "Is it not written in your law, 'I said, you are gods'? If he called them gods to whom the word of God came (and scripture cannot be broken), do you say of him whom the Father consecrated and sent into the world, 'You are blaspheming,' because I said, 'I am the Son of God?'" (John 10: 34–36).

According to Hinduism, *Atman* is considered the very core of existence, that essential spirit that provides humans with a purpose to live; it is the true self within us that is considered divine. *Atman*, however, does not equate with the Western concept of the soul. Bansi Pandit explains: "In the Western view, the soul is created by God. In the Hindu view, the Atman, being eternal, is not created by God. It is a part of God ... this Atman is everlasting, omnipresent, unchangeable, immovable, and everlasting" (63). It is this *Atman* that makes all human beings equal because, after they die, they become immaterial and immortal, a decidedly democratic idea.

Swami Tyagananda further explains: "The Katha Upanishad (2.1.12) says: 'The Self (Atman) is difficult to see because it is lodged inaccessibly deep in the cave of the heart which is itself situated in the midst of misery.' The 'cave of the heart' is the spiritual heart and 'misery' refers to the body and the senses, which are the source of pain and suffering and the consequent misery" (187). Of the Atman, T. S. Saraswathi writes: "The concept of 'real self' in Hindu thought is the Atman, a nonmaterial or metaphysical self, as opposed to the material, experiential forms of the empirical self, involving sensations, desires, and thoughts" ("Hindu Worldview" 44). The *Upanishads* describe the human body as "foul-smelling and insubstantial," but the *Bhagavad Gita* describes it as the chosen vehicle of "the perpetual, imperishable and incomprehensible body-dweller" in which the *Atman* breathes and from which it radiates (qtd. in Maitra, "From Selfhood" 28). So, according to Hinduism, the physical body is a trap or a temporary prison that tests and instructs, and death prepares the *Atman* for its final release from any type of physical form.

In many religions and philosophical discussions, the soul is defined as an immaterial essence that is immortal and that connects to the divine while retaining the personality or particular characteristics of the person. Alternatively, Hinduism believes that these personality traits are temporary, and do not transfigure into the eternal Atman. Hindu's Atman refers to a particular essence of the human being, the self without ego or masque, the authentic spirit. Albahari quotes Karel Werner, that "No Indian school of thought has ever regarded the human soul or the carrier of human personal identity as a permanent substance." Albahari then concludes "That the Atman is not to be understood as a Cartesian thinking substance,[1] or eternal soul, or individual agent of cognitive acts..." (7). Hinduism's perception of the *Atman* is clearly distinct from Western ideas, as exemplified in the *Sixth Meditation* where Descartes tries to prove that his thinking mind and his extended body are distinct substances, and a human's essence and nature resides in an immaterial consciousness:

I then considered attentively what I was; and I saw that while I could feign that I had no body, that there was no world, and no place existed for me to be in, I could not feign that I was not; on the contrary, from the mere fact that I thought of doubting [*je pensais a douter*] about other truths it evidently and certainly followed that I existed. On the other hand, if I had merely ceased to be conscious, even if everything else that I had ever imagined had been true, I had no reason to believe that I should still have existed. From this I recognized that I was a substance whose whole essence and nature is to be conscious [*de penser*] and whose being requires no place and depends on no material thing. Thus this self [*moi*], that is to say the soul, by which I am what I am, is entirely distinct from the body, and is even more easily known; and even if the body were not there at all the soul would be just what it is [qtd. in Anscombe and Geach 32].

The self in Hinduism varies from being an eternal servant of god to being identified as god; Hindus believe the soul-self is eternal, so the eternal essence of god can inhabit temporary, corporeal, reincarnated human bodies (Flood, "Hindu Concepts"). So the *Atman*, or immaterial soul that enlivens humans, takes part in a human experience, but at death humans have a spiritual experience. When the soul disposes of the material body, it becomes endowed with a special consciousness, and eventually, after serving time in the underworld, assumes another form based upon the thoughts and actions of the self during material existence.

Hinduism propounds that the *Atman* or human soul was neither created nor can it be destroyed; like the concept of the eternal god, the individual soul has no beginning or end. Hindus believe that the soul controls the body; consequently, the soul will reap the aftermath of past actions when reincarnated into a new living form. The immaterial movement of the *Atman* from a past body to a new form is referred to as *transmigration*,[2] and the kind of living form the soul inhabits next is determined by *karma*, the deciding point that judges past actions from previous existences and determines the soul's future fate; karma is quite simply the moral law of cause and effect that is grounded in complete personal responsibility (Huston 48). Christian doctrine more than echoes this idea of cosmic, retributive reciprocity, as Galatians records: "Be not deceived; God is not mocked; for whatsoever a man soweth, that shall he also reap" (6:7); and "Judge not, that you should be judged. For with the judgment you pronounce you will be judged, and the measure you give will be the measure you get" (Mathew 7:1, 2) Of karma, Michaels explains: "The doctrine of karma is a theodicy, an explanation of the suffering and unjust earthly world as a result of previous acts, and an eschatology, a doctrine of liberation" (156; Kaufman, "Karma" 15). However, there is a strong differentiation in karmic meaning in Christian doctrine, as there is no belief in reincarnation; according to the New Testament: "And inasmuch as it is appointed unto men once to die, and after this cometh judgment" (Hebrews 9:27). The question remains, however, how long after this one death comes the judgment, and could it be possible that souls transmigrate during eons between the death of a person and the final resurrection and judgment? Hinduism says yes.

There are discrepancies in the New Testament, as Christian theorists have proposed that after death, judgment is immediate and souls are either sent to heaven, hell, or from the Catholic perspective, purgatory or limbo. But, there is the doctrine of resurrection from the dead, and this is the second judgment when human souls face their final destination, but has not this destination already been determined before resurrection at the moment of death? A series of crimes in a human's life and rejection of God will give you a ticket to the lake of fire or the second death, and no one want to die again in Christianity, so they reject the cyclic material births and deaths of reincarnation. However, the second death might be total extinction, a permanent nonexistence, as opposed to a conscious suffering in an eternal hell, which is, in all actuality, the telos of Hinduism. There are critics of the theory of transmigration who generally view it as a perceptions management technique to control people's minds through fear; they view these religious philosophies as offering an escape from the horrors of living on earth. Slater cites the anticleric Principal Fairbairn of Oxford: "...the dogma of transmigration grew up in an age of priestly tyranny and darkness ... transmigration did for the Eastern priesthood what purgatory did for the Western. It strengthened the authority of priest craft by means of terror" (qtd. in Slater 239). Henry Haigh wrote: "Whatever may have been the origin of the transmigration theory, it is undoubtedly an attempt to interpret suffering. The burden that oppresses the Hindu is not sin, but existence and its attendant miseries" (13).

Hinduism promotes the idea that the immortal *Atman* survives after the material body dies, and then enters a new material existence within a variety of species (Gibson 24). The goal is for everyone to achieve *moksha*, the deliverance from cycles of reincarnation (Majithi 231; Huston 50; "Moksha, Freedom"), and this event happens when the soul recognizes its true nature, and unites with Brahman, the divine intelligence, either through a path of duty, a path of knowledge, or a path of devotion. According to the *Bhagavad Gita*, death does not destroy the essence of a living being, but simply discards old bodies to take on new ones; this original essence can never be destroyed (Miller 32). One has then arrived at immortality (Kishore 40), but since there is no beginning to the soul, according to Hinduism, all existence is then immortal, so the only situation a soul needs is release from the *karma-sam-sara*, or the cycles of reincarnation, to achieve a state of nothingness. Elan Divon writes:

> In order to transcend the physical world, and experience a reunion with the Divine ... the Hindu tradition constructed four stages for the individual religious practitioner to assail.... Each of the four life stages prepares the seeker for the ultimate destination of human experience known as *moksha*, a condition which signifies a release from the shackles of the physical world and liberation from the endless cycles of suffering, samsara, and karmic debt [90].

Brahman: The Cosmic or Universal Soul

Unlike the personal god of the Abrahamic religions, Brahman is an impersonal entity (Gellman 110). Brahman has nothing to do with the anthropomorphic, male sky god of the Abrahamic religions, who is vengeful and selective about whom he loves. Brahman cannot be classified, and has no gender ascription. Huston Smith observes the eternal and divine buried in every human being in Hinduism: "Underlying the human self, and animating it, is a reservoir of being that never dies, is never exhausted, and is unrestricted in consciousness and in bliss. This infinite center of every life, this hidden self or Atman, is no less than Brahman, the Godhead" (22). Brahman is the chief god in Hinduism, and has many ascriptions that recall names for other gods in other religions; he is the creator, light of the universe, the ruler and the Lord with no beginning or end. Human souls and all of nature are the manifestation of Brahman. "The *Upanishads* describe Brahman as 'the eternal, conscious, irreducible, infinite, omnipresent, spiritual source of the universe of finiteness and change'" (qtd. in "Brahman").

Brahman created all things, and exists in all things; Brahman is the self or *Atman* of all living beings. Hinduism promotes Brahman as the cosmic soul and ultimate divine reality. Brahman is not an individual entity, but is considered as the reality of all existence (Gordon 149). *Atman* is equated with Brahman in that the individual soul is connected to the cosmic soul; we are created in Brahman's image and there is no distinction between us and the ultimate divine reality, so we and all living things are divine manifestations of a status, in which "in actuality, all people are essentially one and all people are one with the rest of the universe" (Oxtoby and Segal 283; Gordon, "The Interconnection" 149). Even though the human ego may sublimate the soul's divinity with jealousy or fear, or with other negative thoughts, emotions, and actions, its true divine self still exists.

While Hinduism is usually referred to as a polytheistic religion, Hindus actually claim a recognition of one God, Brahman, the eternal origin who is the cause and foundation of all existence. From ancient times, perceptions of God were inclined to believe in aspects of God's power; several religions identified aspects of a supreme god with the natural world and its cycles of death and creation. The many gods of the Hindu faith simply represent different expressions or manifestations of Brahman's triune power as creator, preserver (Vishnu), and destroyer (Shiva) (Oxtoby and Segal 290–291). This idea was later echoed in concepts of a Christian Trinity, which perceives different aspects of god, three beings in one; however, this further recollects the much earlier Egyptian notion of the trinity.

Richard A. Gabriel claims that no other contemporary religion but Christianity contains the idea of the Trinity, three gods in one, and that this idea originates from the Egyptian New Kingdom hymn to a trinity: "All gods are three: Amun, Re, and Ptah" (13). Osiris, Isis, and Horus are also the principal trinity of the Egyptian religions (Massey 544, 545). God the Father, Jesus the Son, and the Holy Spirit (not a female as in Egypt) are the Christian trinity. Thomas Inman also affirms the Egyptian roots of the Christian trinity, but is scathing in his theoretical assessment: "The Christian trinity is of Egyptian origin, and is as surely a pagan doctrine as the belief in heaven and hell, the existence of a devil, of archangels, angels, spirits and saints, martyrs and virgins, intercessors in heaven, gods and demigods, and other forms of faith, which deface the greater part of modern religions" (Inman 13). There are, however, inconsistencies in all religions, including Christianity, and Hinduism is no different. For example, although Brahman is professed not to be cast in human image, the *Upanishads* surprisingly poetically describe God in anthropomorphic terms as the supreme entity that is omnipresent and omniscient, a decidedly Christian notion:

> His hands and feet are everywhere; His eyes, heads, and faces are everywhere; His ears are everywhere; He exists compassing all. The heavens are His head; the sun and moon, His eyes; the quarters, His ears; the revealed Vedas, His speech; the wind is His breath; the universe, His heart. From His feet is produced the earth. He is, indeed, the inner Self of all beings [qtd. in Adiswarananda 92].

Discrepancies aside, the movement towards final unification with Brahman includes a cyclical experience during which souls transition and migrate into other living entities before *moksha* occurs. Most religions speak of an intermediary existence, somewhat like a Catholic purgatory, a holding place where a soul atones for sins, that is located between material life and the arrival at final bliss or union with god. Hindus represent this concept with reincarnation of the soul, a unique way to explain this transitional existence. Although this doctrine evades rational explanation and sound evidence, most religions propose some type of explanation for the time period and actions required to unite with the godhead and achieve immortality.

Reincarnation: The Long Voyage to Conditional Immortality

A belief in a cyclical reincarnation of the soul into some type of visible, living form is one of the cornerstones of Hinduism. Death is viewed as a natural aspect of life, and there are many epic tales and sacred texts that theorize the rationale for experiencing death, its required ceremonies, and the possible destinations for human souls. The future in Hinduism depends on a person's past, so a human being needs to achieve pure thoughts and loving actions to leave his or her existence permanently as an observable life form on earth; the soul's tactical objective is to overcome the necessity to return to earth in physical form ever again.

According to Hindu beliefs, the soul travels into many varied life forms until reaching *moksha*, the end and deliverance from cycles of reincarnation. The *Mahabharata* (540–300 BCE) claims that death did not always exist. Just as the Book of Genesis asserts that Adam and Eve were originally created as immortal beings, this Hindu epic about two related, warring families claims that there was a time on earth when all humans were immortal, but because they were human, they over-populated the land and caused chaos. Similarly, as in other religious literary traditions, there was a global holocaust; Brahma, the observer and creator god, "filled the heaven, the sky and the Earth all with fire," and Shiva begged him not to destroy all of creation (Buck 318– 320). The Hebrew Bible blames the woman Eve for mankind's downfall, and this epic has Brahma drawing fire into himself and creating a woman named Death. Brahma commands Death to "Kill all creatures including idiots and priests." Naturally the woman Death resisted his command, so Brahma decided that humans at death would simply meet her instead. Brahma declared, "I will make greed and anger and malice and shame and jealousy and passion." And since they will kill themselves with "disease and war," "only the foolish will weep over what none can avoid" (318–320). Clearly, the negative and destructive qualities of humans fated them to death, just as the presumed original sin brought mortality to humans.

Early Hindu texts include an Adam figure, but unlike the Hebrew Bible, this man becomes a Hindu god of the underworld, the ruler of the departed who determines retribution and directs souls to their next reincarnation. According to the earlier *Rig Veda* (1500 BCE), the first human to meet Death was King Yama, the first man who became god of the dead, who guaranteed that every good person would receive "admission to Yama's paradise and the everlasting enjoyment of all the heavenly pleasures, include the restoration of a sick body, the maintaining of family relations, and the highly desired apotheosis" (Holck 32; Dhavamony 273; Charran 21).[3] After dying, Yama directs souls to their destiny. According to Hopkins, "Yama was an aboriginal earthly king in an earthly paradise, in short, an Adam. He becomes a god in unearthly regions" (xcv; Bendann 167).

In order to meet Yama and for transmigration to occur, the material dead body must be burned during a cremation ceremony, one of the many prescribed *samskaras* or rituals to celebrate life events (Charran 22). For Hindus, only unnamed babies and the lowest castes are buried in the earth; apparently, their souls are condemned to an invisible earthly existence with no possibility of entrance to heaven. The cremation ritual releases the soul from its earthly existence based on the belief that the astral body will linger as long as the physical body remains visible. If the body is not cremated, "the soul remains nearby for days or months" (Charran 22; Kramer 39). To ensure the passage during the soul's voyage to the otherworld, an eleven-day ritual called *Shraddha* is performed (Jain 126); like the Egyptians, those left behind must provide a symbolic food offering (in this case, rice balls or pinda), so that the soul transitions to the heavens or Yama's realm (Parrinder 197). "On the twelfth day, the departed soul is said to reach its destination and be joined with its ancestors, a fact expressed symbolically by joining a small pinda to a much larger one" (Eck 341–42; Vidyarthi 34).

The *Shraddha* is the point of meeting between the living and the dead, and the expression of their interdependence; the ghosts of the departed are believed to visit misfortune on their descendants who do not execute these offerings or secure their passage to their proper realm (Parrinder 197; Jagannathan 47). Those judged morally worthy are sent to a heavenly realm, a type of holding pen like the Catholic purgatory, where they wait to be born into royalty.

VOYAGE FROM ILLUSIONS TO A TEMPORARY HELL

Various religious leaders have used the idea of heaven and hell to entice or frighten people into certain beliefs and behaviors as a means of political or social control. Fear is the most effective weapon in capturing minds and souls. Like other religions, Hinduism promotes the idea that our actions have consequences in this life and future lives; there are universal laws that dictate the reciprocity of behavior in this life, and there are universally held beliefs in the effects of behaviors in the next. These shared beliefs with other religions are all premised on written texts, oral traditions, and faith in what is not seen. The Hindu *Upanishads* (800–400 BCE), philosophical portions of the Vedas, expound on beliefs about the self and afterlife. According to the *Upanishads*, the world is an illusion, and human actions and perceptions respond to this illusion (Paliwal 29; Samples 240; Haught 38).

Brij Lal Shahi writes: "Maya, a Sanskrit word meaning illusion, is a meta-physical concept, which affirms, that all the experiences of whatever nature, in the life of an individual without an exception are illusory" (16). It would be logical to assume that humans are then somewhat not responsible for their actions and behaviors, for they are authentically reacting in a natural way to the provocative illusions of the world—it is just the way they are. So, why would the *Atman* have to be continually provoked by these illusions, and be mandated to repetitively reincarnate if it were an extension of Brahman, the god source? That truly seems like a hellish idea, and that is why Hindus desire to experience moksha and be delivered into nothingness—the nothingness of a deep sleep—a sophisticated concept that responds to the poverty and abysmal lives ancient peoples had to live.

According to Hinduism, Brahman is the supreme existence or ultimate reality in all things that exceed our material, sensory experiences (Brodd 43; Sharma 2; Krishnamoorthy 179). Ignorance of Brahman and deliberate evil actions trigger the incidence of cycles of death and rebirth, but when the soul or spirit realizes that it is Brahman itself, it is delivered from evil and attains *moksha*. Part of *moksha* includes the recognition that the material world holds no value and is the source of all evil (Rinehart 159; Gandhi 127). The constantly changing nature of the material or physical world reveals there is no reality or true substance in what is perceived, but what humans perceive as reality begins to exist only when they actively encounter it with their presence, and react accordingly for good or for evil using free will. Thus, the world we perceive is simply a personal creation.

Hindus believe that the concept of an eternal heaven or hell is illogical, and runs in antithesis to the natural laws of the universe because an eternal result cannot be the product of a finite, transient action. No actions in life have eternal ramifications, and only result in a limited sphere of time during material incarnations (Jacobsen 386). Bansi Pandit writes: "There is no thought of eternal hell in Hindu scriptures. According to Hindu views, love is neither an attribute nor the quality of god. Love is god, and god is love. Love cannot bear to see anyone suffer and, therefore, Hindus believe that eternal hell is an unsound concept" (115). Hindus trust in a loving god who would never condemn any person to an eternal hell, as god would be a tormentor and undeserving of devotion (Bahadur 131). According to Hinduism, sinners have opportunity to redeem themselves, and have another shot at a new material existence. People who have committed bad deeds and accumulated negative karma are sent to a temporary hell to purify their souls; this hell is a place of sorrow and time spent there depends on the gravity of one's actions while in the previous material body (Achuthananda 95; Sharma 191; "Religious Comparisons" 43; Sheler, "Other Faiths" 64). After purification, the soul transmigrates into another incarnation that could be human or animal.

For Hindus both heaven and hell are not, however, the ultimate goal: "...it can only be a prelude to a better incarnation which will bring a man nearer to final liberation" (Sharma 192). The crossing of Hinduism's moral boundaries results in different types of temporary hells (Firth 44; Bonazzoli 174); the type of hell Hindus receive for breaking the boundaries depends on either their social class or the type of immoral actions they engaged in while alive. Upper caste Brahmins who lie or murder cows are sent to what is referred to as the "Terrible" hell. Adulterers, fornicators, and land thieves must endure a shallow pit filled with hot coals that is a temporary purification of sins until they are released into a different hell designed to further purify (Doniger-O'Flaherty 117–18). J.L. Sheler describes fanciful notions of the Hindu hell and the types of reincarnated, material entities that souls may experience after leaving hell's temporary abode:

> In Hinduism, with its belief in reincarnation, hell is merely one stage in the career of a soul as it passes from one life to the next. Unlike the hells of Christianity and Islam, the Hindu hells—there are 21 of them in all—are temporary abodes where bad karma, the evil that one commits during a lifetime, is burned away. Once purged, the soul is recycled to a higher state in the next life. In the hierarchy of Hindu hells, some are more unpleasant than others. As spelled out in ancient writings called the Puranas, the soul whose karma is not so bad may simply be reborn as an animal. Stealers of meat, for example, may return as vultures, and thieves of grain may be reborn as rats. Worse sinners may come back as grasses, shrubs or other inanimate objects. The very wicked face condemnation to the lower hells where they may be scorched in hot sand, boiled in jars or devoured by ravens. There is no Judgment Day in Hinduism [64].

After the *Atman* or spirit escapes torment in the Underworld, it is reborn into a life where it resumes its life lessons. After many incarnations as animals, as handicapped, or lower caste people, and after the soul is filled with excellence, then the person begins to climb socially, eventually reaching the stage of Brahman (Doniger-O'Flaherty 120). Those who lead a life of kindness, self-denial, and meditation and grace can look forward to the possibility of reaching *Brahmaloka*, the world of Brahma, the creator, from which there is no return to mortality (Bryant 643). According to Nikhilananda, "This is a place of intensely spiritual atmosphere, whose inhabitants live free from disease, old age, and death, enjoying uninterrupted bliss in the companionship of the Deity." There is no need for them to return to earth because they have freed themselves "from all material desires," and experience oneness with Brahma (34). For Hindus, immortality is not desirable, but they believe in reincarnation as a process that eventually leads to reunion with the infinite that achieves a state of nothingness.

Drinking and Eating Immortality

Hallucinogenic drugs have been a major part in the development of some religions; the study of this issue is known as the *entheogen* theory, which analyzes the use of psychoactive substances for religious or spiritual reasons, and the rituals involved with drugs to facilitate ecstatic, religious experiences. There appears to be correlations between neurochemical activities in our brains and various experiences, sacred or secular (Richards 380). Users believe that they experience a more primal and unmediated spirituality than those not using them, but, in reality, they are basing their experience on the material plant world and the effects of its ingestion within the physical body. Frederick R. Dannaway writes: "A very logical method of investigation would be to note the effects of burning a plant to judge its smoke in terms of aromatic and magical (psychoactive) qualities, noting more toxic examples whose inhalation could be lethal. A plant's effects on the mind and body would be remembered and enshrined as holy, or as containing a god or the means of communicating with the spirits" (486). As Carl Jung observed: "The peculiar nature of introverted intuition, if it gains the ascendancy, produces a particular type of man: the mystical dreamer and seer on the one hand, the artist and the crank on the other" (qtd. in Rush 531). Moreover, if all mortal life is an illusion, then the mental introversion that accompanies drug experiences must be an illusion as well, and a product of the unconquerable ego.

The idea that psychotropic drugs can deliver a spiritual experience is hardly a novel one, and there has been a great deal of speculation concerning the actual identity of drugs used for religious purposes in the ancient world. For example, in ancient Greece there was nepenthe, the "drug of forgetfulness," mentioned in *The Odyssey*, that Helen had used to comfort her guests when they were distraught over the protracted absence of Odysseus: "Then Helen, daughter of Zeus, took other counsel. Straightaway she cast into the wine of which they were drinking a drug to quiet all pain and strife, and bring forgetfulness of every ill" (*Odyssey*, Book 4, v. 219–22). Walter Sneader reminds the reader that Helen had learned of these drugs while in Egypt, and that the most likely candidates for the drug were opium or marijuana (18; D. Brown 6). Sneader also repeats the postulation that nepenthe could have been a fanciful creation or simply an allusion to Helen's many physical charms (18).

Drugs and the ingestion of some type of plant appeared all over the ancient world: Gilgamesh searched for the plant of immortality; the connecting aspect of religious drugs in India to other ancient cultures is that Hindus searched for the power to be a god in a plant called *soma*. The *Rig Veda* describes the drug *soma* as a god, a plant, and a beverage extracted or pressed from the plant; if ingested its effects are described as intoxicating or inspiring (Staal, "How a Psychoactive" 745, 752). Hinduism specifies the drugs *soma* and *amrita* were reportedly used by the gods in the ancient Vedas; people who knew the identity of the plant *soma* could use it to become inspired, and to pray or commune more successfully with the gods. In Hindu ancient writings, *soma* is described as a plant that could produce a drink or potion that was consumed by the gods, giving them fantastic powers, and aiding them in their supernatural feats.

Soma was also considered a god, and the ingestion could transform mortals into gods ("Soma, the Rishis"; Elizarenkova, "About the Status" 214). The *Rig Veda* describes the quasireligious and hallucinatory effects of the drug: "We have drunk Soma and become immortal; we have attained the light, the Gods discovered. Now what may foeman's malice do to harm us? What, O Immortal, mortal man's deception?" (qtd. in Bansal 10). Or: "Heaven above does not equal one half of me. Have I been drinking Soma? In my glory I have passed beyond earth and sky. Have I been drinking Soma? I will pick up the earth and put it here or there. Have I been drinking Soma?" (*Rig Veda* X, 119:7–9).

SOMA: HALLUCINATIONS AND A MOMENT OF IMMORTALITY

There is an abundance of speculation regarding the *soma* plant's identity.[4] There were suggestions that it was ephedra, opium, or cannabis; others believed it was a reed grown in water or sugar cane. However, Gordon Wasson theorized that it was *Amanita muscaria*, a large mushroom, and according to Wasson, the soma drink came in two forms: the juice from the plants or the urine of the person who drank it (Ruck 161; Doniger 122; Staal, "How a Psychoactive" 760). There are numerous details provided in the *Rig Veda* suggesting how *soma* was prepared and used, and indicating that Amanita muscaria was the true source of the drug (Ruck 161) (see **figure 4**). Paul M. Gahlinger writes: "Amanita was identified as the Soma of ancient India, and some scholars believe that the worship of this mushroom was the origin of the Christmas tree…. This mushroom contains muscimol, ibotenic acid, and muscarine, which led to the discovery of neurotransmitters" (178). This psychoactive mushroom was chewed, mixed with food, or made into a tea, and created hallucinations (178). The psychedelic properties of the mushroom are also said to have given courage to the Vikings before they went to battle (Kuo and Methven 9).

The drinkable, Immortal, living god Soma is cited in the Hymns of the *Rig Veda* as the preferred drink of both gods and men (Wilson 233), but there is no mention of any human becoming immortal by drinking of its properties.

AGARICUS (AMANITA) MUSCARIUS

Figure 4 Amanita Muscaria. Amanita Muscaria, or the magic mushroom, is considered to be the source of the Soma drink. It is likely that the ingestion of the liquid derived from this "sacred mushroom" caused the mind to believe it was one with the immortal gods, so it was a delusion (Auguste Faguet, Amanita Muscaria).

There are 114 sacred hymns specifically about Soma in book nine of the *Rig Veda* composed by Soma-intoxicated "Seers and Sages" (Teeter, "Amanita Muscaria"). Many of these Soma hymns ring with ecstatic praise of the *soma* plant/god/drink. Some of the hymns are poems describing the red or gold look of the *soma* plant in its mountainous environment (Teeter 17). Other hymns detail the process of making the *soma* plant into the *soma* drink, and a few Hymns refer to healings and to the increased life spans of *soma* users (Teeter 19). In the ancient past, *soma* played an important part in ceremonial worship, and was used as an offering and then drunk by the priests. Prayers were offered to the god Soma for healings and material wealth, as shown in the following verses from the *Rig Veda*:

> For thee, O Lord of Light, are shed these Soma-drops, and grass is strewn. Bring Indra to his worshippers. May Indra give thee skill, and lights of heaven, wealth to his votary. And priests who praise him: laud ye him [*RV* 8.82.25].

The belief was that when humans drank this elixir of the gods, they would experience a feeling of immortality, a deeper understanding, and a more heightened connection to the immortal gods. According to Wendy Doniger, Hindu poets drank *soma* for a feeling of exhilaration or ecstasy before writing the *soma* hymns (123). At the same time, the following verse from the *Rig Veda* also implies that mortality may be a deception; after all, Hindus believed that all interaction with material existence is an illusion, and that human souls are already immortal, and all destined for union with god after achieving *moksha*:

> We have drunk Soma and become immortal;
> We have gone to the light; We have found the gods.
> What can hatred or the malice of a mortal do to us now? [8.48.3; 123].

Amrita: Another Type of Ambrosia

The terms *soma* and *amrita* have been generally conflated in meaning, but *amrita* holds connotations other than a plant for food or drink (Williams 53). There are many other references to *amrita* across Hindu, Zoroastrian, and Indo-European texts; ambrosia, the food of immortality of the Greek gods, is analogous with *amrita*. They come from the same Indo-European root, *n-mr-to*, roughly translated as *non-death*. Similarly, the Greek drink of the gods, nectar (Nektar), literally translates to achieving immortality: Death (*Nek*) Overcoming (*Tar*) (Appel, "5 Ancient Legends"). There are startling Yogic claims that the human body is a capable source of *amrita* during deep meditation. Mark Rogers states: "In yogic philosophy, Amrita is a fluid that can flow from the pituitary gland down the throat in deep states of meditation. It is considered quite a boon: some yogic texts say that one drop is enough to conquer death and achieve immortality" (26; Quinn 25).[5] So, *amrita* is considered to be the liquid secreted while in ecstasy during a divine encounter, or when a human assimilates with god; *amrita* can also manifest while having such an experience during meditation, and is the substance that carries the soul to a special state of consciousness.

According to Hindu texts, *amrita* began in the chaos of creation, and was invented as a cosmic immortality drink when the gods or *devas* agitated the Ocean of Milk (Milky Way) with a serpent for a thousand years (Bentley 19; Quinn 25). Afterwards, the gods collected the cream to give them immortal life, but the gods forbade humans to eat of this cream. *Amrita* features in this galactic, ocean-churning Hindu legend that describes how a mad or crazed mystic cursed the gods, and they lost their immortality (Quinn 25; Krupp 46, 47). Assisted by their mortal enemies, the *Asuras*,[6,7] they churned a great ocean to create the wondrous *amrita*, the nectar of immortality. The *Asuras* are powerful evil beings; they are referred to in translations as demons or giants and in other cases as gods or as enemies of the devas[8] (Wilkins 437). Hindu legends say those who drank of *amrita* literally could not die, and Madame Blavatsky concurs: "The ambrosial drink or food of the Gods; the food which gives immortality. The elixir of life churned out of the ocean of milk in the Puranic allegory. An old vedic term applied to the sacred Soma juice in the Temple Mysteries" (Blavatsky 20).

> Narada said,
> Salutations to thee, O God of gods ... who is Amrita (nectar),
> Who is called Immortal... [Vyasa 761].

Mystic sustenance is spoken of throughout scriptures in all the world's great religions. In Judeo-Christianity, it is called manna, milk and honey, living water (Exodus 16:31; Judges 15:9; Psalms 36:8), and in the East it is referred to as ambrosia, *soma*, *amrita*, or the divine food of the gods. However, the *soma* and *amrita* of Hinduism's concept of immortality differs greatly in function from the Greek and later Christian doctrines of immortality in relation to a specific food or drink. The Greek's ambrosia was strictly reserved for gods and demigods, and anyone who tried to steal ambrosia and give it to mortals was punished severely; for example, the mythical Greek demigod Tantalus was punished by the gods, and whatever he tried to drink evaporated and whatever he tried to eat disappeared (Shoham 69). In Christianity, it is the Eucharist or Host and the wine representing the body and blood of Jesus Christ that promises the faithful immortality after death and resurrection, if they partake in the communion ritual and believe in the doctrine of transubstantiation. While these ideas differed, it is possible that Hinduism influenced the ideas of a material substance that could be consumed allowing a person to live forever. Of course, the earliest Sumerian versions of *The Epic of Gilgamesh* date from as early as the Third Dynasty of Ur (2150–2000 BCE), and the earliest Akkadian renditions date to the early second millennium (Segal 83), so this is likely the first text and archetypal story to speak of a physical substance that grants immortality, as Gilgamesh sought and found the plant of immortality in the sea.

Liberation from Existence and Immortality

There is a type of immortality in Hinduism, but ironically immortality is not the goal of the Hindu soul; reincarnation becomes a type of physical immortality, but ends with *moksha* when the soul unites with the godhead from which it came, and in which it is simply a divine aspect. The actual goal of Hinduism is to attain a state of nothingness. The difference between the claims of Christianity and Hinduism are irreconcilable, as Christians believe they live on as themselves in fellowship with God, while Hindus are absorbed into the supreme godhead and have no personal identity within this absorption (Steinkraus and Mitias 186). Hinduism does have a more realistic outlook and acceptance of life's impermanence, and, certainly, Hinduism's no-permanent-hell doctrine is appealing to those indoctrinated in the fear of eternal torture. The question remains, however, is this state of nothingness after *moksha* a type of immortality? After all, if a supreme deity exists, and the soul is absorbed into and becomes a permanent part of this supreme deity or ultimate reality called Brahman, then a brand of immortality does exist after all. If Brahman causes the universe and all beings to emanate from itself, then it is a type of existence that cannot be denied, as Brahman is the creator, preserver, or transformer and re-absorber of everything. Hindus view God as All in All; if the goal of human existence is to lose the self, transcend the material world, and become one with God, then how can there be nonexistence if Brahman is acknowledged to exist as the ultimate reality?

As there are no specific data that inform readers about how, why, and by whom pre–Hindu and Hindu beliefs originated, there is no proof authenticating the accuracy of these beliefs. Subjective experience is the analytic means by which Hindus understand the truth of their religious views, but if all life experience is an illusion, then how could an individual attain *moksha* based upon the illusory nature of material existence? Hinduism's unknown origins in 1500 BCE, its dependence upon subjective experience, and its lack of unbiased and verifiable evidence make it difficult to accept the claim that the ultimate goal of being is not immortality but, ironically, a state of nonexistence.

5

Judaism: Questioning
the Essence of Immortality

If a man dies, will he live again? (Job 14:14)

An attempt to tie threads of Hinduism into the Hebrew Bible's belief system yields surprising connections: afterlife rewards and punishments, ideas of *moksha* and nirvana, and human life as a divine emanation are similar; however, these universal ideas appear to be active in almost every religious system of thought since ancient Sumer. As a distinct system, Judaism is the foundational Abrahamic religion for the later Christianity and Islam; Christianity began as an offshoot sect of Judaism with the original followers meeting in synagogues, and Islam merged ideas from Judaism, Christianity, and local, cultural conventions to create a new, monotheistic faith. Judaism begins with the great Patriarch Abraham circa 2000 BCE, but does not become an official religious system of laws until the Exodus under Moses in 1290 BCE.

The study of immortality, the afterlife, the human soul, and corporeal resurrection in Judaism is complex, as these issues evolved during various historical eras, and were further complicated with philosophical and supplemental teachings and interpretations at later intervals. The concept of an immortal soul distinct from the corporeal body did not exist in Judaism before the Babylonian Exile (598–596 BCE), but later developed as a result of interaction with other philosophies and religious influences, particularly those from Egypt and Greece, and from the culture in which they found themselves in exile. Jewish adherents generally embraced the idea that condemned souls would be annihilated, but there was no such event as eternal punishment in a place like hell, which had been earlier conceptualized by the Egyptians and the Greeks; as C.W. Emmet writes in his classic book on immortality: "Egyptian religion ... had developed its view of the weighing of the soul and of judgment after death; the condemned, however, were destroyed, and not punished indefinitely. The Greeks had their well-known myths of tortures in Hades, and theories of future punishments were carried further in the Orphic Mysteries ... the Olympian religion was too easy going to believe in eternal punishment" (qtd. in Streeter, Emmet, and Hadfield 183–184).

L. Arik Greenberg includes a valuable statement from T.F. Glasson regarding the Jews' rejection of Orphism,[1] but their acceptance of retribution and immortality: "The Jews did not accept the doctrine of repeated reincar-nation and a succession of earthly lives, nor did they regard the body as a prison-house. But some of them accepted the doctrines of punishments and rewards under the ground; while others held to the immortality of the human soul. One is as Greek as the other" (qtd. in Greenberg 34).[2] The Jewish idea that human actions during lifetime would be judged by higher, supernatural authorities after death also found its roots in Egypt, as the famous British Egyptologist, Sir Ernest Alfred Wallis Budge, affirms: "The belief that the deeds done while in the body would be subjected to analysis by the divine powers after death belongs to the earliest period of Egyptian civilization" (Budge 110). Richard E. Wilde insists on the Greek influence on later Jewish texts; he writes: "Some Greek philosophy can be found in the *Wisdom of Solomon*, a book of the *Apocrypha* written in 150 BCE, where the ideas of cre-ation and of immortality and the afterlife are strictly Platonic" (128).

Judaism has traditionally supported faith in an afterlife, but the charac-teristics that this belief has adopted, and the ways in which this faith has been expressed, have fluctuated from era to era. Immortality concepts are articulated in the Hebrew Bible, in the eschatological literature of the Sad-ducees, Pharisees, and Essenes (530 BCE to 70 CE), in the Talmud (200 to 500 CE), in the *Midrash* of the Post-Temple era (400 to 1500 CE), in Kabalistic lit-erature (1200 -1300 CE), and in current Jewish theology. During the fifth cen-tury BCE, Greek doctrines inspired Jewish theories of the soul's immortality, and by the first century CE, Jewish theologians largely concurred that the soul did not expire when the body died. Pharisees and Sadducees, however, vehe-mently argued this issue. The Pharisees imagined a physical resurrection when humans would re-animate for eternity; by contrast, the Sadducees rejected the idea of corporeal resurrection, opting only for the existence of an immortal soul. Jewish sects generally accept some type of eternal afterlife for the human soul, but the varied sects of Judaism still dispute the nature of this afterlife. Contemporary Jewish theologians mostly concur regarding an immortal soul, but factions continue to conflict on corporeal resurrection with the exception of Orthodox Jews. Egyptian and Greek teachings clearly influenced the development of Jewish thought regarding immortality, and these same teachings later influenced Christian and contemporary secular attitudes towards death.

The Hebrew Bible: Interpretations of She'ol and the Rapture Theory

Jewish belief in an afterlife grew via cultural and historical events within what is known as the Hebrew Bible,[3] but these scriptures are ambiguous regarding the destiny of a person after death. According to Hebrew scriptures, the dead go down to She'ol, a kind of Hades, where they live a ghostly existence (Numbers 16:33; Psalms 6:5; Isaiah 38:18); however, She'ol was neither a place of punishment nor was it a place where any type of individual existence continued. The concept of She'ol became a partitioned abode: it was at times considered an intermediate abode for the departed whence all of Israel would be resurrected, but it also became a type of hell where souls were destroyed. One of the very oldest concepts of She'ol denoted merely an earthly burial place, but Elizear Segal definitively states that an old meaning of She'ol as a literal grave or hole in the ground is not accurate: "When we examine actual passages in which the word *she'ol* appears, we find few, if any, that cannot plausibly be understood simply as 'pit' or (by extension) 'grave,' which became a figurative equivalent of death" (qtd. in Coward 14).

Shaul Bar questions whether both the righteous and the wicked descend to the same place, as some Jewish scholars believe that all human beings descend to She'ol, while others believe it is reserved only for the wicked. For example, "Heidel writes that 'there is no passage which proves that Sheol was ever employed as a designation for the gathering place of the departed spir¬its of the godly'" (Bar, "Grave Matters" 147; Heidel 86). The Hebrew Bible and the New Testament views of the afterlife are distinctive and contradictory, for in the Hebrew Bible both the good and the bad are destined for She'ol, but in later Jewish texts and Christian scriptures, the righteous and the unrighteous are destined for separate places (Johnston 16). These interpretative discrepancies of final afterlife locations continued in Christianity (with purgatory and limbo) with ambiguous and confusing meanings: do souls go to hell directly after death, or do they simply wait for the final hell or "Lake of Fire" that reportedly occurs after resurrection from the dead and final judgment?

Interpretative disagreements and creative theories continued within later factions of Christianity; for example, there are fantastic stories in the Hebrew Bible that directly influenced certain Christian sects' belief in the Rapture theory, when believers will be caught up alive to heaven before tribulation and the apocalypse. These Christian beliefs are based upon the reported "taking up" of Enoch and Elijah, and on Paul's description of the Great Harvest. The Hebrew Bible chronicles that it is possible for a living body to be brought up to heaven, as it is written that Enoch "walked with God, and he was not;

for God took him" (Genesis 5:24), and that Elijah was carried heavenward in a chariot of fire (II Kings 2:11):

> Then Elijah took his mantle, and rolled it up, and struck the water, and the water was parted to the one side and to the other, till the two of them could go over on dry ground. When they had crossed, Elijah said to Elisha, "Ask what I shall do for you, before I am taken from you." And Elisha said, "I pray you, let me inherit a double share of your spirit." And he said, "You have asked a hard thing; yet, if you see me as I am being taken from you, it shall be so for you; but if you do not see me, it shall not be so." And as they still went on and talked, behold, a chariot of fire and horses of fire separated the two of them. And Elijah went up by a whirlwind into heaven. And Elisha saw it and he cried, "My father, my father! the chariots of Israel and its horsemen!" And he saw him no more [2 Kings 2:8–12].

Are these fanciful stories from ancient writings, or are they meant to provide clues about the nature of the relationship between God and human beings? These "chariots" are also described as a supernatural air force that protected Elisha and his servant from being killed by the King of Syria's army, and which struck the King's infantry with blindness (2 Kings 6: 11–19). Elisha, who inherited the mantle of Elijah, was able to relay everything the King of Syria said in private; when the Syrian King became aware of Elisha's abilities, he became a wanted man. These biblical verses are filled with high drama, but they provided assurance to the Hebrews that God would always protect Israel.

Second Temple Literature: She'ol, Resurrection and Immortality Evolve

Changes in Jewish belief in an afterlife were a result of the miseries inflicted on the Hebrews during the Babylonian invasion in the early part of the sixth century BCE, the destruction of the Temple of Solomon, the exile in Babylon, and their subsequent homecoming to Israel. These events dramatically altered earthly karmic concepts of rewards, punishments, and justice, and influenced the idea that justice would only be rendered by God after death within the framework of an afterlife. As Simcha P. Raphael explains: "These socio-political circumstances were reflected in a radically transformed conception of the postmortem underworld. What surfaced at this time was a philosophical notion envisioning chastisement, even decimation, of Israel's enemies in Sheol.... Sheol came to be seen as a place of punishment for the enemies of YHWH and of Israel" (60). This spirit of hopeful revenge was born of sorrows suffered in defeat, so it was natural to think that YHWH had abandoned them while living, but there would be a new world of the dead where justice would be rendered. George Mendenhall writes,

If God could not be relied on to render blessings and curses within the framework of mortal existence, how, then, could God be regarded as a source of justice and righteousness?... The paradox ultimately was resolved by projecting the realization of the divine rewards and punishments to a dimension other than that of normal earthly experience and history [qtd. in Obayashi 78].

Jewish thinkers had begun to question God's active role in people's lives, but this thinking was dangerous, as people could question God's existence, and that would be unacceptable. Thus, the most rational avenue of thought was to make God an invisible force who would judge the enemies of Israel. You could not see God's army, but it could kill you. Whether or not these scriptures were written as propagandistic ventures to ward off Israel's enemies, or whether it is a factual account, the stories are epic accounts of human relationships with God.

There have been other controversies and theories in Judaism, and foremost among them is corporeal resurrection; many later Jewish scholars and sects rejected the doctrine of resurrection from the dead based upon Hebrew Scriptures. For example, in the story of Adam's expulsion from the Garden of Eden for eating from the tree of the knowledge of good and evil, Genesis 3:19 reads: "In the sweat of your face you shall eat bread till you return to the ground, for out of it you were taken; you are dust, and to dust you shall return." This passage reveals a harsh punishment on humans who are seen as dirt, and death is final, absolute, and irrevocable, so there is no afterlife. George Mendenhall validates the claim that there is no afterlife when he writes, "Most of the scholarly world agrees that there is no concept of immortality or life after death in the Old Testament" (qtd. in Obayashi 68). There are biblical references that do, however, speak of the spirit [or soul] of a human reuniting with God. In a startling manner, where there is also no hint of resurrection, the third-century BCE Book of Ecclesiastes 12:7 suggests a sort of polarity between the body's decay and an indwelling spirit that almost references the Hindu concept of *moksha* and nirvana, when the material body ceases to exist and the spirit reunites with the Creator; the Teacher in Ecclesiastes writes, "The dust returns to the earth as it was, and the spirit returns to God who gave it."

In opposition to these ideas, the Hebrew Bible actually provides a clear statement on the controversial resurrection subject, but does not mention what happens between death and the resurrection. In the second-century BCE Book of Daniel, the scripture states: "And many of those who sleep in the dust of the earth shall awake, some to everlasting life, and some to shame and everlasting contempt" (12:2). The Book of Isaiah (800 BCE) also records: "Thy dead shall live, their bodies shall rise" (26:19), and, during his exile in Babylon, the sixth-century BCE prophet Ezekiel dramatically writes about the quickening of the dead in the valley of dry bones:

And he said to me, "Can these bones live?" And I answered, "O God, thou knowest." Again he said to me, "Prophesy to these bones, and say to them, O dry bones, hear the word of the Lord.... Behold I will cause breath to enter you, and you shall live. And I will lay sinews upon you, and will cause flesh to come upon you, and cover you with skin, and put breath in you, and you shall live; and you shall know that I am the Lord" [37:3–6].

Second Temple Judaism (520 BCE to 70 CE), was an era in which Persian and Hellenistic ideas influenced Judaism, and ended with the destruction of the Temple; evolving ideas of the afterlife and corporeal resurrection were Persian, and the philosophy of the soul was Hellenistic (Wilde 128). Some scholars dispute the idea of any Persian influence, but according to Clifford and Johnson, "…resurrection of the dead is unknown in pre-exilic times and emerges late in Israel's history" (258). Hellenistic influences at this time, however, are less controversial because they influenced Jews to think about the here and now, and replace gloomy, supernatural hypotheses with a practical outlook on life based upon knowledge of the Torah.

Jews took a clue from Aristotle who believed that happiness is the objective of human life; one of Aristotle's most significant texts is the *Nicomachean Ethics*, in which he asks, "What is the ultimate purpose of human existence?" Aristotle believed that in order to be happy and live a meaningful life, a person must only choose that which is desirable in itself—nothing else should matter.[4] Aristotle proposed that human beings could be happy, virtuous, and wealthy during their entire lives.[5] According to Aristotle, desirable choices that lead to happiness are: health, wealth, virtue, knowledge, and friends, as all improve and perfect the human condition. This analysis of happiness is evident in Jewish texts, particularly in those written during the Middle Ages by Moses Maimonides discussed later in this chapter. Judaism fully embraced the rational thought that the requisite path to follow to thrive as a human being was inseparable from the relationship with God as revealed in the Torah. Psalms 1, 19, and 119 make it clear that the study of God's Torah alone creates the life in which humans can best thrive and be happy (see Appendix).

The concept of resurrection from the dead in Jewish thinking did not fully emerge until the second-century BCE; definite references to corporeal resurrection are found in I and II Maccabees and the Book of Daniel. In the eschatology of the apocryphal literature of the Second Temple period, Judaic thinking centered on a divine immortality and resurrection from the dead for all of righteous Israel, but immortality and resurrection concepts competed for attention. The Hellenistic IV Maccabees, guarantees eternal life to Jewish martyrs, but never mentions resurrection from the dead (Hogeterp 87). II Maccabees, however, places significance on resurrection (and damnation for their enemies), but some of these verses are wishful thinking in the light of Jewish persecution; for example, II Maccabees 7:14 declares:

After he had died, the soldiers tortured the fourth one in the same cruel way, but his final words were, "I am glad to die at your hands, because we have the assurance that God will raise us from death. But there will be no resurrection to life for you, Antiochus!" [II Maccabees 7:14].[6]

Aware they had drifted from God's laws in the Torah (the basis of their salvation), II Maccabees 7:23 provides assurance that not only will the souls of their enemies be punished and annihilated after dying, but Jews will be forgiven for backsliding, and raised from the dead: "Therefore the Creator of the world, who shaped the beginning of man and devised the origin of all things, will in his mercy give life and breath back to you again, since you now forget yourselves for the sake of his laws." Suffering under foreign oppression, Israel was weak in resources but strong in psychological retribution for their oppressors after death; there was no other logical recourse than to construct an afterlife where only Jews would be resurrected from the dead. Simca Paul Raphael considers that specific sociohistorical conditions led to Jews' embracing resurrection theories; he writes: "Second Maccabees, chapters 6–7, and an early text dating from circa 100 to 40 BCE, speaks of resurrection. The emphasis here is clearly on resurrection only for the Israelite ... interestingly enough, it is likely that the Maccabean Revolt of 167 BCE was the historical context that led to the rapid emergence of concept of resurrection" (110). This same resurrection doctrine later becomes a vital component of the canon of later Christianity.

During the Second Temple Period, resurrection theories also evolved when apocalyptic literature appeared in the *Apocrypha* and the *Pseudepigrapha*, which both contain many references to the resurrection. The *Pseudepigrapha* was a collection of pseudonymous Jewish writings ascribed to various biblical patriarchs and prophets, and written within a 400 year period between 300 BCE and 100 CE. The *Apocrypha* were written in the early Christian era, but neither collection were considered canonical scripture but rather part of a literary form that flourished from 200 BCE to 100 CE. The Jews of Palestine suffered during this historical period under the rule of the Greeks and later of the Romans, so the apocalyptists wrote in visionary and prophetic terms. Jeff S. Anderson writes: "The reason for such an interest in resurrection may have been due to the marginalization of the Jews by other nations during this period. Belief in resurrection may have provided the only real hope for Jewry in dire circumstances" (193). These apocalyptic texts, written during the Second Temple Period and ending around 100 CE, became part of Christian doctrine, and many Christian sects today rely on the terror of Revelation's imagery and the fear of final judgment as a recruitment tool.

While the belief in resurrection was a prime concern, the focus of the apocryphal books was also directed at the immortality of the human soul.

The influence of Hellenistic dualism on Jewish thinking about the individual and death during the Second Temple period did not extend to a general adoption of a Platonic belief in the immortality of the soul. Resurrection beliefs at this time did not emphasize the soul, or the reunification of the soul with the body, but underscored the actual risen body of the person; however, this vein of thinking would also evolve. Richard Bauckham, in his book *The Fate of the Dead: Studies on the Jewish and Christian Apocalypses,* addresses the thinking of this period regarding this topic:

> Since death was not conceived as the separation of the person from his or her body but as the death of the bodily person, so resurrection was not the reunion of person and body, but the resurrection of the bodily person. The notion is not the resurrection of the body so much as the bodily resurrection of the person ... older ways of thinking and speaking of resurrection, simply as the return of the dead from She'ol, persisted alongside newer, dualistic ideas of a reunion of soul and body [275, 276].[7,8]

SADDUCEES, PHARISEES, ESSENES: VARIED VIEWS OF THE AFTERLIFE

During the time of Jesus of Nazareth there were three different sects of Judaism with varied views of the afterlife. The Sadducees, the social and religious elite, rejected any concept of an afterlife, and did not accept any evidence of such outside of the Hebrew Bible, while the Pharisees believed in the resurrection of the body (Setzer, "Resurrection" 67).[9] The Jewish historian Josephus claimed that the Pharisees believed in the corporeal resurrection of the righteous and in eternal imprisonment for the wicked.[10] The Essenes were a branch of the Pharisees who believed in the resurrection, in immortality, and in divine punishment for transgressions.

At the beginning of the Common Era, the elite Sadducees were wealthy and powerful aristocrats who held influential positions as chief priests and high priest (Cohen 147; Acts 4: 1; 5:17), and they occupied the majority of the 70 seats of the Sanhedrin, who "...represented the entrenched religious hierarchy who controlled the practice of the religion through their role as Temple officials and priests of the Temple" (Pasachoff and Littman 63). They accommodated Roman rule, did not relate well to the common man, opposed change and innovation (63), and were unpopular with the common man who related better to the Pharisees. Jonathan Klawans writes: "It is frequently asserted that the Sadducees resisted the afterlife trend that was gaining momentum all around them in the ancient world. It is frequently asserted that the Sadducean denial of the afterlife is reflection of their satisfaction with their socioeconomic status ... the only immortality one should wish for is to be remembered for good, by plenty of progeny" (105, 106). They rejected fate in favor of free will, did not believe in angels or demonic spirits (Orr

2659; (Mattison 56; Acts 23: 8), and they denied any concept of immortality, fate, or unwritten legal traditions (Mattison 56; Capes 261). The Sadducees embraced the good life through financial and religious supremacy.

While the Sadducees held religious-political power in the Sanhedrin, they had to cede clout to the Pharisaic minority because of its popularity with the common people. The Sadducees were conservative fundamentalists who considered only the written Word of God in the Torah; however, some of their doctrines contradicted scripture: they rejected the idea of God's involvement in everyday life; they rejected any concept of resurrection from the dead (Terry 540; Saldarini 14; Matthew 22:23; Mark 12: 18–27; Acts 23:8). They rebuffed the idea of an afterlife because they believed the soul no longer existed at death, so there was nothing after death but a great void or abyss. According to Walter Balfour:

> The Sadducees treated the "traditionary law" of the Pharisees with contempt and adhered to the written law. The chief tenets of the Sadducees were these: "All laws and traditions, not comprehended in the written law are to be rejected as merely human inventions. Neither angels nor spirits have a distinct existence, separate from the corporeal vestment. The soul of man, therefore, does not remain after this life, but expires with the body. There will be no resurrection of the dead, nor any rewards or punishments after this life" [307–308].

The Sadducees ceased to exist in about 70 CE. Since this party existed because of their political and priestly ties, when Rome destroyed Jerusalem and the temple in 70 CE, the Sadducees retained little power or importance.

In contrast to the Sadducees, the Pharisees[11] were mostly middle-class merchants who communicated directly with the common man (Cohen 147). They believed scripture to be the inspired word of God, but they also promoted oral tradition as authoritative, and claimed these stories originated with Moses and augmented God's word, but these claims and additions were forbidden in scripture (Deuteronomy 4:2) and held in disdain by the Sadducees. However, Pharisees believed, like the Greeks, that God controlled the lives of humans, yet they believed in an element of free will that impacted a person's life. Pharisees believed in the resurrection of the dead (Acts 23: 6), and in an afterlife where humans were rewarded or punished, and where evil souls were held in an eternal prison (Nadler 56; Rubin 130). Unlike the Sadducees, they believed in the existence of angels and demons (Acts 23: 8).

All of the aforementioned beliefs, with the exception of reincarnation, became the cardinal principles of the new Christian religion, but reincarnation was actually part of Jewish thought during the time of Jesus; the great historian Josephus suggests the Pharisee's acceptance of a type of reincarnation, when he writes in *War* 2.163 that the Pharisees maintain "...that every soul is imperishable, but the soul of the good passes into another body, while the souls of the wicked suffer eternal punishment" (qtd. in Klawan

106). Pharisees believed in the soul's immortality, but human responsibility for actions in this life would determine the soul's fate. Unlike Hindu doctrines of reincarnation, and according to Josephus' interpretation, Pharisees believed that only the good could assume a new body, that virtuous souls do reincarnate, but first receive recompense in a place "under the earth"; in *Antiquities* 18.14, Josephus also writes that "...souls have the power to survive death and that there are rewards and punishments under the earth for those who have led lives of virtue and vice: eternal punishment is the lot for evil souls, while the good souls receive an easy passage to a new life" (qtd. in Klawan 106; Brocas 56). After the destruction of Jerusalem in 70 CE, the Pharisees continued to exist, perhaps because they were against the rebellion and made peace with the Romans. The Pharisees were also responsible for the compilation of the *Mishnah*,[12] the oral tradition of Jewish law, and an important document for the continuation of Judaism beyond the destruction of the temple in 70 CE (Houdmann 649).

Unlike the Sadducees and Pharisees, who were often motivated by political and social pressures to perform practical rituals and duties, the Essenes were an ascetic offshoot of the Pharisees who obeyed the strict regulations of Levitical purity while seeking the highest degree of holiness (Chalcraft 68; Ginsburg 7; Kohler, "Essenes"); ritual bathing was a key feature of the sect. Descriptions of the Essenes' lifestyle run startlingly close to the later Catholic priesthood that embraced celibacy. Essenes lived, worked, and studied in a commune, but eschewed conjugal intercourse or any type of sensual or earthly pleasure; they believed that denial of the flesh would enable them to understand sacred mysteries and prompt the Messiah to appear. The Essenes personified the sun as God, were said to have the ability to predict the future, were largely celibate, lived communally, and wore white clothing: to be admitted into this fellowship took three years and a period of probation afterwards (Collins 137–146). The Essenes believed in the immortality of the human soul and the resurrection of the dead, and in an immediate judgment after death (Ellis 101; Klawans 111; Boccaccini 174). According to the *Jewish Encyclopedia* of 1912:

> Particularly firm is their doctrine of Resurrection; they believe that the flesh will rise again and then be immortal like the soul, which, they say, when separated from the body, enters a place of fragrant air and radiant light, there to enjoy rest—a place called by the Greeks who heard [of this doctrine] the "Isles of the Blest." ... [F]or they affirm that there will be a Judgment Day and a burning up of the world, and that the wicked will be eternally punished [Singer and Adler 230].

There has been a debate over whether the Essenes subscribed to Greek notions of an immortal soul's journey after the death of the body. Josephus claims that the Essenes had a Greek dualistic notion that the soul was imprisoned within the material body, and was released upon death where it waited in a pleasant but fixed animation[13]:

> For the view has become tenaciously held among them that whereas our bodies are perishable and their matter impermanent, our souls endure forever, deathless: they get entangled, having emanated from the most refined ether, as if drawn down by a certain charm into the prisons that are bodies. But when they are released from the restraints of the flesh, as if freed from a long period of slavery, then they rejoice and are carried upwards in suspension [8.11: 154–155].

Unimpressed with Josephus's records, Eliezer Segal points out that "there do not appear to be any texts among the Qumran documents (the 'Dead Sea Scrolls' commonly attributed to the Essenes) that reflect such a view of the afterlife" (qtd. in Coward 19).

The fatalistic and uptight Essenes believed in predestination, and taught that human fate is unalterable because God's fixed decrees are unchangeable (Schafer 72; Fleuser 12). There was an odd snobbery within the Essenes, as they believed they were God's chosen or the "elect" and everyone else was condemned; of course, this stratified system of thinking causes social fracture zones, and continues today within feuding sects of many religions. Magen Broshi claims that this doctrine separated them from normative Judaism, influenced Christianity's later predestination dogmas of the Protestant Reformation, particularly Calvinism, and caused deep hatreds within strict, theopolitical and social divisions (275): "In such a world, where no repentance is possible and the wicked are to stay forever in their despicable status, it is only natural that those whom God has despised and cursed should be hated, despised and cursed by the elect as well" (276).

The Postbiblical Talmud: Resurrection and Temporary Punishment

Jewish thought about an immortal afterlife continued during Rabbinic or postbiblical Judaism in the origination of the rabbinic Talmud,[14] comprised of the *Mishnah* and *Gemara*,[15] which solidified the required dogma of corporeal resurrection that became a type of scare tactic to improve Jewish participation in religion. Goldenberg writes, "By the time of the Mishnah … the hope for resurrection had become one of the few dogmatic requirements of the Jewish religion; the Mishnah appropriately warns that those who deny resurrection will indeed be excluded from the joys of the World to Come" (qtd. in Obayashi 101). Acceptance in Resurrection beliefs was mandatory for salvation, and had firmly taken root, but theories of the soul continued to be questioned. Rabbi Elie Kaplan Spitz confirms that the Rabbis' fundamental belief in the Talmud embraced immortality and corporeal resurrection, but the belief in an independent soul is also present in the Talmud, so that "... immortality of the soul and resurrection are 'fused and confused'" (181). Another idea surfaced regarding how the resurrected body would be rebuilt, but there had to be bodily remains.

According to the *Mishnah* with regards to resurrection, the dead body never completely vanishes and a new resurrected body is created around the Luz (101), a bone at the base of the spine. According to Goldenberg, this is why Jews did not practice cremation. Of this Luz, Julius Preuss writes: "King Hadrian once asked Rabbi Joshua ben Hananiah: from which part of the body will man in the world to come sprout forth? He answered: 'the Luz of the spinal column'" (65). So, Jews at this time embraced a sophisticated medical-scientific theory that something small in the human body could not only be enlivened, but could spontaneously regenerate from the original; today, medical science researchers experiment with re-growing teeth and body parts from DNA cells, so the rabbi had great foresight.

Rabbinical Judaism has been the main form of Judaism since the sixth-century BCE after the Babylon Talmud was codified; Rabbinism embraced immortality, and shunned any notion of an eternal hell or eternal place of suffering. According to the Talmud, the body and the soul are on conditional loan to every human being, but there have been disputes whether the impious suffer a total destruction of the soul or only temporary punishments (Petavel-Olliff 106). Like Hinduism, Rabbinical Judaism denied the theory of an eternal hell because that would deny the immortal or divine-emanating substance of the human soul that causes us to live. According to Hamburger's *Talmudic Dictionary*: "The Talmud adheres strictly to the biblical doctrine of immortality, rejecting categorically, on the one hand, the opinion that denies all immortality, and on the other hand, that which makes immortality a consequence of the nature of the soul, as though that were of divine essence. The Doctors of the Talmud have declared formally against the eternity of torments" (qtd. in Petavel-Olliff 107).

Resurrection and Judgment at the End of Time

Rabbinical Judaism influenced Christianity and Islam with the belief in end of days prophesies and faith in resurrection and final judgment. Rabbis, however, were divided on these issues: some believed everyone will be judged, but only the righteous will be resurrected; others believed that everyone will be resurrected to stand judgment. There is evidence in the *Mishnah* that post-biblical or Rabbinic Judaism[16] had incorporated the concept of the afterlife and a final judgment into the Jewish faith. One tractate of the *Mishnah*, translated as *Ethics of the Fathers* (*Mishnah Pirkei Avot*), claims that Rabbi Eleazar ha-Kappar (170–200 CE) is said to have preached resurrection and final judgment:

> He also used to say: They who have been born are destined to die. They that are dead are destined to be made alive. They who live are destined to be judged, that men may know and make known and understand that He is G-d, He is the maker, He is the creator, He is the discerner, He is the judge.... And let not your evil nature assure you that the grave will be your refuge: for despite yourself you were fashioned, and despite yourself you were born, and despite yourself you live, and despite yourself you die, and despite yourself shall you [be] destined to give account and reckoning before the supreme King of kings, the Holy One, blessed be He [*Ethics of the Fathers* 4:29].

Transformational Thinking during Medieval and Enlightenment Periods

Robert Goldenberg emphasizes that Jewish traditions regarding death, resurrection, and the afterlife have never been fully solidified as an "authoritative dogmatic scheme"; that contemporary Jews would be surprised that ideas of heaven and hell originated in ancient Judaism, and that "...classic Jewish sources are full of references to the fate that awaits us after we die" (qtd. in Obayashi 98). Despite the historic unanimity of scholarly opinion on basic tenets of Judaism, agreement on the essential beliefs on the afterlife, immortality, and resurrection from the dead continued to be ambiguous and diverse. Jewish writers, such as the famous Sephardic philosopher Maimonides (1135–1204 CE) and the German Moses Mendelssohn (1728–1786 CE), attempted to settle the disparities in Jewish thinking regarding the soul's afterlife, but most Jews continued to believe in traditional concepts: the souls of the dead continue living after the body decomposes, and the character of the soul after death depends on a person's morality during life.

MAIMONIDES: THE ULTIMATE REWARD

Medieval Jewish philosophers debated notions of immortality and resurrection. For the religious rationalist and antiliteralist Maimonides (1135 - 1204 CE), who became the head of the Jewish community in Egypt, immortality of the soul was his dominant concern. During the Middle Ages, the Jewish canonical view was that of bodily resurrection. Maimonides accepted resurrection from the dead, and believed that resurrection is the beginning of the World to Come. Maimonides succinctly deals with resurrection somewhat in his *Commentary on the Mishnah: Introduction to Pereq Heleq*: "The resurrection of the dead [who lived righteously] is one of the cardinal principles established by Moses our Teacher" (13). There was some confusion, however, about Maimonides' real belief in resurrection, as there is mention that he believed resurrected bodies would die a second time, and only the "intellect" and not the soul would survive. It is believed that Maimonides equated the human intellect with the soul. Joel L. Kraemer writes: "Maimonides had asserted in *Introduction to Sanhedrin* that resurrection of the dead is a foundation of the law accepted by consensus within the religious community, which must be believed by all who adhere to it. Yet, the true end of human life is immortality of the soul in the world hereafter. Maimonides taught that after resurrection people would die (again) and only their intellects would survive" (419; Nadler 56). Maimonides posited that corporeal resurrection from the dead was a transitory phase for the human soul, and was followed by a second death when righteous souls lived forever; there was no further existence for the wicked. On this point, Maimonides writes:

> The punishment that awaits the evil man is that he will have no part in eternal life. He will die, and will be completely destroyed. He will not live forever, he will perish with his wickedness like the brute; it is a death from which there is no return … the retribution of the wicked will be to be deprived of the future life" [qtd. in Petavel-Olliff 110].

Maimonides and other medieval Jewish philosophers claimed that immortality was not innate, but a soul's immortal existence depended on the righteous behavior of living mortals, and that it would be arrogant to deny God's power to destroy the soul.

MENDELSSOHN: IMMORTALITY FOR ALL

By the 18th-century Enlightenment period, Moses Mendelssohn (1729–1786 CE) reasoned that all human souls were eternal and believed the human soul to be imperishable. Like the Deists, he claimed that reason could discover the reality of God, understand divine providence, and accept immortality of the soul. An advocate of religious tolerance, he contended that every human soul would experience a heavenly immortality, and the wicked would receive punishments after death for a brief correctional time (Jospe 170–171). Mendelssohn trusted that God's love for His creation would ensure eternal happiness for everyone; virtuous acts were desirable, but faith in God's promises were more important. He abhorred popular teachings about the afterlife based on threats or promises (180–181). Mendelssohn was responsible for the emergence of the "Enlightened Jew" within the pluralistic, 18th-century German society where morality and rationality prevailed to promote common interests (Kaplan 355).

Moses Mendelssohn revived the Platonic doctrine of immortality of the soul in his *Phaedon;* ideas in his text created Reform Judaism, but did nothing to encourage acceptance of resurrection. Martin D. Yaffe writes: "Overall the *Phaedon* intends to prove immortality on the basis of immutability. Immutability (or imperishability) refers to the soul's mere persistence as an individual substance. Immortality, on the other hand, includes the soul's ongoing awareness of its individual past and present" (265). Henceforth, Judaism, particularly Reform Judaism, emphasized the doctrine of immortality in its religious instruction, but the dogma of resurrection was gradually discarded in the Reform rituals and eliminated from the prayer-books.

There is still divergence of opinion about life after death among Jewish sects. According to Segal, Orthodox Jews believe in corporeal resurrection, but the Reform sect reject this doctrine (qtd. in Coward 27). Conservative Jewish sects generally deny concepts of an afterlife, but some conservative Jews hold Maimonidean views of God, which profess there is an afterlife. Taking a more practical approach to life, non–Orthodox sects have the notion that Judaism should be more focused on this world rather than the next, just as had the Sadducees; as Segal states, "...discussions of the afterlife are almost entirely absent from non–Orthodox twentieth-century religious discourse, which has focused on the absolute commitment to this world as the setting for the encounter with the divine, the covenant between God and Israel, and the obligation to serve humanity" (qtd. in Coward 27).

Kabbalistic Literature: the Divine Immortal Soul and Reincarnation

Strikingly similar to Hindu theology, Kabbalistic eschatology conceives of a soul separated into parts, whose origin is divine emanation, and whose incarnation is designed to accomplish a specific mission—returning a part of the divinity back to the all-embracing Divine. Byron L. Sherwin writes: "By recognizing himself as an effect of God rather than a cause in himself, by cultivating his soul thorough observance of the commandments, and by loving God with the love that God has given us to love God, the human being can be reunited with God. The soul that comes from God that is from the realm of the *sefirot,* can be returned to and reunited with God, the source of all" (90). So the essence of God as the primordial source and the essence of the human soul as an elemental emanation are the same; our soul is simply a part of the creative powers of God (Berke and Schneider 341). While medieval philosophy dwelt on the intellectual, moral, or spiritual nature of the soul to prove its immortality, the Kabbalists endeavored to explain the soul as a light from heaven, as previously described in scriptures: "The spirit of man is the lamp of the Lord, searching all his innermost parts" (Proverbs 20: 27), so that the soul's immortality was a return to the celestial world of pure light through its "divine-like creative ability" (Fishbane, "A Chariot" 397–398).

Gilgul or reincarnation first appeared in the 12th century CE and became a major doctrine of Kabbalah, and, according to Gabriella Samuel, this doctrine provided a reason for the injustices and sufferings in the world (115). The main purpose of the doctrine was to provide temporary punishment for those who violated God's law; rather than descend to hell, this provided humans another opportunity to live righteously. After the 14th century, reincarnation or transmigration of evil human souls into animals, plants, or stones appeared in Kabbalistic literature (Samuel 116; Meyers 272). Jewish mystical literature of the *Zohar*[17] and the *Kabbalah* teach that souls exist before birth and after death (Fishbane 391–392). Kabbalists believe that there is a preset time when the soul joins the corporeal body; after existing with the body, the soul eventually leaves to undertake a new existence in corporeal form, or it returns to the god-source. The *Zohar* states, "It is the path taken by man in this world that determines the path of the soul on her departure. If a man is drawn towards the Holy One, and if filled with longing towards him in this world, the soul in departing … is carried upward towards the higher realms by the impetus given her each day in this world" (qtd. in Sonsino and Syme 47). Thus, it is our actions while we live on Earth that determine how rapidly our souls will rise up the ladder of the spiritual world to return to God. Eitan P. Fishbane writes: "The discourse of reincarnation is interwoven seamlessly with the drama of self-formation, insofar as the individual self works on the gradual improvement of that identity over the course of numerous physical lifetimes" (389). The pain that people feel in this world may in fact be the consequence of acts committed in a previous incarnation (Sonsino and Syme 47). Kabbalists even claim that some people act like animals because they carry souls of beasts, or that barren women carry the souls of men, or that converts to Judaism carry Jewish souls (47). Souls that fail their missions are considered the wicked, and are purified in a temporary hell to be reincarnated with a chance to fulfill their task; however, some souls are denied hell or reincarnation, and are expelled without further prospects (Giller 95).

Making Sense of Death

In order to make sense of the world, religious systems, as well as philosophical musings, attempt to create answers to mysteries of the unknown. Judaism's evolution into a multibranched religion prompted diverse speculation on doctrines of resurrection and punishment and concepts of heaven and hell; outside cultures that came into contact with Jews influenced new ways of thinking about these mysteries. Ideas regarding the afterlife in Judaism did not emanate from the Torah, but evolved because of later socio-historical events, and exegetical and dialectical elaborations and debates. Distinct from the Jewish belief in the soul's immortality, their belief in resurrection focused on a nationalistic rather than personally unique optimism—the hope of a national rebirth and ascendancy.

Christianity inherited Judaism's apocalyptic beliefs, and early Christian believers were Jews with deep spiritual roots in the mother religion; as centuries progressed, non–Jewish Christians could not deny the contribution that Judaism had on their faith, and the Jewish apocalyptic tradition became a vital part of the new off-shoot religion. The early Christian hope for bodily resurrection is clearly Jewish in origin; the Hebrew Pharisee and later Christian evangelist Paul of Tarsus believed in the Jewish doctrine of resurrection that was strengthened by the reported resurrection of Jesus: "If the Spirit of the God who raised Jesus from the dead dwells in you, he who raised the Messiah Jesus from the dead will give life to your mortal bodies also through his Spirit who lives in you" (Romans 8:11). But Paul had to compete with many popular, mystery religions in existence, such as the Persian-influenced and Roman-embraced Mithraism that worshipped the sun god, Mithra; other pagan mystery cults such as the Syrian cult of Adonis and the Egyptian cult of Osiris had profound influences on the new religion, so that Christianity partially became an absorption of mystery religions and Jewish religious philosophy (Robertson 23, 32, 36, 39, 72). The early Church fathers denied these pagan connections, and dismissed them as the devil's mimicry, but many traditions and beliefs associated with these cults still continue today in Christian worship.

6

Christianity: Belief and Hope in Eternal Life

So when this corruptible shall have put on incorruption, and this mortal shall have put on immortality, then shall be brought to pass the saying that is written, Death is swallowed up in victory. O death, where is thy sting? O grave, where is thy victory? (1 Corinthians 15:52–55)

Religious and philosophical antecedents from Egypt, Greece, and Israel heavily persuaded Christian immortality concepts. It is not surprising that most global "immortality" beliefs connect, as humans in every religion have pondered their death and fate in the afterlife, and almost all preceding religions believed in some type of conscious continuation of life in eternity. The Christian belief system is based upon salvation through Jesus Christ, a risen and living messiah, and its main tenets focus on life after death, corporeal resurrection, and the promise of immortality in a heaven where believers will never again suffer. Christians believe their bodies will become immortal when Jesus Christ returns; some Christians imagine a rapture of believers before Christ's Second Coming, and the particular generation during which this reportedly is to happen will not taste death, but will be taken up to heaven to avoid the tribulation.[1] Most Christians trust that in the end God will judge and send them to eternal life or to eternal damnation; the promise of everlasting life is the assurance of immortality for the chosen "saints" who will exist in a new glorified body that will not age, decay, or feel sorrow or pain. Nonbelievers will be sent to the "Lake of Fire," and dwell forever in torment with the false prophet and the beast or Antichrist (Revelation 20:15).[2,3] Some people might question whether this system is an industry with a pyramidal business structure espousing political beliefs and affiliations that control human behavior through abject fear with promises of immortality. These promises and hope for eventual immortality might be perception management tools used to make people conform, obey, and not be frightened by the theory that there is no afterlife; however, the road to immortality might actually be a belief and trust in the New Testament gospel, particularly for those who believe in the writings of Paul of Tarsus.

The original Christians, a sect within "apocalyptic Judaism" (McGinn 10–11; Bial 526; Kyle 27; Obayashi 54), trusted in a final judgment day when the kingdom of God would arrive on earth and believers would be raised from the dead; the earliest view of the resurrection espoused a literal bodily resurrection of the dead corpse, which was based upon the reported bodily resurrection of Jesus Christ, as "first-born of the dead" (Rev. 1:5) (see **figure 6**). General Christian theology asserts that everyone will be resurrected, Christian and non–Christian, and all will be judged, but there is the thorny issue of what happens to the souls of those who existed and died before the coming of Jesus. The generally accepted but controversial answer is that when Jesus was in the tomb after His crucifixion and death, he appeared in Hell to preach to the unconverted,[4] but other Christians do not accept this predominately Catholic assessment (Bausch 77). Another unresolved argument centers on

Figure 6 The Resurrection. Christians trust when the kingdom of God would arrive on earth and believers would be raised from the dead; the earliest view of the resurrection espoused a literal bodily resurrection of the dead corpse, which was based upon the reported bodily resurrection of Jesus Christ (unknown Hungarian painter, *The Resurrection*).

the opportunity for salvation for people who were never exposed to Jesus' teachings.[5] There is also a minority view that claims that the damned will simply not be resurrected.

The Christian afterlife has also been hotly debated regarding the time frames for the resurrection and judgment to occur. There are two basic opinions: some believe that judgment transpires immediately upon an individual's death, but the more conventional idea is that death is like a deep sleep, and judgment will happen at Christ's Second Coming when all who have lived will experience bodily resurrection concurrently. At the same time, Christians believe that those who are alive at the Second Coming will be physically transformed; Paul's writing seems to confirm this view in 1 Corinthians 51 when he writes: "Behold, I tell you a mystery: We shall not all sleep, but we shall all be changed." There are other passages in the New Testament that correspond to the death-deep-sleep theory. In Matthew Chapter 9, a leader of the synagogue had approached Jesus to resurrect his dead daughter; Jesus replied, "Leave; for the girl has not died, but is asleep" (9:24).

Another dramatic account about death and resurrection in the New Testament is the Lazarus story. When Jesus heard of Lazarus' sickness, he delayed the family's request for healing for two days, but then announced to his disciples: "'Our friend Lazarus has fallen asleep; but I go, so that I may awaken him out of sleep.' The disciples then said to Him, 'Lord, if he has fallen asleep, he will recover.' Now Jesus had spoken of his death, but they thought that He was speaking of literal sleep" (John 11:11–14). A further question then remains: if Lazarus was resurrected, is he still walking the earth today, or did he have to die a second time? Or was the writer John relating a story that prophesied the future final moment when Christ returns? John gave hope of Jesus' promises to the skeptical, as the reported promise from Jesus' lips was, "I am the resurrection, and the life; he that believes in me, though he were dead, yet shall he live: And whosoever lives and believes in me shall never die" (John 11:35). Dianne Bergant reminds the reader of the important lesson and faith issue from the story: "Death has no power when there is faith" (39). But for most people today, the element of faith eludes them.

Most conservative and fundamentalist Christians have accepted and rely on Paul's explanation of death, resurrection, and judgment in his First Letter to the Thessalonians, which lays out the framework for the most important concepts: death is like sleeping, and people alive at the Second Coming will follow the resurrected and saved after they are taken up into the sky. Paul's passage below seems to imply that the saved will indeed have some type of corporeal resurrected bodies that will be collected by the "angels," as Mark confirms: "And then they will see the Son of Man coming in clouds with great power and glory. And then he will send out the angels and gather his elect from the four winds, from the ends of the earth to the ends of heaven" (13: 26, 27). Paul writes further about the scenario of Jesus' return in First Thessalonians 4: 15–18:

> For this we declare to you by the word of the Lord, that we who are alive, who are left until the coming of the Lord, shall not precede those who have fallen asleep. For the Lord himself will descend from heaven with a cry of command, with the archangel's call, and with the sound of the trumpet of God. And the dead in Christ will rise first; then we who are alive, who are left, shall be caught up together with them in the clouds to meet the Lord in the air; and so we shall always be with the Lord. Therefore comfort one another with these words.

The scenario that Paul describes is quite intergalactic, as "angels" collect humans to meet God "in the clouds … in the air." So, if this is true, and if Jesus Christ is alive today, what kind of God do Christians really worship? Paul was knowledgeable in the Torah's story of Elijah, so this idea of being taken off the earth in a "chariot," or some type of flying vehicle, might not have seemed all that strange to him. Paul's writings are either describing a real event at some future time, or they are merely metaphorical ruminations offering hope to humanity.

Inherited Concepts Influencing Christian Immortality

EGYPT: DEATH, JUDGMENT, BURIAL AND IMMORTALITY

The doctrine that espouses that the souls of the dead separate from the body at death and carry on living in heaven or hell because the soul is supposedly immortal is not a Christian innovation. Clearly presaging concepts of heaven and hell, Egyptian judgment came in the form of rewards and punishments, where some souls experienced reversals of fortune according to their deeds on earth; a divine or mystical power transports souls either to a realm of happiness or to a region of torment. Ancient Egyptians observed the repetitious cycles of nature and associated these patterns of life, death, and rebirth to human existence. Ancient Egyptians worshipped the pharaoh as a living god who would exist beyond death. A millennium after the Old Kingdom fell, the right to immortality included the common people in what historians describe as "the democratization" of the afterlife; the common person in Egypt embraced belief in immortality, and state religion taught that everyone became Osiris in death. The New Kingdom's (1550–1070 BCE) democratization of death, resurrection, and immortality was a brilliant strategy that also ensured loyalty to pharaoh as a divine god incarnate who could influence a person's destiny in this life and in the life to come. This idea clearly referenced inspiration from Sumerian, Akkadian, and Babylonian earlier canons that incorporated a celestial hierarchy of gods, demigods, and immortals. The good news for Egyptian royals was that common people could never become a god, but their souls or spirits could become immortal after dying.

The Osiris myth created the possibility for a democratized idea of immortality after death, and anyone could hope to join Osiris in heaven. It was believed that each night the sun descended down into the underworld or *Duat,* and met with the mummified Osiris. Energized by each other's presence, they both arose again the next day. The Egyptians believed that each person followed a similar cycle. After Osiris was murdered by his brother Seth, his wife Isis gathered the body parts and used them to create the first mummy, after which Osiris, through elaborate ritual, was resurrected as the god of the dead and the underworld (Wegner, "Gateway to the Netherworld" 50; Reid 32, 33). In his epic work *The Golden Bough,* James G. Frazer noted that Egyptian commoners copied the ritual ceremonies Isis had followed as "a representation of the divine mystery" that would bequeath to them life after death. Frazer writes:

> In the resurrection of Osiris the Egyptians saw the pledge of a life everlasting for themselves beyond the grave. They believed that every man would live eternally in the other world if only his surviving friends did for his body what the gods had done for the body of Osiris. Hence the ceremonies observed by the Egyptians over the human dead were an exact copy of those which Anubis, Horus, and the rest had performed over the dead god. At every burial there was enacted a representation of the divine mystery which had been performed of old over Osiris... [327a].

A respectful funeral was one of the conditions for a fortunate afterlife, and the mummified corpse served as a house, sanctuary, or place of rest for the spirit, so mummification became a supernatural, religious ritual that sustained and safeguarded the soul. The cagey priests of the Osiris-Isis religion made money on the Osirian religion by offering immortality by initiation; of course, their teachings would cost, and not everyone could afford to pay (Donadoni 145, 146). These ancient Egyptian traditions are still kept alive in Catholic funeral masses and burial rites, and in reverent Christian funerals. Preservation of the body and respect for the dead in Christianity and in all Abrahamic religions has never included burning the corpse, as was the Hindu custom—Christians only allowed cremation in times of plague.

There has been endless speculation that the story of Jesus might parallel the myth of the Egyptian Isis, Osiris, and Horus. There are claims that the Jesus story is simply a reincarnation of the earlier Egyptian myth contained in the 5000-year-old *Egyptian Book of the Dead,* which has led to the following comparisons: Horus was born of the virgin Isis on 25 December in a cave, and his birth was announced by a star in the East and attended by three wise men; the infant Horus was carried out of Egypt to flee the Typhon's[6] ire, while Jesus was carried into Egypt to escape the wrath of Herod; Jesus had the same titles as Horus, such as the way, the truth, the light, the Messiah, God's anointed Son, the Son of Man, the Good Shepherd, the Lamb of God, the Word, the Morning Star, the light of the world. This is culturally similar to the titles that ancient goddesses, demigoddesses, and queens were ascribed, so Jesus may have been given these same titles because he was a typology of Horus but not actually a mythic continuation of Horus (Coulter-Harris 111–112). Osiris and Horus were both solar deities; Osiris signified the setting sun, Horus symbolized rising sun; Jesus has always been known as the Morning Star, which has well-known associations with Venus, and his resurrection signifies a rebirth or a rising sun. The pharaoh was considered to be an incarnation of Horus, also known as "Amen-Ra," the sun god. In the same way, Jesus is considered the incarnation of his heavenly Father (Massey 442, 446, 488, 497, 498, and 505).

Biblical writers had to be aware of the Horus myth and might have simply transferred the attributes of the old god to the new because their ideas were rooted in Egyptian religious literature, or because Osiris and Horus became "archetypes of Jesus Christ" (Enuwosa, "African Cultural" 91) Tom Harpur, an author, journalist, Anglican priest, and theologian, argued that all of the essential ideas of both Judaism and Christianity came primarily from Egyptian religion (5). Harpur writes in his book: "Massey discovered nearly two hundred instances of immediate correspondence between the mythical Egyptian material and the allegedly historical Christian writings about Jesus. Horus indeed was the archetypal Pagan Christ" (85). Richard A. Gabriel also claims that the "Principles and precepts of the Osiran religion in Egypt are virtually identical in content and application to the principles and precepts of Christianity as they present themselves in the Jesus story" (2). Gabriel further maintains that no other religion but Christianity contains the idea of the Trinity, three gods in one, and that this idea stems from the New Kingdom hymn to a trinity: "All gods are three: Amun, Re, and Ptah" (13), but Osiris, Isis, and Horus are also the principal trinity of the Egyptian religions (Massey 544, 545). God the Father, Jesus the Son, and the Holy Spirit are the Christian Trinity. Thomas Inman also affirms the Egyptian roots of the Christian trinity: "The Christian trinity is of Egyptian origin, and is as surely a pagan doctrine as the belief in heaven and hell, the existence of a devil, of archangels, angels, spirits and saints, martyrs and virgins, intercessors in heaven, gods and demigods, and other forms of faith, which deface the greater part of modern religions" (Inman 13).

Most Christians would likely shun these aforementioned connections, but others might postulate that any Egyptian influence on Christian precepts, rituals, and customs are not necessarily evil, but they strengthen awareness of how Christianity is so rich in history and ancient in origin. The Roman Catholic Church established the doctrine of the Trinity nearly 1800 years ago during the Council of Nicaea in 325 CE, but was this concept wholly original to Christianity? Some might also speculate that the Egyptian trinity was rooted in the Sumerian trinity of father-son-son with Anu, Enki, and Enlil; of course, we must not forget the Babylonian trinity of father-mother-son in Nimrod, Ishtar, and Tammuz. This would make the concept of the Christian Trinity a protraction of thought from the very earliest civilizations on earth. Readers should: either take great comfort from the fact that ideas about gods, so ancient in human belief, might strengthen the hypothesis that there is a god; or, become puzzled by why humans still believe the same way as did their progenitors over 7000 years ago, and propose we are all living under an ancient delusion based upon the earth's natural cycles and forces.

GREEK AND CLASSICAL IDEAS PERMEATE CHRISTIANITY

Hundreds of years before Jesus, Greek culture and religious beliefs exerted a global influence; theories included Plato, Aristotle, Epicurus and the Stoics who all worked out complex hypotheses, which have since influenced much of Western philosophical and religious thought. Homer's view of the soul and eternity was pessimistically simplistic. In speaking of the Homeric poems from the eighth-century BCE, Henrik Lorenz notes, "The [Greek] soul is, on one hand, something that a human being risks in battle and loses in death. On the other hand, it is what at the time of death departs from the person's limbs and travels to the underworld, where it has more or less a pitiful afterlife as a shade or image of the deceased person" ("Ancient Theories of Soul"). When Christianity proliferated, Greek influence on the faith created an integrated view of the afterlife, one which embraced the dualistic, platonic Greek view that the spirit or soul was independent of the physical body.

Werner Jaeger[7] proposes that the soul's immortality was one of the basic principles of Platonism that was in some measure embraced by the Christian church; he states: "The most important fact in the history of Christian doctrine was that the father of Christian theology, Origen, was a Platonic philosopher at the school of Alexandria. He built into Christian doctrine the whole cosmic drama of the soul, which he took from Plato, and although later Christian fathers decided that he took over too much, that which they kept was still the essence of Plato's philosophy of the soul" (qtd. in Partee 55). Origen Adamantius' (185–253 CE) teachings contradicted St. Paul and the apocalyptist John, as Origen taught the pre-existence of souls and the subordination of the Son of God to the Father God, and somewhat believed in resurrection of a nonhuman body. Because he was influenced by Platonic and Gnostic thought, he taught other unorthodox ideas: he denied that scripture was completely historical; he believed in transmigration of souls or reincarnation; he taught universalism (the belief that all will eventually be saved because all souls are naturally immortal); and denied that Jesus was raised from the dead in a physical body. Later church councils declared his teachings to be heretical (Ashwin-Siejkowski 119; Edwards, "Further Reflections on the Platonism of Origen" 322–323).

Greek philosophical thinking regarding the soul's essence and future broadened in the sixth and fifth centuries before Christ. At the start of the fourth century, the soul had acquired emotions, cognitive qualities, and the power to strategize. The origins of the idea of the immortality of the soul comes from Greek philosophy, expounded upon particularly by two of the chief Greek philosophers: Socrates and his student Plato. The Platonic belief in immortality was later regarded as an anticipation or prefiguration of the Christian resurrection. In Plato's *Phaedo*, Socrates proclaims the soul to be immortal and cognizant, capable of discerning thought. In his Cyclical Argument, or Opposites Argument in the *Phaedo*, Socrates relates that Forms (ideas) are eternal and unchanging, and as the soul always brings life, then it must not die; it is necessarily imperishable and merely trapped in the prison of the body (Karasmanis, "Soul and Body" 2, 3; Plato 14, 15, 20; White 63, 64).

Plato reasons that as the body is mortal and subject to physical decay and death, the soul should be its imperishable opposite. Of Plato's *Phaedo*, Lorenz avers that Plato never proved his hypothesis that the soul remains cognizant after the body's death: "Socrates says not only that the soul is immortal, but also that it contemplates truths after its separation from the body at the time of death. Needless to say, none of the four main lines of argument that Socrates avails himself of succeeds in establishing the immortality of the soul, or in demonstrating that disembodied souls enjoy lives of thought and intelligence" ("Ancient Theories"). That said, Plato's speculative concepts of immortality influenced Church Fathers, such as Justin Martyr and Augustine, and this doctrine of immortality was subsumed with other Greek theoretical ideas and traditions, and authorized as Christian. Plato's student Aristotle, in *De Anima*,[8] described a relationship among all physical lives, such as human, animal or plant, and the animating motion of the soul; the body was corporeal, but the soul was not a body or a physical thing (19–22; 27). While Aristotle agreed with Plato's thinking that souls are different from bodies, he did not agree that the soul could exist apart from the body.

Greek philosophers inspired later Christian writers, such as the Catholic bishop Hippolytus (170–235 CE) and Augustine of Hippo (354–430 CE), who conceived new opinions of the soul. Hippolytus was a third-century controversial, schismatic religious leader in the Christian church in Rome who taught that Jesus needed to come in order to grant immortality to humans, and He would not have to do that if humans were inherently immortal. In his famous treatise, *On the End of the World*, Hippolytus quotes from the prophets Daniel and Isaiah to prove his theory: "For concerning the general resurrection and the kingdom of the saints, Daniel says: 'And many of them that sleep in the dust of the earth shall awake, some to everlasting life, and some to shame and everlasting contempt.' And Isaiah says: 'The dead shall rise, and those in the tombs shall awake, and those in the earth shall rejoice.' And our Lord says: 'Many in that day shall hear the voice of the Son of God, and they that hear shall live'" (Chapter XXXVI; qtd. in Roberts and Donaldson 251). Here was a perfect example of the doctrine of the exclusivity of Christian faith—believe in Christ or be damned. Lutheran doctrine appears to be influenced by Hippolytus' earlier denial of the soul's inherent immortality; Lutheran Pastor Billmeier states, "Lutherans do not see humans as innately immortal. Life is a gift bestowed by God. It has a beginning and an ending in death. Eternal life is also a gift of God given to those who receive God's grace through faith in Christ Jesus. Lutherans believe that we cannot lay claim even to faith as our means to eternal life. It is all gift. There is no earning immortality" (Billmeier).

There were other Hellenistic schools of thought that taught the corporeality or physicality of the soul. The Epicureans, founded in 307 BCE by the philosopher Epicurus, believed everything was composed of atoms, including the soul, so when the mortal body died the mortal soul did likewise; they did not believe in divine intervention (O'Keefe 64; Rist 74). James Warren writes that Epicurean arguments included one that proclaimed, "The soul is so fragile and composed of such small and mobile atoms, that it dissolves immediately at the point of a living thing's death" (243), so there is an everlasting nothingness (244). Epicureans believed that religion is the result of irrational human fear, and that "gods" do not need humans to worship them (Moore 42). The Epicurean assessment would be a radical form of materialism; this type of belief leaves no hope for the future, but is more cognizant of this life and what it has to offer; of course, this echoes the philosophy of the Sadducees and the ideas of post-exile Judaism.

The idea that the soul was composed of some type of physical element was also embraced by the logical Stoics, founded by Zeno of Citium (333–262 BCE) in Cyprus, who believed that the soul was separate from the material body, and had a limited consciousness after the body died; they said that the soul was composed of a divine substance, and either pre-existed before birth, survives briefly after death, or both, but they did not believe that the soul was immortal (Lewis 97, 98; Canright 50; Graeser 45). Charles Spring writes: "According to the Stoics, God is a living fire, unlike, however, the common fire. … [T]he soul is a fiery air, being a portion of the soul of the world, but, like every individual being, corporeal and perishable" (12). For Stoics, "… only the World Soul was immortal" (Litwa 139).

As materialists, Stoics rejected chance, believed that there was a rational order to the universe, and taught that religion was also a rational system patterned after nature (Barnes 117; Engstrom and Whiting 14; Koester 144). They agreed with the Epicureans that the Gods do not interfere in human affairs, but "…they proposed reverence for the divine principle of rational order that dwells in all the universe and in which humans participate as rational beings" (Barnes 117). The Christian apologist Eusebius, Bishop of Caesarea in 314 CE, elucidated the Stoic conception of the afterlife when some souls would endure for a time and when others would be destroyed:

> They [Stoics] say that the soul is both generated and mortal. But it is not immediately destroyed upon being separated from the body. Rather it remains for some time by itself—that of the diligent remains until the dissolution of all things by fire; and that of the foolish remains only for a limited time. About the endurance of the soul they say this: That we ourselves remain as souls which have been separated from the body and have been changed into the lesser substance of the soul; whereas the souls of irrational beings are destroyed along with their bodies[9] [Lewis 97; qtd. in Malcolm 252].

Eusebius later decided that the soul will be active at the Second Coming, and God will destroy the bodies and souls of the "irrational" [nonbelievers], a terrifying concept.

Hellenized Jewish Influence

Hellenized thinking deeply influenced interlacing Jewish and Christian doctrines. The Jewish and Christian concept of corporeal resurrection and immortality was conditional, and based upon the righteousness of the human soul, which depended on the grace and power of God to reward the soul for good behavior, a decidedly Greek notion. In *The First and Second Apologies*, Saint Justin Martyr writes: "Christianity was born within a Jewish cradle and it was natural that the earliest attempts at a theological formulation of its doctrines should have been expressed in Jewish terms" (1). Justin Martyr also states that the Hellenistic ideas that penetrated Jewish society also influenced Christianity as well, and according to Alan F. Segal, "The most long-lasting Greek contribution to Jewish culture was from the aristocratic, Platonist intellectual elite of Greek society that said that the soul was immortal. In return for a life of moderation and intellectual development, the soul went upward to receive its astral rewards" (702).

That the immortality of the soul doctrine is something foreign to the Scriptures and primarily came into Christian dogma via Greek ideas that blended Egyptian mysteries, is referenced and clarified in the *Jewish Encyclopedia*: "The belief that the soul continues its existence after the dissolution of the body is ... nowhere expressly taught in Holy Scripture.... The belief in the immortality of the soul came to the Jews from contact with Greek thought and chiefly through the philosophy of Plato its principle exponent, who was led to it through Orphic[10] and Eleusinian mysteries[11,12] in which Babylonian and Egyptian views were strangely blended" (Kohler, "Immortality"). William West also believes that any notion of the soul's immortality is not a scriptural theory, and he uses the *International Standard Bible Encyclopedia* to defend his point: "We are influenced always more or less by the Greek, Platonic idea that the body dies, yet the soul is immortal. Such an idea is utterly contrary to the Israelite consciousness and is nowhere found in the Old Testament" (qtd. in West 588).

Christianity accepted Jewish belief in resurrection and immortal life based upon Old Testament prophecies about human resurrection after death. For example, the prophet Daniel writes in 12: 2–3: "And many of those who sleep in the dust of the earth shall awake, some to everlasting life, and some to shame and everlasting contempt. And those who are wise shall shine like the brightness of the firmament; and those who turn many to righteousness, like the stars for ever and ever." The prophet Isaiah writes: "Thy dead shall live, their bodies shall rise. O dwellers in the dust, awake and sing for joy! For thy dew is a dew of light, and on the land of the shades thou wilt let it fall" (26:19.) But there are also contradictory passages that argue against after-death resurrection. One clear example is in Job 7:7–9 when he says: "Remember that my life is a breath; my eye will never again see good. The eye of him who sees me will behold me no more; while thy eyes are upon me, I shall be gone. As the cloud fades and vanishes, so he who goes down to Sheol does not come up." While this passage represents Job's pessimistic view of his future while suffering physically, mentally, and economically, this passage should never be accepted as proof certain that there will be no resurrection.

In the first-century CE, the Pharisees clearly did have an evolving belief in physical resurrection, but competing Sadducees disputed the theory (White 116). After the ascension of the Pharisaic viewpoint, this belief made its way into many Rabbinic-era texts and was eventually embraced by Christians. So, there were two major competing schools of thought coming from two major Jewish groups in the early first century which indicate that "resurrection ideas" existed in the cultural environment from which Christianity arose, and the Christian view was firmly rooted in the Pharisaic, rather than the Sadduceean, tradition (Viviano 130; White 116). Some scholars argue that

Christianity also has pagan roots in the ancient worship of Mithra, which began in 1400 BCE and ended around 400 CE in Persia, and had followers during that time period in Babylon, India, Rome, and Greece; this was an especially popular mystery cult among Romans during the rise of Christianity that barred women from membership (Morse, "Mithraism" 33; Ferguson, "The Competition" 34). However, a careful review of the similarities between Mithraism and Christianity generates skepticism towards any close connections or influence.

Jesus' Teachings on Immortality and Resurrection

Christianity placed more importance on corporeal resurrection from the dead than it did on immortality of the human soul; at the end of history, souls would reunite with bodies in a transformed and indestructible state that would then be transported to a new heaven and a new earth. As Nancey Murphy writes, "...the apostle Paul notes that the whole creation waits in eager longing to be set free from its bondage to decay (Rom. 8:19–23)" (81). Jesus never directly addressed the idea of the immortality of the human soul, but rather taught people how to achieve the condition (West 590; Jones 184). He maintained that the dead who were saved continued to live in some type of existence, "for they cannot die anymore, because they are equal to angels and are sons of God, being sons of the resurrection" (Luke 20:36). Jesus claimed that every living human would be resurrected and be judged according to their lives on earth, as he stated: "Marvel not at this: for the hour cometh, in which all that are in the tombs shall hear his voice" (John 5: 28). Future immortality was a certainty and strictly tied to human interaction with God (Ross 196), but the codicil to this immortality claim was a belief that Jesus was the Messiah. Jesus affirms, "I am the resurrection and the life. Those who believe in me, even though they die, will live, and everyone who lives and believes in me will never die" (John 11: 25, 26). In this case, immortality is at once a future promise and a gift received only for believers (Horton 223).

Jesus asserted that not all human souls are immortal; he confirmed that souls can and will be destroyed: "And do not fear those who kill the body but cannot kill the soul. But rather fear Him who is able to destroy both soul and body in hell" (Matthew 10:28). Logic informs us that, according to this theory, if souls were truly immortal, then they could not be destroyed, but if God truly created our souls, God can destroy them. Jesus wanted human interaction and obedience to God the Father, and warned that salvation would only be given to a chosen few. Jesus stated, "Enter by the narrow gate. For the gate is wide and the way is easy that leads to destruction, and those who enter by it are many. For the gate is narrow and the way is hard that leads to life, and those who find it are few" (Matthew 7:13). This statement is an absolute validation that Christianity did not believe that all humans innately possessed immortal souls, but Christianity was more concerned with saving souls for their future resurrection after death.

In the Lazarus narrative, Jesus also taught that death was like sleep: "He said to them, 'Our friend Lazarus sleeps, but I go that I may wake him up.' Then His disciples said, 'Lord, if he sleeps he will get well.' However, Jesus spoke of his death, but they thought that He was speaking about taking rest in sleep. Then Jesus said to them plainly, 'Lazarus is dead'" (John 11:11–14). Death then becomes the nothingness of sleep, the unconscious abyss, and immortality for Christians arrives at a later time, in an age to come, as Jesus declares, "Assuredly, I say to you, there is no one who has left house or parents or brothers or wife or children, for the sake of the kingdom of God, who shall not receive many times more in this present time, and *in the age to come everlasting life*" (Luke 18:29–30). Thus, early Christians generally believed that humans do not inherently possess immortality, death is like an unconscious sleep state, and only those who accept Jesus as Savior will awaken to eventually gain everlasting life in an incorruptible new body.

THE APOSTLE PAUL

Early Jewish traditions embraced the belief that the dead went to She'ol, where existence was, "dim, lethargic, and unenviable" (Coward 36). As Judaism developed, certain groups like the Pharisees believed in a physical resurrection of the dead.[13] The Apostle Paul, referred to also as Saul of Tarsus, was a Pharisee who persecuted Christians. According to the New Testament, he converted to Christianity after seeing a ball of light on the road to Damascus. After his conversion and his evangelization of gentiles in Asia Minor and Greece, he was responsible for standardizing the Christian view of resurrection. In 1 Corinthians 15:50–52, Paul preached that the saved would be resurrected in a new type of form and existence that would be immortal and not subject to decay. He writes, "Flesh and blood cannot inherit the kingdom of God; nor does corruption inherit incorruption.... For the trumpet will sound and the dead will be raised incorruptible, and we shall be changed."

There was a great debate between Paul of Tarsus and the Greek philosophers regarding immortality: Paul preached the promise of immortality, when saved souls would resurrect at the Second Coming of Christ; for Hellenized believers, that was at odds with the idea that all humans were immortal because they possessed an immortal soul, which would not necessitate a belief in a particular savior god. Paul had to fight against both ingrained Platonic notions and contemporary Greek thought on the soul. As Sir William Smith writes: "The doctrine of the resurrection, as taught by St. Paul, exposed him to the mockery of the Epicureans and Stoics; it must therefore have been a resurrection of the body, for the immortality of the soul would have been no theme of mockery to any school of Greek philosophers" (2711). Plato believed that the soul was an element that preexisted and united with the body before birth; it is the soul that directs the body, lives in the body for a period of time, and leaves at death to dwell in other bodies, until purified, when it returns to the world of the Ideas and attains a conclusive immortality. The very idea of a rebirth of some type highlights the direct Eastern influence on the Greeks, and Paul would have been aware of their reincarnation theories, but Paul's theory of corporeal resurrection from the dead of a single original body was distant from an elemental soul inhabiting a string of corporeal bodies. Paul was, however, influenced by the Platonic idea of the soul's immortality, as R.R. Hardford proposes in his essay, "St. Paul, Plato and Immortality":

> ...Paul would not have countenanced any interpretation of his words, which amounts to saying that the *natural* immortality of the soul is plain because we have a spiritual side to our nature. He would have insisted that immortality or rather "eternal life" must be related to the profound doctrine of the spirit which he sketches in his epistles [74].

Paul's primary message was that all Jews or Gentiles were doomed to die because all had "sinned, and come short of the glory of God" (Romans 3:23). He postulated that Gentiles who had "sinned without law," must "perish without law" (Romans 2:12), while Jews who had sinned under the law must be judged by the law. Paul also presented a hopeful message of salvation through belief that Jesus was the Messiah, hope that "...to them who by patient continuance in well doing seek for glory and honor and immortality, eternal life" (Romans 2:7). To believers, Paul says:

> What fruit had ye then in those things whereof ye are now ashamed? For the end of those things is death. But now being made free from sin, and become servants to God, ye have your fruit unto holiness, and the end everlasting life. For the wages of sin is death [the second death]; but the gift of God is eternal life through Jesus Christ our Lord [Romans 6:21–23].

Immortal life was thus the core of Paul's message. Those who believe in Christ are "led by the Spirit of God" (Romans 8:14), and such are destined to be "glorified" (Romans 8:17) through corporeal resurrection (Romans 8:23), and they will not experience the second death of the condemned (Romans 5:16; 2:11). In the Book of Revelation, John writes that, "Blessed and holy is the one who shares in the first resurrection! Over such the second death has no power, but they will be priests of God and of Christ, and they will reign with him for a thousand years" (Revelation 20:6). This verse has led to millenni-alism's view that when Christ returns he will reign for 1000 years on earth with his saints. James Hastings is a scholar who believes that St. Paul's early version of Christianity was greatly influenced by Egyptian and Greek beliefs and mystery cults; he writes: "It has been argued that the form which the belief in the Resurrection took, especially in St. Paul, was determined by these external influences, especially by the existence in various Mystery-cults of the idea of the death of a god and his resurrection.... 'The resurrection of the body and the life of the world to come' is the phrase which crystallizes the growth of the idea of immortality for the popular mind during the early stages of Christianity" (608).

Paul had a difficult time teaching his resurrection ideas, as the Church in Corinth embraced the resurrection of Jesus, but eschewed any idea of the resurrection of the dead (Hastings 513). Paul responded bluntly in his epistle to the Corinthians: "If there be no such thing as a resurrection of dead persons, then is not Christ risen" (1 Corinthians 15:13). So, Paul was appealing to logic because, if Christ's resurrection is not an historic fact, then the power of death remains unbroken; this type of logic, however, elicited belief through fear, but Paul believed that it was inconceivable that human logic could under-stand the gospel, and nonbelievers were too unenlightened to comprehend the mysteries: "The unspiritual man does not receive the gifts of the Spirit of God, for they are folly to him, and he is not able to understand them because they are spiritually discerned" (1 Corinthians 2:14). Paul assured his followers that immortal life is guaranteed through the death and resurrection of Christ. If this guarantee of resurrection did not exist, humans' existence would be wretched as there would be nothing to look forward to after dying. Paul clearly espouses the dualistic concept of body/soul with the soul as a separate entity.

So is it with the resurrection of the dead. What is sown is perishable; what is raised is imper-ishable. It is sown in dishonor; it is raised in glory. It is sown in weakness; it is raised in power. It is sown a natural body; it is raised a spiritual body. If there is a natural body, there is also a spiritual body [1 Corinthians 15: 42–44].

Paul wrote his letters in an apocalyptic genre that present a spiritual rev-elation within a narrative: the revelation has come to the preacher through an otherworldly messenger representing God's intervention in human affairs; God rescues the righteous and destroys the wicked, and then restores or recreates the cosmos to its original pristine condition (Lioy 28). Paul has us on edge by his warnings that when people feel they are safe and secure, sudden destruction would come upon them (1 Thessalonians 5:3). One of the very best ways to win an audience is through a propagandistic plan based on fear, which could maintain law and order, but ultimately limits the growth of human thought. Propagandistic or not, the apostle Paul was convinced that there was hope beyond the grave, and referred to dead believers as those who had "fallen asleep" (1 Corinthians: 6, 18, 20). He wrote that "as in Adam *all die*, even so in Christ all *shall be* made alive"—first Christ, and then "those who are Christ's at His coming" (1 Corinthians: 22–23).

Christian hope for life after death depends on one and only one doctrine: the doctrine of the resurrection from the dead. This canon is based upon stories of two opposite polarities: Adam, originally created as immortal, becomes, as the result of disobedience and weakness, the condemned mortal who dies. Jesus, created as both mortal and immortal, and as the result of His obedience to God, becomes the firstborn of the dead, the first to be resurrected. This is the comparative logic and lesson from the two opposite heroes of the Bible: in order to be resurrected, Christians must be obedient in order to gain immortality. Is this a form of control? Yes. Is this type of control injurious to society? No, unless it leads to social unrest and war.

There has been much debate regarding the concept of a resurrected new body, as some believe a spiritual body cannot be material because flesh and blood decay and cannot be resurrected into Heaven, but Terence Penelhum points out that we could be recreated with an indestructible, material body; he writes, "It does not follow from this that those who inherit the Kingdom will not have physical bodies, only that they will not have corruptible bodies. But this does not entail that it is not spatial, three-dimensional, or material" (qtd. in Coward 38). This statement could be validated by some descriptions of heaven in the New Testament that suggest some type of material or three-dimensional existence; for example, in John 14:2, Jesus states: "In my Father's house there are many mansions.... I go to prepare a place for you," but this scripture could have a symbolic reading, which would cancel out the idea of a physical, three-dimensional heaven, and that only a bodiless spirit or soul continues after death. To speculate upon the types of elements that would constitute and enliven a new type of body does not seem unreasonable today in light of current medical-scientific research and experiments that attempt to discover the cellular switch of the "longevity gene."

Early Church Fathers and Disputed Beliefs

Christianity began as a Jewish sect whose adherents met in synagogues (Ziffer xiii; Lang 237; Kee 18), so it is not surprising that the Christian view of the soul, immortality, corporeal resurrection, and other views of the afterlife included Judaic teachings. What separates Christian from Jews is the belief that Jesus of Nazareth is the Messiah or Christ whose death on the cross absolved humans of "original sin," and made possible the promise of salvation and eternal life for all. "Original" sin is a doctrine based on the belief that all humans are born as sinners and destined to die because of Adam and Eve's disobedience; Adam and Eve were originally immortal beings (Dunderberg 40; Anderson and Swinton 266; Fitzgerald and Cavadini 445), but because of their "sin" all humans became undeserving of God's grace, and could only be "saved" and achieve immortality through belief and baptism in Jesus Christ. Jesus' death offered a means to be absolved of original sin and achieve eternal life, but this concept is based upon old beliefs that the sins of the father still rest in the children. While this doctrine has been accepted by mainstream churches of the Catholic and Protestant persuasion, there has been dispute among some Protestant factions who believe in predestination, so that a person's afterlife has already been determined by God (Buis 87; Hillerbrand 217).

The Lutheran position on original sin agrees with Roman Catholicism; Pastor Martin E. Billmeier writes: "The *Augsburg Confession* states the Lutheran position on original sin is thus, 'It is also taught among us that since the fall of Adam all men who are born according to the course of nature are conceived and born in sin. That is, all men are full of evil lust and inclinations from their mother's wombs and are unable by nature to have true fear of God and true faith in God. Moreover, this inborn sickness and hereditary sin is truly sin and condemns to the eternal wrath of God all those who are not born again through Baptism and the Holy Spirit.' So, original sin is the condition with which every human is born that destines them to commit individual acts of sin" (Billmeier). Other earlier factions have denied the doctrine of original sin; this is the dogma of "Pelagianism"[14] that imagines humans are inherently good, morally unaffected by the Fall, and can attain moral perfection through free will, and because they are already forgiven by Jesus' sacrifice, they may warrant God's grace through free will, without the sacrifice of Jesus (Hindson and Caner 392).

While original sin was later rejected by Christian sects, such as the Baptists and its fundamentalist offshoots during the Reformation in Europe, later disputes continued regarding physical resurrection theories. The *Church of England Catechism*, published in 1876, claims that French liberal Protestant factions denied corporeal resurrection, imagining instead that once the body dies, the saved human soul ascends to heaven (11). According to *The Westminster Review* from 1864, doubts about resurrection began in the early Church in Corinth (72), and in response to these early doctrines Justin Martyr, a second century CE Christian apologist stated, "For I choose to follow not men or men's doctrines, but God and the doctrines [delivered] by Him. For if you have fallen in with some who are called Christians, but who do not admit this [truth], and venture to blaspheme the God of Abraham, and the God of Isaac, and the God of Jacob; who say there is no resurrection of the dead, and that their souls, when they die, are taken to heaven; do not imagine that they are Christians" (276). Here, Justin Martyr asserts that dead souls do not go to heaven; they must await resurrection. Perhaps the suffering involved in a dead spirit is that the soul cannot enjoy either this life or the next because it is in a state of hovering where it died, frustrated that it cannot participate, while longing to meet the Divine.

Another Christian apologist was Tertullian, a second century religious leader in Carthage, who lectured against heresy and Gnostic ideas; he is often referred to as "the founder of Western theology" (Gonzalez 91–93). Tertullian wrote that the soul is corporeal, and exists at the moment of conception, and is sprung "from the breath of God, immortal" and "evolved from one archetypal soul," so if man's essence is the soul, a preserver of God's spirit, then man is like God (Karamanolis 197; Potts and Devanno, "Tertullian's Theory" 210–211). Tertullian advocated for corporeal resurrection for two reasons: scriptural evidence, and the fact that the Christian faith could not possibly rest upon vagueness or doubt (Lehtipuu 97). Tertullian reasoned that just as the flesh of Jesus died and was resurrected, so also would human flesh share in this same resurrection (Dunn 25). About the resurrection and the changed corporeality of the re-enlivened body, Tertullian writes to validate Paul's teachings and to provide a logical connection between the mortal body and the incorruptible body:

> The resurrection is first, and afterwards the kingdom. We say, therefore, that the flesh rises again, but that when changed it obtains the kingdom. "For the dead shall be raised incorruptible," even those who had been corruptible when their bodies fell into decay; "and we shall be changed, in a moment, in the twinkling of an eye. For this corruptible"—and as he spake, the apostle seemingly pointed to his own flesh—"must put on incorruption, and this mortal must put on immortality." in order, indeed, that it may be rendered a fit substance for the kingdom of God. "For we shall be like the angels." This will be the perfect change of our flesh—only after its resurrection. Now if, on the contrary, there is to be no flesh, how then shall it put on incorruption and immortality? Having then become something else by its change, it will obtain the kingdom of God, no longer the (old) flesh and blood, but the body which God shall have given it. Rightly then does the apostle declare, "Flesh and blood cannot inherit the kingdom of God"; for this (honour) does he ascribe to the changed condition which ensues on the resurrection [qtd. in Roberts and Donaldson 451].

The prominent church fathers, Irenaeus[15] and Augustine, had differing views on immortality, but both embraced the idea of original sin (Jeffrey 17). Irenaeus believed in a "conditional"[16] immortality that depended on the grace of God upon accepting Jesus Christ as savior; he believed that nonbelievers were deprived of the gift of immortality (Thiselton 250; Briggman, "Irenaeus' Christology" 543, 544). Augustine believed in the human soul's natural immortality (Fudge 21), or an "unconditional" immortality with souls headed either to "eternal bliss or eternal torment" (qtd. in Thiselton 250). St. Augustine demonstrates the immortality of the soul in *Soliloquy* II, XIX, 33 by showing that it possesses truth; truth is immortal because it can never be untrue; therefore, the soul in which truth dwells cannot die. Augustine writes: "Therefore the soul is immortal; believe in the truth; it cries out with a loud voice that it abides in you, that it is immortal, and that, whatever the death of the body might mean, her dwelling (the soul's) cannot be separated from you" (Augustine 106). Differences aside, both Irenaeus and Augustine merged the nonbiblical idea of an immortal soul with the biblical promise of resurrection; this interpretation accepts that the soul lives on after the body dies, and at the resurrection unites with a new, spiritual body. These varied beliefs in an immortal soul signified that all humans are either endowed with immortality at their creation, or immortality is a gift given to believers through the death and resurrection of Jesus Christ. The message of the Bible is that we are not immortal, but that God wants to give us immortality: "For the wages of sin is death, but the gift of God is eternal life in Christ Jesus our Lord" (Romans 6:23).

Today's Christians

Most contemporary Christians blend the nonbiblical idea of an immortal soul with the scriptural assurance of resurrection, and thrash out their own conception of immortality, which assumes that after the body dies, the soul lingers reuniting with an incorruptible, spiritual body at Christ's Second Coming, a gift through the death and resurrection of Jesus Christ. Today, these ideas are still popularly juxtaposed with the nonreligious view that all humans are imagined to possess an immortal soul, this latter theory being a post–Christian, humanist perception that there is no need for a redeemer, intermediary, or God to intercede on their behalf at death, as humans innately have immortality, and govern their own fate.

Clearly, as Christianity progressed throughout the Mediterranean region, apologists and theologians who accepted immortality at resurrection modified their teaching on immortality to blend with Greek and Jewish philosophies. By the time of Augustine, dogmas on body-soul dualism and immortality of the soul were strongly embedded as Christian principles. This hybrid account produced the theory that when the body dies, saved souls journey to heaven, and at the end of time, on resurrection day, souls will reunite with transformed, indestructible bodies that will eternally live in a paradisiac state.

The New Testament built upon Hebrew Scriptures regarding final resurrection and judgment, "...for an hour is coming when all who are in the tombs will hear his voice and come out, those who have done good to the resurrection of life, and those who have done evil to the resurrection of judgment" (John 5:26–29). From Egypt, Greece, and Rome, concepts of the soul, judgment, and resurrection would eventually influence and construct the Islamic religious consciousness. Greek philosophy would influence Muslim philosophers' conception of the soul, and Christian concepts of judgment, resurrection, and heaven scarcely changed in the new religion of Islam.

7

Islam Declares the Final Revelation on Immortality

On that day [the unbelievers] shall be sternly thrown into the fire of Hell....
But in fair gardens the righteous shall dwell in bliss, rejoicing in what
their Lord will give them. Their Lord will shield them from the scourge
of Hell. He will say: Eat and drink to your hearts' content. This is the
reward of your labors. (Qur'an 52:13–24)

Immortality refers to existence after death in some type of subjective consciousness, but as in all religions there has been controversy about the elusive nature of eternal life, there being no real proof what happens to people after death; humans' reliance on hope and faith in a resurrection, a coming kingdom, and an eternal paradise could be considered tenuous or speculative. However, religions provide an element of hope for a better existence, but people must have faith in a power beyond what is mortal; skeptics would say that life in this world is all there is, but the question becomes—why have all civilizations claimed otherwise?

Islam is the last of the great Abrahamic religions, and its conceptual development of an eschatological doctrine was a recursive editing of global beliefs and an original embrace of a new or final revelation. There is neither a pantheon of immortal gods, nor is there a son of God in Islam; there is one immortal god only—Allah. For Muslims, immortality is not a right, but humans become candidates for immortality, and this condition must be achieved through concentrated, spiritual and moral effort (Iqbal 95; Ahmed 130). Islam presented righteous people with immortality in exchange for submission, just as Christianity had offered immortality in exchange for belief in Jesus Christ as the Messiah, and just as some sects of Judaism had conferred immortality in exchange for adherence to the law. Immortality in the Abrahamic religions enforces a righteous code of conduct and a surrender to a force greater than man's private ego, and preaches that humans will become immortal only at resurrection. Islam amalgamated reason and revelation with Greek theorists and Judaic and Christian eschatological ideas, and presented universally inspired hypotheses about death, soul, afterlife, resurrection, and heaven that Muslims believe are final and conclusive.

The Heavens of Islamic Cosmology

Directly in centuries following the emergence of Islam, traditional Islamic cosmology included seven earths and seven heavens with God's throne above everything, so this was a universe that contained a hierarchy and grades of being (Janos 27). These seven distinct heavens in Islam are not final, afterlife destinations for the dead, but are regions distinct from earth (Qur'an 2:29; 65:12). Muslims do not consider the seven heavens to be an event after the Day of Judgment, but the seven heavens are "...an institution of the time until Doomsday" (Luling 477). In religious-mythological cosmology, seven heavens generally have signified seven sectors where immortal beings live, and have often referred to the sun, moon, planets and stars (Hetherington 267, 401). Islam partially adopted the idea of seven heavens from apocryphal Jewish writings; according to traditions, Mohammed passed through these seven heavens during his night journey (Hughes 170).[1] In Islam, the varied altitudinal heavens are separated by gateways guarded by angels, which can be opened if the Muslim was observant in following prescribed practices on earth: jihad, charity, fasting, and the Hajj to Mecca. Vincent J. Cornell writes: "Having passed successfully through the gates of the seven heavens, the soul celebrates its arrival at the Uppermost Heaven where it sees its name inscribed on the register[2] that is kept until Resurrection Day.... Here, the soul attains its closest proximity to the Divine Presence" (158).[3] This biographical register is directly referenced in the Qur'an as the record that will either condemn or save:

> And every man's fate we have fastened about his neck: and on the Day of Resurrection will we bring forthwith to him a book which shall be proffered to him wide open: Read thy book: there needeth none but thyself to make out an account against thee this day [17:13–14].

This Islamic register or record recalls many passages from the Hebrew Bible and the New Testament that refer to the "Book of Life," which is reportedly a record of the names of those who will be saved. Psalm 69: 28 records: "Let them be blotted out of the book of the living, and not be written with the righteous." The prophet Daniel speaks of the last day when the saved who are recorded in the Book will be rescued: "Now at that time Michael, the great prince who stands *guard* over the sons of your people, will arise. And there will be a time of distress such as never occurred since there was a nation until that time; and at that time your people, everyone who is found written in the book, will be rescued"(Daniel 12:1). In the gospels Christ says, "...but rejoice that your names are recorded in heaven" (Luke 10:20). One of the most dramatic passages regarding the Book of Life is found in Revelation 20:12, which also alleges that there is a record of personal human activities, and those who led righteous lives and believed in the Gospel of Jesus Christ would be saved: "And I saw the dead, the great and the small, standing before the throne, and books were opened; and another book was opened, which is *the book* of life; and the dead were judged from the things which were written in the books, according to their deeds." Both the Qur'an and the Holy Scripture of the Jews and Christians agree that this Book will appear at the Resurrection, and will be used to identify the saved.

The Qur'an briefly references Mohammad's passage through the seven heavens, but Hadith literature[4] explains the account in more detail. The angel Gabriel appeared with Buraq, the heavenly steed of the prophets, while Mohammad was at the Sacred Mosque in Mecca. Buraq took Mohammad to the Western Wall in Jerusalem, and after prayers and varied tests, Mohammad was taken on a tour of the heavens. Mohammad claimed to have met famous biblical characters while ascending to the seventh heaven; however, this story is not original, as many religious stories are based upon more ancient texts, and the mythology of seven heavens is ancient—at least as old as ancient Sumer (Arnold 12).

The ancient Sumerian netherworld, administered by the Annun'aki gods, was constructed like a city with seven walls and seven gates, but before passing through these gates, the deceased had to cross the demon-infested steppe lands and the river Huber (Walton 318). In *Ascent to Heaven in Islamic and Jewish Mysticism*, Algis Uzdavinys quotes professor Vita Daphna Arbel about the structure of ancient Sumerian temples for Anu and Antu: "The temple structure included significant symbolic features. It had three gates which open outwards and seven courts around a courtyard in which the shrine of destinies is found.... Thus, seven heavens or palace courts had to be crossed before the worshipper comes face to face with the enthroned deity of cosmic destinies" (qtd. in 93). Wayne Horowitz also corroborates the Sumerian origins of the seven heavens: "A number of Sumerian incantations may preserve a Sumerian cosmographic tradition of seven heavens and seven earths..." (208).

In a Zoroastrianism story in the *Book of Arta Viraf* that predates Islam by almost 1000 years, the priest Arta Viraf is said to have travelled through the seven heavens in a dream-journey to speak with Ormazd, the great deity of the whole universe (Clare 91; Rawlinson 272). Originally, the number seven may have been taken from the celestial bodies that are nearest to earth, but in subsequent mythologies, the heavens symbolize distinct levels of paradise for pious humans. While these ideas originated in ancient Mesopotamian religions, similar beliefs are found in Hinduism, Judaism, and in Christian sects such as Catholicism (Josi 172; Schwartz 185; Arnold 12).[5] The Qur'an does refer to "seven heavens," but doesn't explain the thinking behind this particular number, leaving the features of heaven open to creative interpretation.

Islamic Concept of God

In all Abrahamic religions, there is one immortal God. In Islam, God is the only Divine being, the omnipotent and omniscient creator, all-merciful, and judge of the universe; humans must submit to God's will, and the human will is very limited as human actions are controlled by divine law (Esposito 22; Pelikan, "The Only Source" 18). God is singular, inherently one (*ahad*), and, unlike Christianity, not a trinity[6] of being (Esposito 88). Zulfiqar Ali Shah writes about God's interaction with humans and their dependence on God for success in life: "The True God is the True Sovereign. He helps whomsoever He pleases, benefits whomsoever He wants, and causes harm to whomsoever deserves so, 'There is no victory except from Allah, the Exalted, the Wise'" (492; Qur'an 3:126). According to this view, God's relationship with the world is to test humans, and make sure that they are obedient to his laws and faithful in their worship. God in Islam is not only majestic and sovereign, but also a personal god who morally guides and protects humans. Most Muslims today believe that the religion of Abraham, which is now split into Judaism, Christianity, and Islam, are of one source, which is the Almighty God.

In ancient times, humans named god or gods with different titles or designations that described a list of powers or qualities of temperament: "Sky God," "Thunder God," "Lamb of God," "the Compassionate," etc. Allah is imbued with being merciful, all-seeing and all-knowing; according to the Qur'an, Allah has 99 names, and each name evokes a characteristic, and among these names, Allah is most often referred to as "the Most Gracious" (*al-rahman*) and "the Most Merciful" (*al-rahim*) (Moghul, "Allah" 41); nothing is truly divine but God, nothing truly real but the Real, nothing truly merciful but the All-Merciful (Chittick, "Love" 232). Just as in Judaism and Christianity, Islam believes in an Omniscient Being whose power and intelligence are beyond man's intellectual ability to comprehend. According to the Qur'an,

"No vision can grasp Him, but His grasp is over all vision. He is above all comprehension, yet is acquainted with all things" (6:103). Islam contends that humans will never understand the fundamental nature of God, but can come to know God's disposition through memorizing and studying God's 99 names. David Bentley writes: "A great Muslim Theologian, Al'Ghazali, expressed what has become a fixed theological position. He stated that while it is impossible to know God's essence, it is possible to know the attributes of God as expressed in the 99 names" (xiv). A Hadith from Abu Hurayra (678 CE), the closest companion of the prophet, asserts: "God has 99 names, one hundred minus 1, and whoever memorizes them will enter Paradise" (qtd. in Campo 515). Muslim theologians have divided the names into words reflecting God's essence and words designating God's qualities (Allah and Al-Rahman 515).

Unlike Christians who have statues and paintings of God, Jesus, and the Holy Spirit,[7] Islam forbids the fashioning of an image of God or the prophet Mohammad. According to Veli-Matti Karkkainen, "As in the Bible, there are occasionally anthropomorphic metaphors of Allah such as the face of God (2:115; 92:20) or the hand(s) of God (48:10; 5:64), although in general, Islam is very cautious about picturing Allah" (368). God cannot be described in human words or by human language; the Qur'an only employs language that is allegorical and symbolic to describe God, as it is a great sin in Islam to portray God in art (Byrne 94; "The Path of Allah" 5).

Belief in Magical Beings: Angels and Jinns

ANGELS IN ISLAM

Like many previous religions, Islam embraces a belief in spiritual or supernatural beings, such as angels, Jinns, and the one God; from earliest history, religious ideas abounded with stories of immortal beings, or about humans, primarily demi-gods, who became immortal. Very much like every religion since ancient Sumer and Egypt, Islam agreed that all humans possess the ability to attain immortality, but they have to die first. This is evident beginning with the *Epic of Gilgamesh*, and ending with the story of Jesus Christ who was "the first-born of the dead"[8] (Colossians 1:18; Revelation 1:5).

Most religions from ancient civilizations to the current times believe in angels, another global and unified concept that should encourage people to dwell on their similarities rather than their differences. One of the six Sunni articles of faith is the belief in immortal angels or *malaekah* or *mala'ika* who were created from light (*nur*), who obey god in all matters, and always do good. Muslims share belief in some of the same high-ranking angels as Christians and Jews: the angel Gabriel or *Jibreel* reportedly appeared to Mohammad over a period of twenty years; Michael or *Mikhael* is the angel of mercy who brings rain and thunder. Other angels in Islam are Izrafil or *Izrael*, the angel of death, as well as the angel who blows the trumpet or horn signaling Judgment Day; angels Munkar and Nakir are angels who question people when they are lowered into their graves (Helminski 92; Webster 96).

Somewhat like Medieval Christianity's division of angels into spheres, Islam set a hierarchy and category of 14 angels defined by the jobs God assigns to them, such as guardians, protectors, recorders of deeds, intercessors, etc. According to Catholic teaching, there are basically nine divisions of angels: seraphim, cherubim, thrones, dominions, virtues, powers, archangels, principalities, and angels (Nowell 26). The order of archangels is the highest order of angels referred to in the Qur'an and in the Bible (Surat az-Zumar, 75; Surat as-Saffat, 164–166; Jude 9; 1 Thessalonians 4:16); according to God's commands regarding job categories (Surat an-Nahl, 49–50), archangels may belong to more than one hierarchy of angels, such as St. Michael Archangel,[9] who is a princely seraph.[10] The archangels have a unique role as God's messenger to people at critical times in history and salvation as in the Annunciation, the Apocalypse, and the revelation to Mohammad (Surah Hud, 69–73; Surah Al 'Imran, 39–41; Surah Al 'Imran, 42–47; Tobit 12:6, 15; John 5:4; Revelation 12:7–9).

As in Islam, Roman Catholic and standard Christian teachings describe angels as closest to the material world and human beings; there has been a preponderance of stories in all religions of unusual visitors who bring revelatory messages, announcements, warnings, and comfort to humans, and Islam is no different. For example, angels visited every Hebrew prophet in the Bible and every important biblical character who would change history, or alter the course of belief in a new revelation; there are many instances in the Qur'an that mention the Angel Gabriel's visitation to Mohammad (Surat at-Takwir, 19; Surat an-Najm, 4–6; Surat an-Najm, 13–18). Christianity and Islam upended history, with Christians believing Jesus is the Son of God, Messiah, and Savior, and with Islam claiming God's final revelation from the final prophet who is Mohammad (Knitter, "Islam and Christianity" 560). Muslims also believe in Jesus as a prophet whose message became a great part of Islam, but they do not believe God has a son, nor do they believe that Jesus was crucified because God would never kill His own son. These religions believe that angels relay people's prayers to God, and they will assist believers in escaping any type of harm, so this comforts people knowing they are not alone in the world.

Just as in other religions, and although mentioned only a few times, the Qur'an describes the angels as having wings: "Praise be to God, who created (out of nothing) the heavens and the earth, who made the angels messengers with wings—two, three, or four (pairs) and adds to Creation as He pleases: for God has power over all things" (Fatir 35:1; I'Tiqad-Nama 27). S.R. Burge writes of the aforementioned verses that "The opening of Q. 35:1 (Sūrat al-Malāika or Sūrat al-Fāṭir) attests to the creative power of God and describes the angels as winged messengers, the only aya where angels are portrayed in this way in the whole of the Qur'an ... it is one of only a few which describe the relationships between God, humans and angels" (50).

That Islam would depict beings who were able to fly is not a new idea; as far back as in Sumerian pictographs, wings represented a god or goddess who could fly; in *The Secret Teachings of All Ages,* Manley Hall recounts a legend that, at the beginning of earth's history, "winged serpents" were actually the demigods who predated all known historical civilizations of every nation (LXXXVIII). Angels are described in anthropomorphic form in a multitude of biblical stories; every patriarch and prophet met these angels face-to-face. They appeared to Abraham and he called them "Lords," and made a feast for them and they ate; later two of them visited Abraham's nephew Lot in Sodom, a city they later destroyed. The prophet Elijah not only saw the Divine Chariot of the angels, he lifted off from earth in it (2 Kings 2:8–12).

The Sumerians did not believe that the gods answered prayers, and so developed a system of angelic personal gods or intercessors through which people achieved salvation. Even today, angels and saints are prayer intercessors to God on man's behalf; this is an ancient custom that continues today in the Roman Catholic Church. Flying angels in Islam is not a new concept, but angels became a metaphorical image, as Muslim tradition maintained that "wings" connote transcendence, freedom, and speed in time and space; their wings attest to their pure spirituality (El-Zein 50). Therefore, Islam attests to supernatural immortality through revelation, angelic visitation, and through the word of God, just as does its Abrahamic brother religions: "As Al-Shahrastani stated of Al-Ash'ari's doctrine: 'The sentences and words which are revealed through the tongues of angels to the prophets are signs of the eternal word: the sign itself is created and originated, but what is signified is eternal'" (qtd. in Halverson 132).

ANGELS IN HELL

Most religions use rhetorical strategies to frighten potential or existing adherents to obey and believe what is taught, or to frighten others into believing prescribed doctrines; these strategies include horrifying descriptions and metaphors of hell to manage their listeners' or readers' perceptions in order to regulate their thinking, and ultimately control their behavior. Unlike the

Christian conception of hell, which does not allow anyone at any time to escape the fires and torments, Muslims believe there are angels in hell who are there to cleanse humans of spiritual errors. Islam's hell is meant as a temporary place of punishment, except for polytheists and nonbelievers, who will be punished forever; no one will come out of Hell except remorseful, sinful humans who believed in Allah and the Prophet Mohammad. As well as the Qur'anic seven gates, in the body of the Hadith, hell has seven levels with the least severe as Gehenna (Khalil 150; Vance 73). According to the Qur'an, there is a bridge that damned souls must pass across to enter the seven gates of hell with each gate as an entryway for a specific group of sinners (15: 33–34; Kaltner 229). Naeem Abdullah writes that "The prophet Mohammad is reportedly to have said, 'The seven gates are shown in the human body as his two eyes, two nostrils, his mouth and his two ears, these are the gates on the human being that will lead him to Paradise or hell" (32). So, humans' use of their bodies' physical components during temporal life determines what gate they pass through; any sins prompted by their senses will need to be purified.

Malik is known as the angel of hell to Muslims who consider him an archangel. Malik is in charge of maintaining *Jahannam* (hell), and carrying out God's command to punish the people in hell. He supervises 19 other angels who also guard hell and punish its inhabitants (At-Tahrim 66:6; Mehar 13; Oliver and Lewis 233). For Muslims, as well as for Christians, Hell is a real place for sinners, criminals and nonbelievers, for those who defy God's laws, and for those who reject His messengers; Hell is neither an existential state of mind, nor is the place an imaginary location. Oliver Leaman writes about the Islamic hell: "It is an eschatological place of punishment, physical torture, mental anguish and despair" (259). According to the Qur'an, hell is the ultimate place of loss and degradation:

> Our Lord! Surely, whom You admit to the Fire, indeed You have disgraced him, and never will the wrongdoers find any helpers [Qur'an 3:192].

> Know they not that whoever opposes God and His Messenger (Mohammad), certainly for him will be the Fire of Hell to abide therein? That is the extreme disgrace [Qur'an 9:63].

MAGICAL, MYSTICAL JINN

Muslims also believe in semi-immortal, shape-shifting Jinn,[11] who are creatures somewhere between angels and humans; like humans, Jinn possess intelligence, free will, and are capable of salvation. According to Dawn Perlmutter, "Jinn provide Islamic explanations for evil, illness, health, wealth, and position in society as well as all mundane and inexplicable phenomena in between" ("The Politics" 85). According to the Qur'an, Jinn were invoked and worshipped in pre–Islamic Arabia (6:100; 37:158; 34:41; Islam and Camp-bell, "Satan Has Afflicted" 231). In Arabian and Muslim folklore, Jinn are somewhat like demons with supernatural powers, which they can grant to others; this sounds very much like the belief in praying for angelic protection. Jinn are believed to live thousands of years, and they eat, drink, procreate, and eventually die. According to Annemarie Schimmel in *Introduction to Islam*, "Their [Jinn's] existence is officially acknowledged in the Qur'an (Sura 72), so much so that even the possibility of marriage between humans and Jinn is discussed among scholars" (83). While angels live in the celestial realms, Jinns live in the sublunary or earthly realm (El-Zein 50).

The word Jinn or Genii derives from *janna* meaning covered, concealed, hidden, or protected. In the Qur'an, Jinn are mentioned as good and evil spirits who influence humans to be righteous or to sin; their origins are said to be in fire and some of them are said to be evil geniuses (Qur'an 15:27; 55: 15; Hughes 134), and it is they who entice men to low passions and desires. Some scholars propose the Jinn are the adepts, or the Sons of Fire referred to in various mystery schools. In Arabic folktales the Jinn fly, just as in the Sumerian and Babylonian tales of flying demons (El-Zein 50); however, Islam makes a differentiation between Jinn and demons. Other Arabic stories claim that God created the Jinn 2000 years before Adam; Thomas P. Hughes writes, "It is commonly believed that the preadamite Jinn were governed by forty kings, to each of whom the Arab writers give the name of Sulaiman (or Solomon)" (134). Legend has it that King Solomon possessed a ring, probably a diamond, with which he called up "Jinns" to help his armies in battle. The concept that this king employed the help of Jinns may have originated from 1 Kings 6:7, which describes the magically built house of interlocking stones that was constructed without tools: "And the house, when it was in building, was built of stone made ready before it was brought there, so there was neither hammer nor axe nor any tool of iron heard in the house, while it was in build-ing" (Coulter-Harris 10).

In Islam, Jinn are "fiery" spirits (Qur'an 15:27) associated with the desert who can shape-shift or take on human and animal forms to manipulate human actions and decisions; according to Heffner, they are quick to punish those indebted to them who do not follow their many rules. There are several myths concerning the home of the Jinn. In the *Arabian Nights*, Jinn or genies came from Aladdin's Lamp, so they come from a metal vessel that gives light, just like in the ancient Sumerian tales of "dragon" gods who descended to earth in flying vessels that gave light. Persian mythology depicts some of them as living in a place called *Jinnistan*. Ancient Persians held the popular belief that Jinnistan was an imaginary country where lived the Jinn who sub-mitted to King Solomon. Others say Jinns live with other supernatural beings in the Kaf, mystical emerald mountains surrounding the earth (Hefner, "Jinn"; Coulter-Harris 11). Hughes provides an ancient story of the preadamite Jinns as told by al-Qazwini: reportedly, the Jinn were a race that covered the earth and were granted many favors from God, but they turned unrighteous and were destroyed by an army of God's angels, "...who took possession of the earth, and drove away the Jinns to the regions of the islands, and made many of them prisoners," one of whom was Azazil who was later called Iblis (134). Iblis grew up around angels and became the leader of the Jinns "...until the affair with Adam happened," or until he refused to worship Adam. In the Qur'anic creation story, angels lose in a battle of wits with Adam, so they all prostrate themselves before him, with the exception of Iblis, who refused because he considered himself superior to the "clay creature" (Chipman, "Adam" 138). Iblis fell in stature from being an angel to that of a fallen angel or Jinn, and was reduced to tempting humans to sin (Qur'an 15:28–43; Nigosian 97).

Greek Influence on Concepts of the Muslim Soul versus Traditional Beliefs

Plato developed the theory that the human soul is an entity that exists with divine and incorporeal beings, so that the soul existed before attaching itself to a body, which simply becomes a tool for the soul in the material world. Plato explained that the soul returns to its original abode after the body dies. When Socrates was asked how he should be buried, he replied: "As you please, provided I remain still with you, and do not make my escape elsewhere ... as soon as the poison has operated I shall remain no longer here, but be transported to the mansions of the blest..." (qtd. in Mendelssohn 205). Islamic scholars rejected Greek-Hellenistic philosophy, and considered its influence as evil and pagan, but by the ninth century CE the rationalist theologians or Mu'tazilites, such al-Kindi and al-Razi, acknowledged Greek philosophy as a method of questioning instead of blindly accepting dogma. Just as Plato had divided the soul into parts, Abu Yusuf ibn Ishaq al-Kindi (800–866 CE), the Father of Islamic Philosophy, believed in an immortal soul with three parts: intellectual, passionate, and desirous (Abboud 53). Hamid Naseem writes: "As to the nature of the soul, al-Kindi opposes any material-istic conceptions ... regards man as a soul and body is its instrument, and the souls is substance not the body, and the substances don't depend on bodies ... al-Kindi finds no difficulty in explaining the immortality of the human soul. Having descended from the world-soul, and being independent of body, it is an uncompounded, simple, imperishable substance" (67, 68).

The later Medieval Muslim scholar, Ibn Rushd (Averroës) (1126–1198 CE), however, believed that the rational soul[12] is not separate from matter, so the soul must also be material and have a temporal beginning (Craig 43; Fortney and Onellion 150). The rational soul, as defined by Muslim thinkers, has no beginning or end—it is eternal. The rational soul is not aware of anything material, including its body, but is aware of its own existence. For Ibn Rushd, the theoretical intellect is the rational soul; in the end, he reconciled ethical theory and religious orthodoxy with obvious contradictions between human reason and religious faith (Borrowman, "The Islamization" 354; Fortney and Onellion 149). Influenced by ancient Greek philosophy, Ibn Rushd, inspired by Aristotle, reasoned that immortality could only be understood as the absorption of the individual mind into the greater whole of the universal intellect (Craig 43). He agreed with Aristotle that individual souls cannot exist apart from material bodies, but stuck to the Qur'anic concept of corporeal resurrection (Kak 38). Ovey N. Mohammed writes:

> The understanding of the soul/spirit as of a material nature influenced many [Muslim thinkers] to claim at the resurrection the soul will be part of the revivified body, and not a separate spiritual substance joined to it.... Others, such as those influenced by Greek philosophy, denied that the spirit (or soul) was in any way material. They held that it was a purely spiritual substance and so immortal by nature [32].

Ibn Rushd, like the earlier ibn Sina and al-Ghazali, was part of an important movement to try to combine Aristotle's scientific description of the world with religious views to create a unified idea of the world. Ibn Rushd also thought that the human soul was divided into two parts: one part personal, and the other part divine, so that when a person died, the personal soul died, but the divine soul merged into the universal divine soul (Averroës 103). In his famous *Reviving Religious Knowledge*, Al-Ghazali advocated for a "science" of the Way of the Afterlife, a teleological devotion to prepare the individual soul to meet the Divine, which he believed was the ultimate event in every human life (Gianotti 597).

Plato's theory regarding the existence of the human soul before creation of the material body is accepted among many Muslim mystics and philosophers; even so, the theory that the incorporeal soul is eternally severed from a material body is unacceptable to them. Just as in Christianity, the return of the soul without any material body at the Resurrection was not acknowledged by Islam. Therefore, various Muslim philosophers accepted spiritual-material resurrection because of their faith in divine revelation. Neoplatonism greatly persuaded Islamic philosophy, but Islamic philosophers were constrained by Muslim theology, which imagines that the individual character or nature of a person inhabits the soul, without free will, but is accountable to God at final judgment (Wilde 141).

The nature of the soul—or *nafs*—is immortal in traditional Islamic thought, and Muslims firmly believe that the soul comes into existence at the moment of conception; if a fetus is aborted, the soul of that fetus will be a witness on the Day of Judgment against those who destroyed it (Picken, "Tazkiyat Al-Nafs" 101; Norcliffe 122). Muslims believe that at the moment of death, the person's soul travels to an afterlife of happiness until the day of judgment when the soul reunites with a perfect, corporeal body at which point the person achieves immortality, and is destined to heaven or hell. Muslims think that the body and its physical actions reflect the soul, either good or evil. Nerina Rustomji writes: "Islamic eschatology provides an afterworld, while Christian eschatology focuses on an afterlife.... Christian texts in general present the quality of future lives through relationships with humans, angels, and the divine. By contrast, Muslims enjoy an afterlife within the parameters of a physically described afterworld" (xvii, viii).

Resurrection, Judgment and Paradise

For Muslims, believing in corporeal resurrection from the dead affirms God's sovereignty, and encourages a person's accountability to God (Swanson, "Resurrection" 248). God determines how long each individual lives, and, according to the Qur'an, the deceased must wait for the Day of Judgment when everyone will be culpable for their actions: "Then as for he who is given his record in his right hand; he will be judged with an easy account.... But as for he who is given his record behind his back; He will cry out for destruction" (84: 7–8, 10–11). In Islam it is, "...an article of faith that there is a Day of Resurrection and of Judgment on which the living and the dead shall answer for their thoughts and actions..." (Coward 56). The faithful will be saved, but the wicked will be sent to hell, where they will, "Burn in a blaze" (Qur'an 84:12), just like the fiery hell of Christianity.

There are a multitude of other similarities between Islam and Christianity regarding eschatological beliefs, such as the false messiah or antichrist figure, called the Dajjal,[13] who will appear, but be defeated upon the return of Christ, son of Mary, who will accompany the Mahdi, or Divinely-Guided One," a kind of Muslim Messiah who is sometime identified as Jesus[14] (Corfield, "The End" 37; Livne-Kafri, "Jerusalem in Early Islam" 383). In the Hadith-Bukhari 9.504, it is said that the Dajjal will be blind in the right eye, and his left eye will look like a rotten grape (Al-Bukhari 1872, Book 93). Varied Hadiths say the Dajjal will terrorize believers, and will appear in Iraq or in Iran (Kabbani 217). According to Oliver Leaman, the Dajjal will deceive multitudes of people, just as is predicted in the description of the Antichrist in the Book of Revelation: "The Dajjal is successful, he revives the dead, he is very powerful, he leads a large army, and so his claim to be the representative of the divine has some strength to it" (165). This is reminiscent of the description of the Antichrist in Chapter 13 in Revelation: "It works great signs, even making fire come down from heaven to earth in the sight of men[15]; and by the signs which it is allowed to work in the presence of the beast, it deceives those who dwell on earth, bidding them make an image for the beast which was wounded by the sword and yet lived" 13:13–14).

The Muslim paradise also sounds much like the Christian description of heaven in Revelation 21:4: "And God shall wipe away all tears from their eyes; and there shall be no more death, neither sorrow, nor crying, neither shall there be any more pain: for the former things are passed away." The Muslim heaven is where the saved will have everything they ever desired: four fruit-filled gardens with four streams or rivers where the saved lounge, "…on beds whose linings are of silk brocade and the fruit of the two gardens is hanging low" (Qur'an, 55: 50, 54; 61:12; 76:13; 98:8). It is a place where the saved live with angels, prophets from the Hebrew Bible and enjoy the presence of God, and where there will be no hatred or weariness (Rustomji xiv; Qur'an 15:47; 35:35; 15:48). The difference in description between the Muslim and Christian paradise is Islam's promise of a sensual and sexual paradise, whereas in Matthew 22: 30, Jesus stated that, "For in the resurrection they neither marry, nor are given in marriage, but are as angels in heaven." The Qur'an, however, promises both sex and marriage in the afterlife: "Within gardens and springs, Wearing [garments of] fine silk and brocade, facing each other…. We will marry … fair women with large, [beautiful] eyes" (Qur'an, 44:52–54). "In them [the gardens] are women limiting [their] glances, untouched before them by man or Jinni—As if they were rubies and coral" (Qur'an, 55:56, 58). Other than this major difference, Christian and Jewish conceptions of heaven did influence Islamic thought through local customs and conversions. Fairchild D. Ruggles writes: "But Islam, born in the seventh century, flourished in the eastern Mediterranean where Roman and Byzantine Christianity as well as Judaism also flourished, and both the material culture and the religion of Islam owe much to these neighboring peoples (and indeed, many of the early Muslims were converts whose cultural formation had been as Jews, Christians, and polytheists" (89–90).

Barzakh, Purgatory and the Resurrection

A further influence of the Christian Church on Islam was the concept of Purgatory that emerged as the Islamic doctrine of Barzakh; purgatory originated with Christian Hermas of Rome[16] who authored a popular book in the second century CE called "The Shepherd,"[17] and the concept was solidified as fact by Pope Gregory the Great in the fifth century CE (Walker 193). The early church taught people to pray for souls in purgatory, and later traditions during the 12th century CE were hyperbolic in their imaginings of the fires of purgatory and the suffering of souls. Catholics believed purgatory was a post-mortem period of purification, forgiveness, and temporary punishment, but purgatory did not really emerge as a popular doctrine until the 12th century CE. The practice of paying for indulgences that allowed Catholics to obtain remission of sins from temporary punishments was a big money-maker for the Catholic Church; abuses of indulgences in the Middle Ages was a key factor in Protestant Reformers separating from the Catholic Church.

The original meaning of purgatory may have been corrupted throughout time, as some scholars believe that the original meaning of purgatory in the very early church meant simply the passage or journey through the heavens to meet God, the "completing the heavenly journey," or "passage through the heavens" (White 84). This original idea aligns perfectly with ancient Egypt's The *Book of Gates*, which is a solar funerary text dating from the New Kingdom (18th and 19th Dynasties, 1500–1200 BCE) that describes the journey of a recently deceased soul into the world of the afterlife; this voyage duplicates the passage of the sun through the abode of the dead during the hours of the night (Murdock 272). Budge asserts that the text was written "in spite of the pretentions of the priests of Amen-Ra," to prove that "Osiris was Lord of the underworld and that his kingdom was everlasting" (85). According to the *Book of Gates*, the soul must clear twelve gates; each gate associates with a particular goddess whom the deceased must recognize. The goddesses listed in *The Book of Gates*, daughters of the sun god Ra and often called "The Hours," control the destinies and life spans of humans; each has different titles and wears different colored clothes, but are identical in all other respects, wearing a five-pointed star above their heads (Hart 76). This book serves as an important source for understanding the fate of the damned in early conceptions of the afterlife, and how closely Egyptian ideas resemble and influenced ideas of hell and inspired other apocalyptic images of later religions including Judaism, Christianity, and Islam.

Some hadiths state that the world of Barzakh has its own heaven and hell in which people are rewarded or punished for their deeds. The Prophet (s) says: "the grave is either a garden of heaven or a hole of hell" (Hadîth Sharîf, Sunan-al Tirmidhî). That would suggest that there are some people whose lives enable them to be in the presence of the divine heaven, while Christian interpretations imply that everyone but saints must spend time suffering in purgatory. The Qur'an regards death as transferal from one type of life to another in Barzakh: "And do not call those who have died in the way of Allah dead; rather, they are alive but you do not realize" (Surah Baqarah 2:154). Islam teaches that the souls of the dead do not disappear after death, but continue to live in Barzakh, a type of Catholic purgatory, waiting for the Day of Judgment or "Qiyamat." Many Qur'anic verses attest to the existence of the span of Barzakh, which is in effect from the moment of death to the Day of Resurrection:

> Until, when death comes unto one of them, he says, "My Lord! Return me! Surely I shall act righteously in that which I have forsook." Never! It is just a word he speaks and behind them is an intermission (Barzakh) till the day they shall be resurrected [Surah Mu'minun 23: 99–100].

So, Barzakh is the state of existence or intermediate realm between this world and the hereafter, or between death and the resurrection, but the term also means that altered state when people participate in varied realities while dreaming, including encountering spirits of invisible entities and spirits of the living and the dead (el-Aswad 110). Essentially, then, Barzakh is that state in which divine revelation, human reason, and imagination collide. During this state, deceased souls can connect and communicate with the living about their lives and future events during sleep through their dreams (Bender and Klassen 194). The Qur'an says that dead people even recognize the visitors to their graves, as God sends their deceased souls to their graves during visiting; the dead can also influence events in the lives of the living (Wherry 129).

THE DISEMBODIED BODY

Some Muslim intellectuals regard the human soul without a body in the plane of Barzakh; however, others regard the soul attached to a spiritual body that is similar to the material body of the individual (Smith and Haddad 124). Because humans are an amalgam of body and soul and have partial material perceptions, Muslims believe there is a body that is the essence of every human, which exists in the zone of Barzakh. At the time of natural death, the soul and its attached spiritual body enters the zone of Barzakh, but on the Day of Resurrection, or Qiyamat, the soul will have a new, perfected corporal body that will never decay, a type of facsimile body. "Scholars and experts of scholastic theology have compared the Barzakh body with what one sees in a mirror. Of course, there are two differences. First, the said picture is actual (not a mere reflection) and second, it achieves senses. The facsimile body is real and it also senses and understands things" ("Barzakh [Purgatory]").

Muslims believe that death brings about a type of metaphysical division of a human being that becomes unified again only at Resurrection when the authentic individual returns after a long physical and supernatural separation. Barzakh is that intermediate period between death and Resurrection, so that the interrelations between the human soul (*nafs*), body (*jasad*), and the breath of life from God (*ruh*) and their composite actions in life, determine their ultimate fate during Qiyamat. The famous, influential 11th century theologian Al-Ghazali, in his eschatological text *Al-Jami Al-durra Al-fakhira* (*The Precious Pearl*), wrote about the interaction of body, soul, and breath components working together to force separation from one another, and describes how this interaction causes great suffering when an unrighteous person is in the process of dying. He writes:

> And when the destiny approaches, that is, his earthly death, then the four angels descend to him; the angel who pulls the soul from the right foot, the angel who pulls it from the left foot, the angel who pulls it from his right hand, and the angel who pulls it from his left hand … the good soul slips out like the jetting of water from a water-skin, but the profligate spirit squeaks out like a skewer from wet wool [Al-Ghazali 21].

Thus, for Muslims, human immortality is physical and spiritual, and human resurrection includes both spiritual and corporeal aspects; on the Day of Resurrection each person's earthly body will be reproduced and reaffixed to the soul, so that judgment will be carried out on the same body that actively engaged in righteous or unrighteous actions. Other Islamic authorities believe that the resurrected or *Akhirat* bodies will not be the same as people's original corporeal bodies, but will only appear similar in form. Ayatullah Husain Dastghaib describes *Barzakh* as an allegorical world and the postmortem body as an allegorical body; he writes:

> Barzakh is called Allegorical World also, because it is just like this world. But is so in shape and form. But it is different and distinct from the viewpoint of its substance and especiality. After our death, we enter a realm which, in comparison, is like this world vis-a-vis a mother's womb. Similarly, our bodies also will be allegorical (Misaali) bodies in Barzakh. This is to say that they will appear quite like our worldly material bodies but, factually, it will not be this body (containing skin and flesh). It will be an elegant, fine and exquisite body. It will be finer than air. There will be no barriers for it which our bodies face in this material world. It (the Barzakh body) can see anything and everything from everywhere everytime [93].

Islam and Christianity: Connecting and Disconnecting Ideas

Islam's doctrine of salvation and immortality is far different from the Christian canon, as Muslims do not believe they have anything to be saved from; Muslims strive for God's forgiveness, but forgiveness is not guaranteed (Greear 61; Abu-Nimer and Nasser, "Forgiveness" 478). Muslims achieve salvation by surrendering their soul to God. Both Muslims and Christians believe that the soul comes into existence at conception, and departs the body at death; both religions assert that life after resurrection from the graves will be physical and not metaphysical or spiritual, and the Qur'an and the Bible contend there will be physical life with physical bodies with functions that are analogous to the original earthly body.

Muslims believe there will be no more death after the last day, but Christian doctrine claims there will be a second death (Revelation 2:11; 20: 6, 14; 21:8); some Christians believe that the first death is the temporary, physical death of the body, but that the second death is a permanent death of the physical, resurrected body, a total annihilation of existence, or a conscious suffering in an everlasting hell. Christians, Jews, and Muslims believe the saved who enter paradise will stay there permanently, but Islam disagrees with the permanent hell of Judaism and Christianity; Islam professes that Hell will be everlasting for particular groups of wrongdoers, but minor offenders will be forgiven and enter heaven after spending a limited time of punishment there. Islam, the last of the great Abrahamic religions, conceived its eschatological doctrine as a recursive editing of ancient global beliefs, and embraced a final revelation.

8

Reviewing Global Doctrines and Analyzing the Human Condition

We live between two darknesses ... starting life with an experience
we forget and ending it with the anticipation of something we cannot
understand. (E.M. Forster, *Aspects of the Novel*)

Humans have been chasing immortality since the beginning of human history; they sought answers to sickness and death, to aging, and to the afterlife, and they questioned what constitutes a human being. Not surprisingly, the effort to uncover the mysteries of immortality did not end in the exploration of the material, corporeal body alone, but philosophers, sages, and priests explored the possibility that a human being was more than an enlivened lump of clay, and further concluded that people had a spirit or soul that caused them to live, and that soul was the essence of a person's personality and character. There have been endless, global debates and speculation over millennia regarding the origin of the idea of God, and more conjecture over the soul's shape, substance, origin, and ability to transmigrate, whether the soul dies with the body, whether it is immortal from conception and birth, or is a natural and immortal emanation of God's spirit become flesh. In addition, there have been persistent discussions and teachings on the ability of God to resurrect the dead, the time when bodies are reunited with their souls. This vast array of scholarship could only lead to the conclusion that we are more than a miraculous and complex combination of minerals, proteins, and atoms, but that we are vessels of some greater love, intelligence, energy, and spirit. However, these concepts could also be simply creative imaginings that relieve anxieties about death and the afterlife; after all, death is the most pitiful condition for humans.

Sun God Worship

Winter is a time for rest in nature when everything goes to sleep until the warm sun arises and brings new life; the ancients studied these cycles of nature and applied them to theories of the human afterlife and symbols of a mysterious power source. Early humans, undiscerning of the scientific basis for heavenly events, likely thought eclipses, comets, and meteorites were signs of the gods. Even before the time of Abraham, people venerated the sun and stars; ancient civilizations in Mesopotamia and Egypt ascribed divinity to sun images (see Chart of the Sun Gods), and so they began to coordinate the perception that their king was like the sun, equating that king with god or a representative of god.

Sun worship derives from (prehistory and) ancient Sumer where Shamash was a sun god and great grandson of Anu, the original father god; Shamah or Shamash in Assyria was depicted as the winged sun-disc (see **figure 8**). The earliest bona fide record of the antiquity of sun worship is an inscription on the foundation stone of the temple of the sun god at Sippara in Babylon by Naram-Sin, son of Sargon, 2300–2200 BCE. Another ancient tablet has a commemorative inscription to an early king of Babylon, on which is sculpted the king and his attendants worshipping the sun god, who is seated on a throne beneath a canopy. The physical description of this sun god bears a striking resemblance to current Christian conceptions of the Father God; and the ancient symbol of the sun god bled millennia later into metaphors of Jesus as the "Sun of Righteousness" or "Light of the World." According to William Tyler Olcott:

> The worship of the sun was inevitable, and its deification was the source of all idolatry in every part of the world. It was sunrise that inspired the first prayers uttered by man, calling him to acts of devotion, bidding him raise an altar and kindle sacrificial flames. Before the Sun's all-glorious shrine the first men knelt and raised their voices in praise and supplication, fully confirmed in the belief that their prayers were heard and answered. Nothing proves so much the antiquity of solar idolatry as the care Moses took to prohibit it. "Take care," said he to the Israelites, "lest when you lift up your eyes to Heaven and see the sun, the moon, and all the stars, you be seduced and drawn away to pay worship and adoration to the creatures which the Lord your God has made for the service of all the nations under Heaven" [143].

During the 11th dynasty in Egypt (2133–2000 BCE), Amun became the powerful sun god of Thebes, where he was worshipped as Amun–Ra; later he was made the supreme god of the entire realm and king of the gods. Sun worship has been a consistent, widely practiced, and universal form of devotion in the history of mankind (Jones, A.T. 2). Ancient Egyptians worshipped the sun gods Ra and Osiris; among the Babylonians and Assyrians, under the names of Bel and Shamas, and by whatever name or form, a female divinity

Figure 8 Shamash the Sun God. In this photograph of a plaster cast of a limestone original, Sin's son, Shamash or Shamah, the grandson of Enlil and great-grandson of Anu, the original father-god, bore the emblem of a "winged" sun. Shamah or Shamash in Assyria was depicted as the winged sun-disc (Daderot, Shamash, the Sun God, Sippar, Early Iron Age, 870 BCE).

Chart of the Sun Gods in Ancient History		
Name	*Nationality and Gender (Ascription)*	*Characteristics*
Shamash or UTU	Mesopotamia (Sun God)	God of light, truth, and justice. In Assyrian iconography, Shamash is pictured as a solar disc with wings.
Ra or Re Osiris Horus	Egypt (Mid-day Sun God)	An Egyptian god shown with a solar disk. Later associated with Horus as Re-Horakhty. Also combined with Amun as Amun-Ra, a solar creator god.
Ba'al	Canaanite (Sun God)	Associated with physical pleasure.
Helios	Greece (Sun God)	Before Apollo was the Greek sun god, Helios held that position. Rides the sky in a horse-drawn chariot.
Apollo	Greece and Rome (Sun God)	Rides the sky in a horse-drawn chariot.
Mithra Mitra	• Iranian/Persian (Sun God) • Roman (Sun God) • Indian (Sun God)	• God of the sun, justice, contract, and war • Mystery cult • Mediator between God and man
Hvar Khshaita	Iranian/Persian (Sun God)	Earlier than Mithras.
Arinna (Hebat)	Syrian (Hittite) (Sun Goddess)	Offers protection from war and disaster.
Surya	Hindu (Sun God)	Rides the sky in a horse-drawn chariot.

was always associated with the sun. Sometimes this female was also the moon or the earth; other times the sun was hermaphroditic (2).

Osiris and Horus were both solar deities; Osiris signified the setting sun, Horus symbolized the rising sun; Jesus has always been known as the Morning Star, which has well-known associations with Venus, and his resurrection signifies a rebirth or a rising sun. The pharaoh was considered to be an incarnation of Horus, also known as "Amun-Ra," the sun god, and, in the same way, Jesus is considered the incarnation of his heavenly Father (Massey 442, 446, 488, 497, 498, 505). The halos or radiances used in portraits of Jesus, Mary, and the saints originate from iconography created by the ancients to depict sun gods like Horus.

The sun god was worshipped and widely known in Axsum, one of Ethiopia's earliest Kingdoms. Sun god worship became widely practiced in

Arabia in Yemen; these particular Arabians were a Cushite Semitic people who migrated across the Red Sea to the South of Axsum, taking with them their sun god and moon worship and other cultures. The Hindu's red sun god, Surya, also crosses the sky like Helios and Apollo, in a chariot drawn by seven horses, and Hindus still place the symbol of the Sun over shops for good luck. The Greeks and Romans traded gods with other cultures, bringing their own brands of belief and worship into new territories, and in some instances creating new gods to appease their customers or captives. For example, Alexander the Great created Ammon-Zeus, a hybrid father god, to merge similarities between Greek and Egyptian cultures' obsessions with the sun and thus gain their trust (Gordon 32).

The Hebrew Bible contains mostly references to the actual sun in the solar system, but there is an odd reference to the sun in Ecclesiastes 7:11, when Solomon writes, "Wisdom is good with an inheritance, an advantage to those who see the sun." Solomon may simply be implying that if a person has knowledge and wealth, and wakes up in the morning to see the literal sun, that person is blessed. There is also the possibility that Solomon is invoking some type of reference to a celestial light, an indication that a person may be enlightened, but oftentimes scripture is opaque, and creates obstacles that make it difficult to discern the author's intention or reference.

The most famous sun god in Greece was Helios, the Titan god of the sun, usually depicted as a beardless, handsome man wearing purple robes and crowned with the shining aureole of the sun, who drove a chariot across the sky each day and night. Homer described it as drawn by solar bulls (*Iliad* 16.779). As time passed, Helios was increasingly identified with the god of light, Apollo, and corresponds to Ra (Re), the ancient Egyptian sun god. Apollo, Dionysus, and even Zeus represented the sun. Some scholars have taken the position that the Greeks were simply referring to the Gods metaphorically at this time in history: Zeus commanded the sky, Hephaistos symbolized fire, Apollo was the sun and commanded the element of human reason and logic, etc. If this is the case, these gods' names would simply be ascriptions that signified nature or natural events and had nothing to do with real divinity and only with the human imagination.

The Canaanites worshiped Ba'al as the sun god and storm god, and like Zeus, he is usually depicted holding a lightning bolt. Ba'al worship was rooted in physical pleasure, and involved ritual prostitution in temples. Ba'al worshippers often conducted a human sacrifice of the firstborn of their children (Jeremiah 19:5), and their priests injured themselves while screaming appeals to their god (1 Kings 18:28). After finally crossing into the "Promised Land," the Hebrews became acquainted with Ba'al worship from Canaanite farmers and observed their religious festivals. These new cultural traditions seeped into the YHWH religions, and contributed to the religious and moral decline of Israel. The Book of Hosea describes the moral and religious deterioration that Baʾal worship produced just before the fall of the monarchy; YHWH became regarded as the supreme god of the Baʾals (Hosea 2: 16). This particularly occurred during the time of King Solomon who, influenced by foreign wives, participated in Baʾal worship, and patterned his temple after the temple of Baʾal. Baʾal worship was not so prevalent after the Babylonian exile, but the Hebrew people there were influenced by Assyrian and Babylonian reverence of stars and planets.

Unfortunately for Christians, some groups in ancient times began to assert that Jesus Christ was in fact a sun god, but this is a false claim. Allegations of Christian sun-worshipping developed early in Christian history, but also remained into the fifth century. St. Augustine addressed this controversy in his "Tractate on the Gospel of John" (34):

> Let us not suppose that the Lord Jesus Christ is this sun which we see rising from the east, setting in the west; to whose course succeeds night, whose rays are obscured by a cloud, which removes from place to place by a set motion: the Lord Christ is not such a thing as this. The Lord Christ is not the sun that was made, but He by whom the sun was made. For all things were made by Him, and without Him was nothing made [qtd. in Murdock and Acharya, "Jesus as the Sun"].

Debate on the Constitution of the Soul

Today most of the religious world believes in an immortal soul that lives on in some form; this is a shared teaching of Hinduism, Judaism, Buddhism, Christianity, Islam, and native and tribal religions throughout Africa, the Americas, and elsewhere. Some say that a soul is a preexistent, immortal entity that will live forever in either a heaven or a hell, or will reunite and reanimate a dead corpse on a Day of Resurrection, and then live forever in paradise with God. Others suppose that after death the soul will reanimate other life forms in an endless cycle of reincarnation through transmigration of souls. There are also those who believe that when the body dies, the soul or spirit dies with the material, as the soul is a material essence. The only certainty within these theories is that, from the earliest human civilizations, humans thought that they were more than just a body, that there was something within them that animated them, which drove them to make conscious behavioral decisions, and connected them to a greater power in and beyond the skies.

In earliest recorded history, the conditions for existence of the soul in the afterlife continued in similar social and economic conditions as the living body had on earth; afterlife beliefs demanded that relatives take care of the soul in the grave through respectful offerings of gifts and prayers, but the soul's circumstances in the afterlife were seen as an economic caste system that depended on chance or luck in the life into which they were born. The Sumerians believed that souls did exist after death, and could even find happiness there, but that a good afterlife depended on those left behind. The Sumerians had not developed a dogma of hell, so the moral state of people's souls had nothing to do with their afterlife circumstances; their social and economic status in this life translated to the next world, as Sumerians burials signified. As people were in life, so would they be in death. Sumerians placed no prohibitions against contacting dead souls, so the living could freely practice necromancy and solicit the dead's assistance (Hays 55). The later old Babylonian religion held a demoralizing vision of the afterlife, where souls entered a shadowy world without hope, and where the conditions of existence in the other world also depended on the livings' generosity and remembrance.

Babylonian beliefs were nowhere as complex as the Egyptian's faith in an immortal spirit or tripartite soul that disconnected from the body at death. Egyptians maintained the individuality or persona of the person, gave the spirit a home in the sky with the gods, and provided a home in its burial chamber. This belief lasted until the sixth century CE, and clearly influenced Judaic and Christian faith in an afterlife and in burial rituals (Reisner 2–3); Christian beliefs, particularly those of the Roman Catholic Church, have continued the respectful Egyptian tradition of honoring the dead through strict funerary practices and beliefs that the soul ascends to heaven where all the tribulations of earthly life end. The Egyptians, however, believed the soul or spirit containing the personality of the individual after death experienced the same anxieties of earthly life. Egyptians reasoned that a human was naturally made of visible and invisible parts: the observable physical body, and the invisible two souls that lived on after the body's death, which they named the *Ka* and *Ba* souls. The ancient Greek historian Herodotus (fifth century BCE) tells us in his *History* that the ancient Egyptians were the first to teach that the soul of man is separable from the body, immortal, transmigratory, and cyclic (Rawlinson 197), a key connection to later Hindu theories of reincarnation. The Egyptians believed in a mystical state where the soul became a divine intelligence in another type of supra-physical world and in an improved state of consciousness after death (Motte 81).

The classical Greek thinkers and authors also argued their developing theories of the human soul that later influenced Judaism, Christianity, and Islam. Plato developed the theory that the human soul is an incorporeal entity that pre-exists before attaching itself to a body; materiality is simply the carrier for immateriality. In Plato's *Phaedo*, the philosopher's teacher, Socrates, asserts the soul to be eternal, knowing, and resurrectionable; the soul was always in conflict with the needs of the body. It was the soul that ruled and regulated the body to participate in virtuous actions and opposed the passions and physical needs of the body (34; Ahrensdorf 156; Shields 131–132). By the end of Socrates' life in the fourth century BCE, the soul had acquired "intelligence, emotion, and appetite" (Allen and Springsted 34).

Homer's epic poems and odes see the soul as something lost when dying in battle, or something that leaves a person's body and travels to the underworld, where it lives as a shadow (Snell 19). According to Aristotle, the form of the soul exists within the form of the body. Aristotle defines the soul as the efficient, formal, and final cause of the living being, and its natural body as the material cause (Leunissen 74–75). Plato conceived that the soul was immortal, pre-existent, and longing for death's release; the soul had no connection to the body except in its prison state. Aristotle's locus vis-à-vis the soul diverged substantially from Plato, as soul was the form of the body, not a distinct substance that inhabited it. According to Aristotle, the form of the soul exists within the form of the body, and the soul did not exist apart from the body, but only differentiated corporeal life from nonexistence. Homer (800 BCE), Hesiod (750 BCE), and other ancient texts debated the nature of the soul that corresponded to a human's personal uniqueness or individuality; immortality for ancient Greeks included an immortal union of body and soul, as the soul would live eternally in Hades. Human life on earth was considered a living death as the soul was trapped within the body; however, the soul was purified when the body died. This belief offered a body-soul duality that emphasized the soul as a nonphysical, divine, and eternal dimension, while the body was judged worthless (Jaeger 135–147).

Hindus believe the soul-self is eternal, so the eternal essence of god can inhabit temporary, corporeal, reincarnated human bodies. Hinduism propounds that the *Atman* or human soul neither was created nor can it be destroyed; like the concept of the eternal god, the individual soul has no beginning or end. Hindus believe that the soul controls the body; consequently, the soul will reap the aftermath of past actions when reincarnated into a new living form. The goal is for everyone to achieve *Moksha*, the deliverance from cycles of reincarnation (Majithi 231; Huston 50; "Moksha, Freedom"), and this event happens when the soul recognizes its true nature, and unites with Brahman, the ultimate god or eternal and divine energy; human souls and all of nature are the manifestation of Brahman. "The *Upanishads* describe Brahman as 'the eternal, conscious, irreducible, infinite, omnipresent, spiritual source of the universe of finiteness and change'" (qtd. in "Brahman").

The concept of an immortal soul distinct from the corporeal body did not exist in Judaism before the Babylonian Exile (598–596 BCE), but later developed as a result of interaction with other philosophies and religious influences, particularly those from Egypt and Greece. During the fifth century

BCE, Greek doctrines inspired Jewish theories of the soul's immortality, and by the first century CE, Jewish theologians largely concurred that the soul did not expire when the body died. Sadducees did not believe that the soul existed when the body died, but Pharisees maintained the immortality of the soul, a type of reincarnation for the righteous, and eternal punishment for the wicked. They believed in the soul's immortality, but human responsibility for actions in this life would determine the soul's ultimate fate.

While Judaism's belief in the soul's immortality did influence Christianity, Jesus asserted that not all human souls are immortal; he confirmed that souls can and will be destroyed when He taught: "And do not fear those who kill the body but cannot kill the soul. But rather fear Him who is able to destroy both soul and body in hell" (Matthew 10:28). Logic informs us that, according to this theory, if souls were truly immortal, then they could not be destroyed, but if God truly created our souls, God can destroy them. Thus Christianity was more interested than Judaism in saving souls for the resurrection from the dead when bodies would be reunited with a new type of perfected body, and live eternally with God.

Early Islamic scholars attempted to combine Aristotle's scientific description of the world with religious views to create a unified idea of the world. Ibn Rushd also thought that the human soul was divided into two parts: one part personal, and the other divine, so that when a person died, the personal soul died, but the divine soul merged into the universal divine soul (Averroës 103). The nature of the soul is immortal in traditional Islamic thought, and Muslims firmly believe that the soul comes into existence at the moment of conception. Because humans are an amalgam of body and soul and have partial material perceptions, Muslims believe there is a body that is the essence of every human, which exists in the zone of Barzakh. Similar to Christianity, at the time of natural death, the soul and its attached spiritual body enters the zone of Barzakh, but on the Day of Resurrection the soul will have a new, perfected corporeal body that will never decay, a type of facsimile body.

Resurrection Progression: From Gods to Humans

From earliest times, only those who were considered gods were able to be resurrected. Death and the search for immortality played a central role in ancient Sumerian religious epics: "after death a god would travel to the 'Land without Return' across the 'Waters of Death' and be magically reborn" (Uttal 93), so death and resurrection of the gods were basic tenets of Sumerian cosmology, and had a metaphorical connection with the solar calendar. These most ancient of beliefs may have influenced the later Osiris story in Egypt, and may have had some influence on the later stories of Jesus. In the Egyptian

Book of Gates there is a series of texts and pictures, which depict magical ceremonies performed in ancient times to reanimate or resurrect the body of the Sun to make it rise each day. This Egyptian resurrection imagery was reinforced with texts about Osiris and later influenced Jewish, Christian, and Islamic belief in resurrection from the dead.

In Plato's *Phaedo*, the philosopher's teacher, Socrates, asserts that the soul is immortal, cognizant, and resurrectionable; the soul was also in constant conflict with the needs of the body (34; Ahrensdorf 156; Shields 131–132). The ancient Greek literary and philosophical tradition contributed significant work that inspired later thinking on the concepts of resurrection and the human soul. There are varied literary examples of gods resurrecting humans and demigods from the dead; these stories might have later influenced the Lazarus story and other resurrection accounts from the New Testament. The Platonic belief in immortality was later regarded as an anticipation or prefiguration of the Christian resurrection.

The study of immortality, the afterlife, the human soul, and corporeal resurrection in Judaism is complex, as these issues evolved during varied historical eras and were further complicated with supplemental teachings at later intervals. While the Hebrew Bible does contain a few scriptures pertaining to resurrection, particularly in writing from the prophets Daniel, Ezekiel, and Isaiah, the concept of resurrection from the dead in Jewish thinking did not fully emerge until the second century BCE; it was not until Roman rule in Israel that the doctrine of resurrection from the dead became a prominent issue. The Pharisees imagined a physical resurrection when humans would re-animate for eternity; by contrast, the Sadducees rejected the idea of corporeal resurrection, opting only for the existence of an immortal soul. Even today, Jewish sects generally accept some type of eternal afterlife for the human soul, but the varied sects of Judaism still dispute the nature of this afterlife. Contemporary Jewish theologians mostly concur regarding an immortal soul, but factions continue to conflict on corporeal resurrection with the exception of Orthodox Jews. Judaism shares end-of-days prophesies and faith in resurrection and final judgment with Christianity and Islam. Rabbis, however, have been divided on these issues: some believed everyone will be judged, but only the righteous will be resurrected; others believed that everyone will be resurrected to stand judgment.

Christianity inherited Judaism's apocalyptic beliefs, and early Christian believers were Jews with deep spiritual roots in the mother religion; as centuries progressed non–Jewish Christians could not deny the contribution that Judaism had on their faith, and the Jewish apocalyptic tradition became a vital part of the new offshoot religion. The early Christian hope for bodily resurrection is clearly Jewish in origin; the Hebrew Pharisee and later Christian evangelist, Paul of Tarsus, undoubtedly believed in the Jewish doctrine of resurrection. The Christian belief system is based upon salvation through Jesus Christ, a risen and living messiah, and its main tenets focus on life after death, corporeal resurrection, and the promise of immortality in a heaven where believers will never again suffer. In Christianity, it is the Eucharist or Host and the wine representing the body and blood of Jesus Christ that promises the faithful immortality after death and resurrection, if they are baptized into Christ and partake in the communion ritual and believe in the doctrine of transubstantiation. In 1 Corinthians 15:50–52, Paul preached that the saved would be resurrected in a new type of form and existence that would be immortal and not subject to decay. He writes, "Flesh and blood cannot inherit the kingdom of God; nor does corruption inherit incorruption.... For the trumpet will sound and the dead will be raised incorruptible, and we shall be changed." The very idea of a rebirth of some type highlights the direct Eastern influence on the Greeks, and Paul would have been aware of their reincarnation theories, but Paul's theory of corporeal resurrection from the dead of a single original body was distinct from an elemental soul inhabiting a string of corporeal bodies.

In Islam, it is "...an article of faith that there is a Day of Resurrection and of Judgment on which the living and the dead shall answer for their thoughts and actions..." (Coward 56). The faithful will be saved, but the wicked will be sent to hell, where they will "Burn in a blaze" (Qur'an 84:12), just like the fiery hell of Christianity. Muslims believe that death brings about a type of metaphysical division of a human being that becomes unified again only at Resurrection when the authentic individual returns after a long physical and supernatural separation. Thus, for Muslims, human immortality is physical and spiritual, and human resurrection includes both spiritual and corporeal aspects; on the Day of Resurrection each person's earthly body will be reproduced and reaffixed to the soul, so that judgment will be carried out on the same body that actively engaged in righteous or unrighteous actions. Other Islamic authorities believe that the resurrected bodies will not be the same as people's original corporeal bodies, but will only appear similar in form. This substantial change in the material essence of the resurrected body echoes the Pauline teachings that resurrected bodies would be changed into unknown, incorruptible substances.

Managing Perceptions: Using Punishment as a Motivator

The human condition is pitiable; there is no concrete evidence to support theories of the soul, immortality, or bodily resurrection—there is only a myriad of speculative and creative theories of the unknown. However, unreliable sensory perceptions should not be the sole factor when excavating the unknown; the old adage "I will believe it when I see it" assumes that the sense of sight can be a determining factor in uncovering mysteries. In opposition, the Abrahamic religions proffered a unique perspective that said, "Believe, then you will see it"; this was the doctrine of faith in the unseen, but those who had "eyes to see and ears to hear" would somehow transition into knowing, completely surrendering to a conviction that lessons people have been taught contain ultimate truths, based upon a myriad of religious texts. There are also people without conviction within these religions who get mired in an intellectual snobbery or righteousness, thinking they are the only chosen religion or sect that will be saved. The endless wars and animosities perpetrated by all religions over millennia have been often based upon disputes over interpretations of celestial bodies and events, characteristics and nomenclatures of God, identification of God's chosen, and notions of punishments and rewards.

Each religion's views of rewards and punishments in the afterlife mirror the shared values, aspirations, and laws of that culture. Mesopotamian religious beliefs included an afterlife of suffering because people suffered within an uncontrollable natural environment, but this original afterlife idea was a type of hell that included more sorrow than punishment. The supernatural land, or "Land without Return," was a transitory stopover not only for gods but for humans as well, "...a place where gods would judge humans and decide how long they would remain" (Uttal 94). The invention of heaven and hell could have been a means of controlling early human behavior, as there is no greater motivator to good behavior than fear of punishment. Clearly presaging concepts of heaven and hell in later religions, Egyptian judgment came in the form of rewards and punishments, and souls experienced reversals of fortune according to their deeds on earth; a mystical power conveyed souls either to a dominion of bliss or to a region of anguish. The Greeks believed that their immortal gods controlled all aspects of nature, and their human lives were totally at the mercy of the will of the gods. Interactions between people and gods were generally considered friendly, but the gods could dispense harsh punishment to mortals who were conceited, arrogant, overly ambitious, or wealthy.

An attempt to tie threads of Hinduism into the Hebrew Bible's s belief system yields many connections: afterlife rewards and punishments, ideas of *moksha* and nirvana, and human life as a divine emanation are similar; however, these universal ideas appear to be active in almost every religious system of thought since ancient Sumer. Jewish adherents generally embraced the idea that condemned souls would be annihilated, but that there was no such event as eternal punishment in a place like hell, which was earlier conceptualized by the Egyptians and the Greeks. According to Hebrew scriptures, the dead go down to Sheol, a kind of Hades, where they live a ghostly existence (Numbers 16:33; Psalms 6:5; Isaiah 38:18); however, Sheol was neither a place of punishment, nor was it a place where any type of individual existence continued. Changes in Jewish belief in an afterlife were a result of the miseries inflicted on the Hebrews during the Babylonian invasion in the early part of the sixth century BCE, the destruction of the Temple of Solomon, the exile in Babylon, and their subsequent homecoming to Israel. These events dramatically altered earthly karmic concepts of rewards, punishments, and justice, and influenced the idea that justice would only be rendered by God after death within the framework of an afterlife. Judaism's evolution into a multi-branched religion prompted diverse speculation on doctrines of punishment, heaven, and hell; outside cultures that came into contact with Jews influenced new ways of thinking about these mysteries.

Catholics believed purgatory was a postmortem period of purification, forgiveness, and temporary punishment, but purgatory did not really emerge as a popular doctrine until the 12th century CE. The practice of paying for indulgences that allowed Catholics to obtain remission of sins from temporary punishments was a big money-maker for the Catholic Church; abuses of indulgences in the Middle Ages were a key factor in Protestant Reformers separating from the Catholic Church. Unlike the Christian conception of hell, which does not allow anyone at any time to escape the fires and torments, Muslims believe there are angels in hell who are there to cleanse humans of spiritual errors. Islam's hell is meant as a temporary place of punishment, except for polytheists and nonbelievers who will be punished forever; no one will come out of Hell except remorseful, sinful humans who believed in Allah and the Prophet Mohammad, and followed the Five Pillars of the faith.

Beginning with the Sumerian civilization, ancient ideas evidenced in literary and visual texts still influence contemporary human rituals and thinking about immortality and the afterlife. These texts are closely woven into the fabric of a human consciousness that has not dramatically changed its conceptions of death, heaven, or hell in six thousand years. These beliefs may also be vestiges of chromosomal memories from antecedents, or might simply have originated as a way of fantasizing about immortality, death, and the afterlife in order to cope with mortality.

It could be argued that, despite what humans know about religions of the past and present, there is still the thorny issue of how and why these beliefs originated and proliferated throughout human history: behavioral control and political domination through fear of future events, explanation of unusual past events in history, and subjugation of the human intellect and imagination through indoctrination are a few theories. Managing perceptions of reality are deliberate actions to convey and/or deny selected information and values to people to manipulate emotional reactions, motives, and objective analysis. This type of control communicates or repudiates particular information in order to produce specific action and obtain agreement favorable to the originator's goals and intentions. Religious doctrines have often used perceptions management techniques to control people's reactions, so that adherents conform and react with a positive response to doctrine. On a deeper level, perceptions management can direct the way people perceive their own culture, as perceptions management combines "truth" projection and psychological manipulation to alter beliefs, attitudes, and values with the ultimate goal of changing behavior and adjusting attitudes towards "others." The first objective of perceptions management is to make people believe in and about something. In *Persuasion: Messages, Receivers, and Contexts,* William Rogers writes:

> Most people have an enormous range of "factual" beliefs about themselves, others, and the physical world observed around them, and a metaphysical world they cannot see. Some of these beliefs can be more easily changed with persuasion than others. You could probably persuade me that the exact recipe used for making Coca-Cola varies in different parts of the world. On the other hand, some of our beliefs are more resistant to change. For example, you could not convince me under any circumstances that on earth the sun rises in the west and sets in the east. But in a whimsical moment you might have a chance to convince me that on the day I die, my name will be written in a cloud [7].

This statement contains a profound truth about religious belief: in a moment of creative thought, the human imagination is susceptible to believing in doctrines of the unknown based upon wishes or desires that calm anxieties about death and the afterlife. While these skeptical opinions are valid considerations, they are not the only compelling arguments able to assess the facts or fictions of afterlife, soul, resurrection, and immortality theories.

Projecting Faith in the Unseen

Scripture informs us that everything that exists is made from things that we cannot see; just as we cannot see atoms with our human lens, atoms exist nonetheless and make up every constituent part of what is material. Paul's Letter to the Hebrews teaches us that sensory perceptions are temporary, but it is what is not seen that is immortal. We cannot see our soul, but that does not mean it does not exist, and was not created at the moment of all creation; the logical conclusion is that human souls are already immortal creations, for all things are made of similar substances that are categorized.

By faith we understand that the world was created by the word of God, so that what is seen was made out of things which do not appear (Hebrews 11:3)

...because we look not to the things that are seen but to the things that are unseen; for the things that are seen are transient, but the things that are unseen are eternal (2 Corinthians 4:18).

Assertion of faith in the unseen within varied religions throughout millennia, combined with testimonies, scriptures, sacred texts, and rituals throughout history, bear witness that all civilizations from the beginning of time believed in God, the soul, the afterlife, and in a type of immortality. Could such a throng of persons be entirely in the wrong? Our ancient ancestors used logic to explain experiential phenomena that was supra-natural, and not easily explained through science or mathematics. For eons in every culture, people have wanted to connect with the unseen through prayers, meditations, and rituals in an attempt to have a deeper vision or understanding of what they cannot see, of what lies beyond sensory perceptions. Believers in the unseen acknowledge there are elements and factual realities in the material world that our senses cannot discern; for example, we know there are particles in the atmosphere that the human eye cannot see, but they exist nevertheless.

Accepting that we cannot understand other dimensions and other realities requires faith; faith fastens itself to the unknown, and accepts what it cannot actualize or materialize. All sacred texts instruct people to believe in the invisible, which makes our own material intellect, which is steeped in western logic, very concerned that faith is a delusional aspect of the limited, human intellect. Augustine eschewed empiricism as a method aiming to prove that sensory perceptions alone should be able to validate the Christian faith, but he assumed that belief in the unseen was a legitimate endeavor. "In Chapters 3–4 (sects. 5–7) Augustine proceeds to the demonstration of theological faith. He takes up the further objections of empiricists, namely that mental knowledge of things unseen is always based on inference from outward signs and indications" (Deferrari and McDonald 447). All knowledge is not derived from sensory experiences; Augustine was thinking about transcendence of the mind or the intellect, and believed the most critical piece of evidence, that man was created and patterned after God, is the rational mind, which is inherently infused with knowledge of God (Herzfeld 16).

For Descartes, the substance of the rational mind and the soul is different from the substance of the body, and is also innately immortal. Descartes defines substance as, "a thing which exists in such a way as to depend on no other thing for its existence" (qtd. in Skirry 27). Descartes rationalizes that the soul and the body are not dependent on each other for existence because they are distinct substances. While the corporeal body decays, the material from which it is made continues to exist. Descartes concludes that the soul does not decay because it is indivisible and made of a pure substance; he also deduces that the mind is immortal by its very nature, and does also not decay (Demsey, "A Compound" 248). So it is the mind or the intellect and the soul that is proposed to be immortal; this claim is not so startling, as, according to William Wordsworth, the human imagination is the divine spark that connects humans to the greater universal, deific source while we are alive.

While faith in the unseen can never give substance to what does not exist, faith does provide a confident expectation, hope, and trust that what has been promised in sacred scriptures and texts will materialize. Faith cannot make what is invisible magically visible, although there certainly are cases in scriptures where visible signs of God have occurred: the burning bush that appeared to Moses, the visible descent of God with his angels on Mount Sinai, the ball of light seen by Paul on his way to Damascus, etc. However, faith is beyond what can be discerned by the physical senses, and is the witness to things not yet seen; we cannot forget that the physical material or substances that we currently see were created from invisible substances already existing before the creation of our universe, world, and human physicality. The unseen or invisible God created that which is visible, and all material substances are subject to the one indivisible, invisible, nonmaterial source.

Chasing Immortality

In the current era of conflicting religious ideas, some concepts of chasing immortality are based upon scientific and medical pathways to extend life, rejuvenate aging cells, and make our faces appear younger than they are; these are only temporary measures that can allow us to be healthier, live longer lives, and look more attractive, but these methods cannot and never will be able to grant immortality to any human, unless of course science and medicine discover how to create a human body that does not decay, or is not susceptible to disease. Aging and death were not natural aspects of early human life, as Adam and Eve were created as immortals. One may recall the story of Adam and Eve who gained immortality by eating of the permissible fruit from the Tree of Life, but would suffer death if they dared to eat from the Tree of Knowledge: "And the Lord God commanded the man, saying, 'You may freely eat of every tree of the garden; but of the tree of the knowledge of good and evil you shall not eat, for in the day that you eat of it you shall die'" (Genesis 2:16–17). Even if the reader believes the Eden story is fictional, it provides us with a lesson about our place in the universe. The death knell for Adam and Eve was they sought knowledge of dichotomies: good and evil.

Why would this cause them to lose immortality? Because once they became aware of their physicality, the knowledge they were naked, and gained a spirit of conscience, they lost their primary, spiritual attributes that bonded them to the source of life; although they were created as immortals, they were not created as gods.

Immortality may be theoretically possible, but no scientifically proven explanation for aging and death is forthcoming. If a cell is provided with the metabolites and nutrients necessary for life, there is no reason why it should not continue to exist and never expire, but impelled by a mysterious and undiscovered cause, cells expire, although many medical scientists have accepted the theory that the ends of chromosomes (telomeres) degrade through time, affecting active genes. Innate, encoded, and non-recognizable cell death transpires, which implies that some type of mechanism regulates cellular mortality, according to an involuntary or intentional schedule (Olshansky and Carnes 69; Brown 13). Corporeal immortality may be achievable through science, if it can crack the genetic code, but success in this endeavor is highly unlikely, unless humans can penetrate the mind of God, the essential core of universal power.

In 1930 and 1931, Carl Jung wrote about his belief in humanity's creative spirit and in the innate human concern regarding the inevitability of death. He stated, "Death is psychologically as important as birth and, like it, is an integral part of life" (qtd. in Gordon, "Death and Creativity" 107). Jung wrote about death as a joyful event, as a type of wedding when the soul attains wholeness ("On Life After Death" 14). This wedding metaphor ignites a metaphysical interpretation of the story of Jesus' Second Coming at "the wedding feast of the Lamb" (Revelation 19.9) when his church (or the saved) would be assembled to meet with God; perhaps death is when we "wed" God, or when we become "one" with God, as a bride becomes "one" with her husband; we return to the original, divine source and are made whole. According to Christian beliefs, resurrection is when we assemble at the "marriage supper of the Lamb" to celebrate the promised victory over death, and finally become immortal in some type of an altered, cosmic body. That may be why the ancient Egyptians believed their pharaohs became stars in the sky after death. Jung believed that death should be something to look forward to because we will experience immortality; he also claimed that humans begin to decline when they reach middle age, although this statement almost seems irrelevant today in light of medical advances.

In his commentary on *The Secret of the Golden Flower*, Jung writes: "As a doctor, I make every effort to strengthen the belief in immortality, especially with older patients when such questions come threateningly close. For, seen in correct psychological perspective, death is not an end but a goal, and life's inclination towards death begins as soon as the meridian is past" (Jung 46). Freud, however, disagreed with Jung that death should be something that is embraced, but "...rather [death is] one more unsavory fact in the litany of such truths regarding the human condition" (Katz 377). Freud also considered that faith in previous lives, transmigration of souls, and reincarnation are psychological creations that compel humans to deny death (Drobot, "Freud on Death").

It is possible that aging and death simply transform us into new types of matter and energy that are invisible, enabling us to travel and exist in another dimension as part of a universal divine soul and intellect. Our invisible substance is what animates us, but later leaves the corporeal body behind while continuing in an alternate dimension that humans are unable to see; this condition is the veil stretched over human understanding, or the darkened mirror that only reflects a glimpse of the supernatural knowledge humans will have of themselves and of their condition: "For now we see in a mirror, darkly; but then face to face: now I know in part; but then shall I know even as also I have been known" (1 Corinthians 13:12). The famous rocket scientist Wernher von Braun also confirmed the idea of a supernatural afterlife; here von Braun endorses the utility of science confirming religious doctrine: "Nature does not know extinction: all it knows is transformation. Everything science has taught me, and continues to teach me, strengthens my belief in the continuity of our spiritual existence after death" (qtd. in Furfaro 29). This idea is comforting, but humans today are generally so devoted to their own physicality and the material world that little thought is spent considering any type of supernatural event in this life or the next; most people have no understanding of a consciousness detached from the world.

Immortality and the Human Condition

There are several issues inherent in concepts of death as a defining feature of the human condition. It seems cruel that when people have reached the height of intellect, accomplishment, and physical prowess, they begin to degenerate and plunge towards aging and death; if God loves us so much, why do we all have to experience this dreadful moment of fear and anxiety? It is because the material word, as beautiful or exciting as it may be, is not representative of who we really are as human beings; a great host of writers, theologians, and thinkers agree that humans are essentially spiritual beings who possess conscience, free will, and an innately immortal soul. As in the story of Adam and Eve, it was not so much that they were banished from paradise for disobedience, but they lost immortality because they made the wrong choices.

Free will, the ability to make choices, determines what the immortal soul's final end will be: a continued immortality or a complete desolation and destruction. The Gospel of Matthew quotes Jesus who makes it clear that God has the ability to annihilate souls: "Do not fear those who kill the body but cannot kill the soul; rather fear Him who can destroy both soul and body in hell" (10:28). Unfortunately, part of the human condition is often an inability to choose correctly because of worldly pressures and enticements, but if this incapacity is part of the natural conditions of human nature, why should God destroy our souls for a psychological feature that humans cannot regulate—why should humans be punished for what they cannot control? This theory of *annihilationism* espouses that destroying souls replaces the traditional doctrine of physical torments in hell, and is related to the doctrine of conditional immortality, which propagated that only the redeemed in Christ would be saved, but no others (Land 71; Hoekema 266). This heretical theory was condemned by the Second Council of Constantinople in 553 CE and by the Fifth Lateran Council in 1513 CE, not for its exclusivity, but for denying torments in an eternal hell; the doctrine of physical suffering in an eternal hell continues to influence people's consciousness today through religious teachings. And probably makes them physically ill. So how do humans transcend their condition?

Nietzsche proposed that humans were willing to give up physical pleasures or even their lives, if they could obtain immortality, which was, for the philosopher, the supreme degree of human power (Kaufmann 249); his plan required discipline and self-sacrifice. Of course, Nietzsche was only thinking of the Super-Men, and excluded most humans from his theory. Nietzsche loathed religious teachings, particularly Christian theories; he considered that notions of immortality of the soul and the soul itself "…are instruments of torture, systems of cruelty by virtue of which the priest became master, and remained master" (qtd. in Magnus 46). Nietzsche alleged that a belief in a personal immortality together with a belief in a day of judgment were propagandistic measures for making people dependent on the priests (Murphy 135). Of course, Nietzsche viewed the history of Christianity as a history of error in which the death of Jesus becomes a crass and vulgar tale of a slave mentality of a "diseased barbarism" that embraces a state of guilt over a state of life (Magnus 46). Nietzsche imagined that the belief in personal immortality is an expression of cowardice and relates specifically to a person's arrogance of ego (Higgins 35). Admittedly, such philosophy arose from religion, albeit a hated one for Nietzsche, in an attempt as a reflective person to understand and explain himself and his role in the universe and in the culture in which he found himself. Nietzsche's theories aside, immortality becomes a faith in humanity, as it developed from a religion of nature to a religion of faith in a God. Any philosophy that maintains that death is not final, and that some human beings will have the chance to live beyond corporeal existence is quite appealing, as it eases the fear of nothingness that westerners have come to dread and dismiss. Death does not negate the fact of humans' existence or of their continued influence. Others, however, dismiss a personal immortality, and espouse that humans at death are absorbed into a "universal mind."

Contemporary thinkers reject many aspects of the traditional Christian view of immortality, especially with regards to resurrection because this presupposes that immortality relies on an immaterial soul controlling the corporeal body: how can something immaterial trigger a material reaction? Scientists conclude that only matter consists of an energy that is able to cause a material reaction. If the soul is immaterial, no reaction is possible. However, the soul could be composed of a substance, unlike known material matter, that is supra-natural, eternal, and unable to be discerned or labeled by modern science, and perfectly able to animate corporeality. As the human mind is finite, full understanding of such mysteries is impossible, unless it can be concluded that belief in immortality is simply a delusion created to bring order, control, and optimism to human lives, and, without such a fantasy, life would be a nihilistic misadventure, an existence that would have meaning only in the material. And would that satisfy the psychological directives that control moral impulses in humans, or would human behavior simply become more brutish and violent? Immortality then becomes a protector of human morality, although many philosophers would deny this, and promote a principle of natural morality within humans that is governed by an innate conscience that has nothing to do with immortality or the soul, and is solely a function of the intellect.

In the end, humans have choices: to believe or not to believe in God, immortality, an afterlife, an immortal soul, or resurrection from the dead. Considering the vast number of texts throughout the millennia that support these possibilities, it would seem more logical to accept that not all of these minds can be in error. There is also the element of faith that has become an object of scorn for many, but a focus of hope for others that this physical life might have meaning and rewards, and an active faith will receive some type of immortal life in the future, just as the Book of Hebrews explains: "Now faith is the substance of things hoped for, the evidence of things not seen" (11:1). This is the human condition: reality does not rely on sight, humans cannot depend on sense perceptions alone for knowledge, and life teaches us that sometimes we must trust in what we cannot prove.

Appendix: Psalms

Psalm 1

¹ Blessed is the one
    who does not walk in step with the wicked
or stand in the way that sinners take
    or sit in the company of mockers,
² but whose delight is in the law of the LORD,
    and who meditates on his law day and night.
³ That person is like a tree planted by streams of water,
    which yields its fruit in season
and whose leaf does not wither—
    whatever they do prospers.
⁴ Not so the wicked!
    They are like chaff
    that the wind blows away.
⁵ Therefore the wicked will not stand in the judgment,
    nor sinners in the assembly of the righteous.
⁶ For the LORD watches over the way of the righteous,
    but the way of the wicked leads to destruction.

Psalm 19

A psalm of David.
¹ The heavens declare the glory of God;
    the skies proclaim the work of his hands.
² Day after day they pour forth speech;
    night after night they reveal knowledge.
³ They have no speech, they use no words;
    no sound is heard from them.

⁴ Yet their voice[b] goes out into all the earth,
   their words to the ends of the world.
In the heavens God has pitched a tent for the sun.
 ⁵ It is like a bridegroom coming out of his chamber,
   like a champion rejoicing to run his course.
 ⁶ It rises at one end of the heavens
   and makes its circuit to the other;
   nothing is deprived of its warmth.
 ⁷ The law of the LORD is perfect,
   refreshing the soul.
The statutes of the LORD are trustworthy,
   making wise the simple.
 ⁸ The precepts of the LORD are right,
   giving joy to the heart.
The commands of the LORD are radiant,
   giving light to the eyes.
 ⁹ The fear of the LORD is pure,
   enduring forever.
The decrees of the LORD are firm,
   and all of them are righteous.
¹⁰ They are more precious than gold,
   than much pure gold;
they are sweeter than honey,
   than honey from the honeycomb.
¹¹ By them your servant is warned;
   in keeping them there is great reward.
¹² But who can discern their own errors?
   Forgive my hidden faults.
¹³ Keep your servant also from willful sins;
   may they not rule over me.
Then I will be blameless,
   innocent of great transgression.
¹⁴ May these words of my mouth and this meditation of my heart
   be pleasing in your sight,
   LORD, my Rock and my Redeemer.

Psalm 119

א Aleph

 ¹ Blessed are those whose ways are blameless,
   who walk according to the law of the LORD.

² Blessed are those who keep his statutes
    and seek him with all their heart—
³ they do no wrong
    but follow his ways.
⁴ You have laid down precepts
    that are to be fully obeyed.
⁵ Oh, that my ways were steadfast
    in obeying your decrees!
⁶ Then I would not be put to shame
    when I consider all your commands.
⁷ I will praise you with an upright heart
    as I learn your righteous laws.
⁸ I will obey your decrees;
    do not utterly forsake me.

ב Beth

⁹ How can a young person stay on the path of purity?
    By living according to your word.
¹⁰ I seek you with all my heart;
    do not let me stray from your commands.
¹¹ I have hidden your word in my heart
    that I might not sin against you.
¹² Praise be to you, LORD;
    teach me your decrees.
¹³ With my lips I recount
    all the laws that come from your mouth.
¹⁴ I rejoice in following your statutes
    as one rejoices in great riches.
¹⁵ I meditate on your precepts
    and consider your ways.
¹⁶ I delight in your decrees;
    I will not neglect your word.

ג Gimel

¹⁷ Be good to your servant while I live,
    that I may obey your word.
¹⁸ Open my eyes that I may see
    wonderful things in your law.
¹⁹ I am a stranger on earth;
    do not hide your commands from me.
²⁰ My soul is consumed with longing
    for your laws at all times.

21 You rebuke the arrogant, who are accursed,
      those who stray from your commands.
22 Remove from me their scorn and contempt,
      for I keep your statutes.
23 Though rulers sit together and slander me,
      your servant will meditate on your decrees.
24 Your statutes are my delight;
      they are my counselors.

ד Daleth

25 I am laid low in the dust;
      preserve my life according to your word.
26 I gave an account of my ways and you answered me;
      teach me your decrees.
27 Cause me to understand the way of your precepts,
      that I may meditate on your wonderful deeds.
28 My soul is weary with sorrow;
      strengthen me according to your word.
29 Keep me from deceitful ways;
      be gracious to me and teach me your law.
30 I have chosen the way of faithfulness;
      I have set my heart on your laws.
31 I hold fast to your statutes, LORD;
      do not let me be put to shame.
32 I run in the path of your commands,
      for you have broadened my understanding.

ה He

33 Teach me, LORD, the way of your decrees,
      that I may follow it to the end.[b]
34 Give me understanding, so that I may keep your law
      and obey it with all my heart.
35 Direct me in the path of your commands,
      for there I find delight.
36 Turn my heart toward your statutes
      and not toward selfish gain.
37 Turn my eyes away from worthless things;
      preserve my life according to your word.[c]
38 Fulfill your promise to your servant,
      so that you may be feared.
39 Take away the disgrace I dread,
      for your laws are good.

⁴⁰ How I long for your precepts!
    In your righteousness preserve my life.

ו Waw
⁴¹ May your unfailing love come to me, LORD,
    your salvation, according to your promise;
⁴² then I can answer anyone who taunts me,
    for I trust in your word.
⁴³ Never take your word of truth from my mouth,
    for I have put my hope in your laws.
⁴⁴ I will always obey your law,
    for ever and ever.
⁴⁵ I will walk about in freedom,
    for I have sought out your precepts.
⁴⁶ I will speak of your statutes before kings
    and will not be put to shame,
⁴⁷ for I delight in your commands
    because I love them.
⁴⁸ I reach out for your commands, which I love,
    that I may meditate on your decrees.

ז Zayin
⁴⁹ Remember your word to your servant,
    for you have given me hope.
⁵⁰ My comfort in my suffering is this:
    Your promise preserves my life.
⁵¹ The arrogant mock me unmercifully,
    but I do not turn from your law.
⁵² I remember, LORD, your ancient laws,
    and I find comfort in them.
⁵³ Indignation grips me because of the wicked,
    who have forsaken your law.
⁵⁴ Your decrees are the theme of my song
    wherever I lodge.
⁵⁵ In the night, LORD, I remember your name,
    that I may keep your law.
⁵⁶ This has been my practice:
    I obey your precepts.

ח Heth
⁵⁷ You are my portion, LORD;
    I have promised to obey your words.

⁵⁸ I have sought your face with all my heart;
    be gracious to me according to your promise.
⁵⁹ I have considered my ways
    and have turned my steps to your statutes.
⁶⁰ I will hasten and not delay
    to obey your commands.
⁶¹ Though the wicked bind me with ropes,
    I will not forget your law.
⁶² At midnight I rise to give you thanks
    for your righteous laws.
⁶³ I am a friend to all who fear you,
    to all who follow your precepts.
⁶⁴ The earth is filled with your love, LORD;
    teach me your decrees.

ט Teth

⁶⁵ Do good to your servant
    according to your word, LORD.
⁶⁶ Teach me knowledge and good judgment,
    for I trust your commands.
⁶⁷ Before I was afflicted I went astray,
    but now I obey your word.
⁶⁸ You are good, and what you do is good;
    teach me your decrees.
⁶⁹ Though the arrogant have smeared me with lies,
    I keep your precepts with all my heart.
⁷⁰ Their hearts are callous and unfeeling,
    but I delight in your law.
⁷¹ It was good for me to be afflicted
    so that I might learn your decrees.
⁷² The law from your mouth is more precious to me
    than thousands of pieces of silver and gold.

יוד Yodh

⁷³ Your hands made me and formed me;
    give me understanding to learn your commands.
⁷⁴ May those who fear you rejoice when they see me,
    for I have put my hope in your word.
⁷⁵ I know, LORD, that your laws are righteous,
    and that in faithfulness you have afflicted me.
⁷⁶ May your unfailing love be my comfort,
    according to your promise to your servant.

⁷⁷ Let your compassion come to me that I may live,
for your law is my delight.
⁷⁸ May the arrogant be put to shame for wronging me without cause;
but I will meditate on your precepts.
⁷⁹ May those who fear you turn to me,
those who understand your statutes.
⁸⁰ May I wholeheartedly follow your decrees,
that I may not be put to shame.

כ Kaph

⁸¹ My soul faints with longing for your salvation,
but I have put my hope in your word.
⁸² My eyes fail, looking for your promise;
I say, "When will you comfort me?"
⁸³ Though I am like a wineskin in the smoke,
I do not forget your decrees.
⁸⁴ How long must your servant wait?
When will you punish my persecutors?
⁸⁵ The arrogant dig pits to trap me,
contrary to your law.
⁸⁶ All your commands are trustworthy;
help me, for I am being persecuted without cause.
⁸⁷ They almost wiped me from the earth,
but I have not forsaken your precepts.
⁸⁸ In your unfailing love preserve my life,
that I may obey the statutes of your mouth.

ל Lamedh

⁸⁹ Your word, LORD, is eternal;
it stands firm in the heavens.
⁹⁰ Your faithfulness continues through all generations;
you established the earth, and it endures.
⁹¹ Your laws endure to this day,
for all things serve you.
⁹² If your law had not been my delight,
I would have perished in my affliction.
⁹³ I will never forget your precepts,
for by them you have preserved my life.
⁹⁴ Save me, for I am yours;
I have sought out your precepts.
⁹⁵ The wicked are waiting to destroy me,
but I will ponder your statutes.

⁹⁶ To all perfection I see a limit,
    but your commands are boundless.

מ Mem

⁹⁷ Oh, how I love your law!
    I meditate on it all day long.
⁹⁸ Your commands are always with me
    and make me wiser than my enemies.
⁹⁹ I have more insight than all my teachers,
    for I meditate on your statutes.
¹⁰⁰ I have more understanding than the elders,
    for I obey your precepts.
¹⁰¹ I have kept my feet from every evil path
    so that I might obey your word.
¹⁰² I have not departed from your laws,
    for you yourself have taught me.
¹⁰³ How sweet are your words to my taste,
    sweeter than honey to my mouth!
¹⁰⁴ I gain understanding from your precepts;
    therefore I hate every wrong path.

נ Nun

¹⁰⁵ Your word is a lamp for my feet,
    a light on my path.
¹⁰⁶ I have taken an oath and confirmed it,
    that I will follow your righteous laws.
¹⁰⁷ I have suffered much;
    preserve my life, LORD, according to your word.
¹⁰⁸ Accept, LORD, the willing praise of my mouth,
    and teach me your laws.
¹⁰⁹ Though I constantly take my life in my hands,
    I will not forget your law.
¹¹⁰ The wicked have set a snare for me,
    but I have not strayed from your precepts.
¹¹¹ Your statutes are my heritage forever;
    they are the joy of my heart.
¹¹² My heart is set on keeping your decrees
    to the very end.[d]

ס Samekh

¹¹³ I hate double-minded people,
    but I love your law.

114 You are my refuge and my shield;
    I have put my hope in your word.
115 Away from me, you evildoers,
    that I may keep the commands of my God!
116 Sustain me, my God, according to your promise, and I will live;
    do not let my hopes be dashed.
117 Uphold me, and I will be delivered;
    I will always have regard for your decrees.
118 You reject all who stray from your decrees,
    for their delusions come to nothing.
119 All the wicked of the earth you discard like dross;
    therefore I love your statutes.
120 My flesh trembles in fear of you;
    I stand in awe of your laws.

ע Ayin

121 I have done what is righteous and just;
    do not leave me to my oppressors.
122 Ensure your servant's well-being;
    do not let the arrogant oppress me.
123 My eyes fail, looking for your salvation,
    looking for your righteous promise.
124 Deal with your servant according to your love
    and teach me your decrees.
125 I am your servant; give me discernment
    that I may understand your statutes.
126 It is time for you to act, LORD;
    your law is being broken.
127 Because I love your commands
    more than gold, more than pure gold,
128 and because I consider all your precepts right,
    I hate every wrong path.

פ Pe

129 Your statutes are wonderful;
    therefore I obey them.
130 The unfolding of your words gives light;
    it gives understanding to the simple.
131 I open my mouth and pant,
    longing for your commands.
132 Turn to me and have mercy on me,
    as you always do to those who love your name.

¹³³ Direct my footsteps according to your word;
    let no sin rule over me.
¹³⁴ Redeem me from human oppression,
    that I may obey your precepts.
¹³⁵ Make your face shine on your servant
    and teach me your decrees.
¹³⁶ Streams of tears flow from my eyes,
    for your law is not obeyed.

צ Tsadhe
¹³⁷ You are righteous, LORD,
    and your laws are right.
¹³⁸ The statutes you have laid down are righteous;
    they are fully trustworthy.
¹³⁹ My zeal wears me out,
    for my enemies ignore your words.
¹⁴⁰ Your promises have been thoroughly tested,
    and your servant loves them.
¹⁴¹ Though I am lowly and despised,
    I do not forget your precepts.
¹⁴² Your righteousness is everlasting
    and your law is true.
¹⁴³ Trouble and distress have come upon me,
    but your commands give me delight.
¹⁴⁴ Your statutes are always righteous;
    give me understanding that I may live.

ק Qoph
¹⁴⁵ I call with all my heart; answer me, LORD,
    and I will obey your decrees.
¹⁴⁶ I call out to you; save me
    and I will keep your statutes.
¹⁴⁷ I rise before dawn and cry for help;
    I have put my hope in your word.
¹⁴⁸ My eyes stay open through the watches of the night,
    that I may meditate on your promises.
¹⁴⁹ Hear my voice in accordance with your love;
    preserve my life, LORD, according to your laws.
¹⁵⁰ Those who devise wicked schemes are near,
    but they are far from your law.
¹⁵¹ Yet you are near, LORD,
    and all your commands are true.

¹⁵² Long ago I learned from your statutes
    that you established them to last forever.

ר Resh

¹⁵³ Look on my suffering and deliver me,
    for I have not forgotten your law.
¹⁵⁴ Defend my cause and redeem me;
    preserve my life according to your promise.
¹⁵⁵ Salvation is far from the wicked,
    for they do not seek out your decrees.
¹⁵⁶ Your compassion, LORD, is great;
    preserve my life according to your laws.
¹⁵⁷ Many are the foes who persecute me,
    but I have not turned from your statutes.
¹⁵⁸ I look on the faithless with loathing,
    for they do not obey your word.
¹⁵⁹ See how I love your precepts;
    preserve my life, LORD, in accordance with your love.
¹⁶⁰ All your words are true;
    all your righteous laws are eternal.

ש Sin and Shin

¹⁶¹ Rulers persecute me without cause,
    but my heart trembles at your word.
¹⁶² I rejoice in your promise
    like one who finds great spoil.
¹⁶³ I hate and detest falsehood
    but I love your law.
¹⁶⁴ Seven times a day I praise you
    for your righteous laws.
¹⁶⁵ Great peace have those who love your law,
    and nothing can make them stumble.
¹⁶⁶ I wait for your salvation, LORD,
    and I follow your commands.
¹⁶⁷ I obey your statutes,
    for I love them greatly.
¹⁶⁸ I obey your precepts and your statutes,
    for all my ways are known to you.

ת Taw

¹⁶⁹ May my cry come before you, LORD;
    give me understanding according to your word.

[170] May my supplication come before you;
    deliver me according to your promise.
[171] May my lips overflow with praise,
    for you teach me your decrees.
[172] May my tongue sing of your word,
    for all your commands are righteous.
[173] May your hand be ready to help me,
    for I have chosen your precepts.
[174] I long for your salvation, LORD,
    and your law gives me delight.
[175] Let me live that I may praise you,
    and may your laws sustain me.
[176] I have strayed like a lost sheep.
    Seek your servant,
    for I have not forgotten your commands.

Chapter Notes

Chapter 1

1. In his book, *Ancient Iraq*, Georges Roux opines about Gilgamesh: "Yet his arrogance, ruthlessness and depravity were a subject of grave concern for the citizens of Uruk (his kingdom). They complained to the great god Anu, and Anu instructed the goddess Aruru to create another wild ox, a double of Gilgamesh, who would challenge him and distract his mind from the warrior's daughter and the noblemen's spouse, whom it appears he would not leave in peace" (114). Roux is correct in his assessment, as Gilgamesh evolves in the story from a wild, immoral, and brutish man to a noble king who treats his citizens with dignity.

2. Purgatory, according to Catholic Church doctrine, is an intermediary state after physical death in which those destined for heaven "undergo purification, so as to achieve the holiness necessary to enter the joy of heaven" ("Catechism"). Catholics have access to indulgences in the form of prayers and monetary offerings that take time off the "years" in purgatory. Purgatory virtually disappeared from Catholic belief after Vatican II. John E. Thiel writes: "The theological and pastoral reception of the Second Vatican Council highlighted the power of God's grace in bringing believers to salvation, and that emphasis undermined the detailed accounting of personal virtue and sin in the Tridentine merit system. This accent on the graciousness of divine love brought about a seismic shift in Catholic belief and practice. Conservatives in the Church would continue the explanation by concluding that the postconciliar theology of God's infinite mercy and compassion tragically eclipsed the preconciliar sense of the power of personal sin. This diminishment of the sense of sin has had repercussions for a host of other mutually related beliefs and practices that explain the contemporary indifference toward purgatory" ("Time, Judgment" 741–742). See also *Theological Studies* 69.4 (2008): 741–785.

3. Steffan Laursen provides the location, and a very detailed description of Dilmun in his article, "Early Dilmun and Its Rulers." He states: "Although its exact geographical extent has been the object of both controversy and fluctuation over time, Bahrain and the adjacent Eastern Province of Saudi Arabia undoubtedly constituted the heart of Dilmun. A predecessor of the celebrated Dilmun polity that flourished on Bahrain has long been recognized in the potential third-millennium centre on Tarut Island, Saudi Arabia (Bibby 1973: 31; Potts 1983: 370; Kohl 1986: 16)" (156). See also Laursen's article, "A Late Fourth- to Early Third-Millennium Grave from Bahrain, C.3100–2600 BC," *Arabian Archaeology & Epigraphy* 24.2 (2013): 125–133; the article details the archaeological excavations in Bahrain that proves it was occupied as early as the late fourth to mid-third millennium BCE.

4. The kings of Mesopotamia believed that by having certain texts inscribed, they

would leave a legacy in perpetuity. However, they also used writing to authenticate their rule while still in command (Galvin 20).

5. Akkadian is a later, unrelated, Mesopotamian language, which also used the cuneiform writing system. An article by Uri Gabbay details about one thousand Akkadian texts that include commentaries, exegetical interpretations of natural phenomena, and letters to kings, etc. See "Akkadian Commentaries from Ancient Mesopotamia and Their Relation to Early Hebrew Exegesis," *Dead Sea Discoveries* 19.3 (2012): 267–312.

6. In pages 81–103 of *The Evolution of the Gilgamesh Epic*, Tigay documents the modifications that took place between the old Babylonian and later versions; changes vary from small alterations such as paraphrasing, addition of lines, and reformation of ideas to larger changes in character, incorporation of different passages, and theological changes (Berlin 130). For more information on variances among the text's different versions, read Tzvi Abusch, "The Development and Meaning of the Epic of Gilgamesh: An Interpretive Essay."

7. Rachel Galvin's article "The Imprint of Immortality" provides a brief history and description of Ashurbanipal's library. She informs the reader: "Modern decipherment of Sumerian was aided by an 1854 rediscovery of a trove of literature in a ruined library at Nineveh, on the east bank of the Tigris river. The Assyrian king Ashurbanipal, who reigned during the seventh century BCE, was a patron of the arts and an avid reader. At the king's command, copyists had compiled more than twenty thousand literary, religious, medical, epistolary, and administrative texts, creating the first cataloged library in the region. A twelve-tablet version of the Epic of Gilgamesh was found at Nineveh, written by the first known author in history, Shin-eqiunninni. The library also contained copies of creation stories and folk tales such as 'The Poor Man of Nippur,' a forerunner of 'The Thousand and One Nights.' Only fourteen years after the king's death, Nineveh was sacked and the library destroyed. It took twenty-four centuries for its treasures to be found again. 'Thousands of the tablets in Ashurbanipal's library were bilingual—that is, ancient scribes translated them from Akkadian into Sumerian or vice versa,' explains Tinney. The bilingual tablets helped scholars crack the ancient language, but as of today, a complete Sumerian dictionary has yet to be published" (Galvin 23).

8. For a recent discussion of the royal status of the flood hero in Mesopotamian tradition, see J. R. Davila, "The Flood Hero." As regards the *Epic of Gilgamesh*, Davila notes "…the Standard Babylonian Gilgamesh epic followed the tradition of the royal Flood hero" (206).

9. Shuruppak became a grain storage and distribution city, and had more silos than any other Sumerian city. The earliest excavated levels at Shuruppak date to the Jemdet Nasr Period about 3000 BCE; it was abandoned shortly after 2000 BCE (Martin 44). Today, the remains of Shuruppak are called Fara, and are located halfway between Baghdad and Basra (Bertman 30).

10. Jager Bernd provides a clear account of the discovery of the Epic in his article "The Birth of Poetry and the Creation of a Human World"; he writes: "When we read the Mesopotamian story of the Flood for the first time we are amazed to discover that we already are familiar with its broad outline and that even in many minor details it resembles the Biblical story of the Flood. Curiously, it was the discovery of this part of the Gilgamesh Epic that caused a sensation in England, when its discovery was announced by George Smith before a meeting of the Society for Biblical Archeology of 1872. His subsequent publication of the Chaldean Account of the Deluge provided the impetus for further excavations at Nineveh which in turn led to the discovery of additional tablets of the Epic (Sanders, N.K. 1960, p. 10). Subsequent archeological work has shown that the oldest extant account of the Flood story appears in the Sumerian 'Poem of Atrahasis,' sometimes referred to as 'The Supersage,' that dates from the seventeenth century BCE (Bottero, J. 1998, 199)" (Bernd 137).

11. Mount Nisir is also called Nimush, and today is called Pir Omar Gudrun and is located in Kurdistan in Northern Iraq.

12. It is worth reading page 32 of Curtis E. Larsen's *Life and Land Use on the Bahrain Islands: The Geoarchaeology of an Ancient Society* (University of Chicago Press, 1984). Also valuable in deciphering the location of Dilmun is "The Dilmun of the Cuneiform Inscriptions," page 234 in Volume 18, *The Expository Times,* edited by James Hastings (Edinburgh: T. & T Clark, 1906).

13. Ancient snake symbolism went beyond ascriptions of wisdom, which complicate analysis of the snake in the Epic. According to Karen Joines, an entire doctoral dissertation was written to prove that the figure of the serpent in ancient Semitic-Sumerian culture represented immortality (18), as well as being a symbol of wisdom, chaos, and evil. Then snake imagery in the story emphasizes that immortality is not for humans or demigods— do not even try to capture it. But the snake in ancient literature and iconography usually represents the ancient gods. In Egypt, serpent worship was the same as sun worship, and "both male and female deities were represented in serpent form" (Wilkinson 220). Snakes images in ancient worship, generally were symbols of goddesses with phallic representations, such as in Hathor's iconography. "Hathor's original name was Nut, and she was referred to 'as the Great Snake Ua Zit, as Maat, and as Hathor, mother of all deities, Queen of Haven, creator and destroyer.... She is the Sacred Cow of Heaven who can become the Great Serpent'" (Leeming 43). According to Baring and Cashford, "Hera may reach back to the Neolithic Snake Goddess who ruled the heavenly waters, and Homer and Plato both connected her name with the air. In the *Iliad* she is called the 'Queen of Heaven' and 'Hera of the Goddess Throne.'" She was also goddess of earth and was personified in ancient times as a cow, recalling legends of the Sumerian Ninhursag and the Egyptian Hathor (311). Karen Joines also states that the idea that "the serpent is also associated with sex, the goddess, and the fertility of the earth carried over into the Persian and Hellenistic Periods" (113). Pictorial representation of serpents have been found in pottery, in funerary vessels, in tombs, sanctuaries, and seals dating from the Chalcolithic, Early Bronze, and Middle Bronze Ages in Mesopotamia, Palestine, Canaan, and Egypt (98–99).

14. See pages 86, 210, 211 in Jeffrey Tigay, *The Evolution of the Gilgamesh Epic* (Philadelphia: University of Pennsylvania Press, 1976).

15. See pages 140–141 in Thorkild Jacobsen. *The Sumerian King List.* Jacobsen suggests the list was first complied by ancient sources during the reign of Utu-Hegal, after the defeat of the Gutian invaders during the late Third Millennium BCE. The Gutian dynasty came to power around 2083 BCE by destabilizing Akkad at the end of the reign of king Ur-Utu or Lugal-melem of Uruk, and reigned for about 100 years. The Gutian people were native to the central Zagros Mountains in western Iran. For a detailed history of this people, please see pages 265 to 267 in Trevor Bryce's *The Routledge Handbook of the Peoples and Places of Ancient Western Asia from the Early Bronze Age to the Fall of the Persian Empire* (London: Routledge, 2009).

16. The star or *dingir* symbol always represented God's name in cuneiform, and the Sumerian word for god always signified the name An (Anu) and heaven; this symbol later became part of the Akkadian Semitic language and meant "god" (Boulay 67; Selin 244).

17. Anu is the original Annun'aki or Sumerian father-god; his other names include Ya, Yaw, and Yam.

18. Aruru is the ancient goddess Ninhursag, the purported creator of humans. She had many names, including Ninmah ("Great Queen"), Nintu ("Lady of Birth"), Mamma or Mami (mother), and Belet-Ili (lady of the gods, in Akkadian) (Dalley 326).

19. *Etemmu* is the main word for ghost in Akkadian. It is the common term for "ghost of the dead" and is the numen repeatedly referred to in the first millennium necromancy incantations from Mesopotamia (Schmidt 157–158). Humans could plead with the *etemmu* for help, and could offer prophetic knowledge; it could attack the living and make them ill. It was not considered as the soul (Hays 43, 44).

20. Campbell explores the theory that important myths from around the world, which

have survived for thousands of years, all share a fundamental structure, which Campbell called the *monomyth*. In a well-known quote from the introduction to *The Hero with a Thousand Faces,* Campbell summarized the monomyth: "A hero ventures forth from the world of common day into a region of supernatural wonder: fabulous forces are there encountered and a decisive victory is won: the hero comes back from this mysterious adventure with the power to bestow boons on his fellow man" (30).

Chapter 2

1. Hathor's original name was Nut, and was referred to "...as the Great Snake Ua Zit, as Maat, and as Hathor, mother of all deities, Queen of Heaven, creator and destroyer.... She is the Sacred Cow of Heaven who can become the Great Serpent" (Leeming 43).

2. *Maatkheru* translates as true of voice. The term *maat* means divine law and balance and by extension truth. The term *kheru* means *to voice, to command.* One who consistently demonstrates the capacity to function as *maatkheru* (female) is one who regularly voices, commands, delivers the divine law, that which is in harmony with divine order. To be *maatkheru* is to have attained spiritual maturity. In the ancient Egyptian afterlife, souls had to be judged morally righteous. Once the soul had passed the test, the "weighing of the heart," he or she was judged to be *maatkheru*, and was allowed to enter the afterlife and not experience the second death (Allen 95; Anthes 50).

3. The *Book of Gates* is also referred to as the *Book of Pylons* and the *Book of Portals* (Murdock 272). This book is a myth about the sun god written during the New Kingdom (1550–1069 BCE). The book is dominated by giant serpents who guard the 12 gates and assist the Sun God through his journey. Pat Remier states that, "Early Christian concepts of hell may have been derived from this theme" (30). For a detailed explanation of each of the 12 Gates, please see pages 30–31 of Remier's *Egyptian Mythology, A to Z.*

4. The Greek scholar Plutarch relates the story of Osiris, a divine man (pharaoh of Egypt) who was resurrected as a god. Osiris had been killed by his brother and his body hacked into 14 pieces, which were scattered about the land. Isis, the wife of Osiris, collected the pieces and brought him back to life. Osiris became the god of the Underworld, and his resurrection created the possibility of an everlasting life for everyone. Patrick V. Reid writes: "According to Plutarch, he made the Egyptians give up their destitute and brutish mode of life, showing them the fruits produced by cultivation, and giving them laws, and teaching them how to worship the gods" (32). Pages 32–34 in Reid's *Readings in Western Religious Thought* are worthwhile.

5. Safkhet (also Sesat, Seshet, Sesheta, and Seshata) was the Ancient Egyptian goddess of wisdom, knowledge, and writing. She was seen as a scribe and record keeper and her name means she who is the scribe, and is credited with inventing writing. She also became identified as the goddess of architecture, astronomy, astrology, building, mathematics, and surveying. These are all professions that relied upon expertise in her skills. She is identified as Safekh-Aubi in some late texts (Wilkinson 166).

6. Maat, the goddess of truth, justice and balance took the form of an ostrich feather. The final trial of the deceased would be to have his heart weighed against Maat. If the person had led a good and decent life, his heart would be in balance and he would pass into the Afterlife. But if the weight of his heart did not balance with Maat, a monster named The Devourer consumed his heart. The heart was identified as "the seat of intelligence and moral judgement, as well as of emotions." The term Maat Kheru is identified with the party at the end of a civil trial that would be declared innocent and true, or "true of voice" or "justified." See pages 201–202 in Patricia Monaghan, *The New Book of Goddesses & Heroines* (Llewellyn Publications, 1997); page 674 in *Britannica Encyclopædia of World Religions* (Chicago, 2006).

7. Reisner, *The Egyptian Conception.*

8. George A. Reisner writes also about the change in funerary rituals after the establishment of Christianity: "When Christianity came into Egypt, all the gaudy apparatus of the Osiris religion was swept out of existence. The body was to rise again and might not be mutilated. Mummification, which destroyed the body in order to preserve a conventional simulacrum, ceased abruptly. Grave furniture was of course unthinkable. But the use of charms did not cease. Crosses were embroidered in the grave cloths; or small crosses of metal or wood placed on the breast or arm; the gravestone bore a simple prayer to the Holy Spirit for the peaceful rest of the soul. But the offering place was still maintained; prayers were recited on the feast days; lamps were allowed to remain at the grave; food was brought, but given to the poor" (74). The reader may wish to pursue the full text by Reisner, *The Egyptian Conception of Immortality* (1912).

Chapter 3

1. "The ancient Sumerian gods, demigods, and their descendants married within the family to keep genetic bloodlines pure, and this tradition continued with the pharaohs and is evidenced today in certain cultures. Bloodlines are strategic in deciphering connections among ancient peoples' political development, in identifying religious affiliations, and in analyzing the names of these specific gods and goddesses and their connections to kings, queens, and pharaohs. Interfamilial marriages among the Annun'aki 'gods' and their half-human 'demigod' offspring created tribes still in existence today; for example, tribes like the Arabian Shammari have a name that harkens back to the ancient Sumerian and Mesopotamian god Shamash, a Sun god and great grandson of Anu, the original father god. Even the patriarch Abraham married his half-sister Sarai, later named Sarah, who was a princess; he dismissed Ishmael's patriarchal succession when Sarah bore Isaac, creating two separate genealogical lines. This practice of interfamilial marriage still occurs among the tribes in Saudi Arabia, Kuwait, Yemen, and other countries in the region, as men prefer to marry their first or second cousins, making this contemporary custom a curious tie to ancient history and tradition" (Coulter-Harris 13–14).

2. The pre–Hellenic Lapiths are a famous tribe from Greek mythology, whose home was in Thessaly. Lapithes was a valiant warrior, but Centaurus was deformed, the product of a sexual union between a "cloud" image of Hera and Ixion. He later mated with mares from whom the race of half-man, half-horse Centaurs or Ixionate tribes came. See Homer, *Iliad* xii.128; Diodorus Siculus iv. 69; v. 61.

3. Metis was one of the original Titans, and was the first great spouse of Zeus. By the fifth century BCE, Metis had become the goddess of wisdom and deep thought, but her name originally connoted "magical cunning," and was as easily equated with the trickster powers of Prometheus with the "royal *metis*" of Zeus (Brown 130–143). Metis also connoted the "intelligence of cunning" and the wisdom involved in practical existence. Michael Shank, *Art and the Early Greek State* (Cambridge University Press, 1999), see p. 137.

4. In Book 8, lines 266–366, the Bard Demodocus sings of the love affair between Ares and Aphrodite and the suffering of Hephaestus (Morford 80).

5. See C. Scott Littleton, ed., *Gods, Goddesses, and Mythology*, Volume 5 (Tarrytown: Marshall Cavendish, 2005), p. 654.

6. See *ApollodorusŌ Library and HyginusŌ Fabulae* by Apollodorus & Hyginus, trans. R. Scott Smith and Stephen M. Trzaskoma (Indianapolis: Hackett, 2007), p. 48. Apparently, Apollodorus states that the remaining daughters of Cadmus rumored that Semele had slept with a human and not Zeus, and that was why she was struck dead with a thunderbolt.

7. The Romans and the modern West refer to him as Hercules; the Romans adopted

the Greek version of his life and works essentially unchanged, but added anecdotal details of their own, some of it linking the hero with the geography of the Central Mediterranean.

8. The most important classical texts dealing with Heracles are Pseudo-Apollodorus, *Bibliotecha* 2.4.8 ff; Diodorus Siculus, *Library of History* 4.8.1.ff; Pseudo-Hyginus, *Fabula* 29–36; Pseudo-Hyginus, *Astronomica*; Hesiod, *The Shield of Heracles*; Euripides, *Madness of Heracles*; Sophocles, *The Women of Trachis*; Theocritus, *Idylls* 24–25; Seneca, *Hercules Furens*; Seneca, *Hercules Oetaeus*; Apollonius Rhodius, *Argonautica Book 1*; Valerius Flaccus, *Argonautica Books 1–3*; and Anonymous, *Megara*. The translated texts of this original material may be found in "Theoi Greek Mythology: Exploring Mythology in Classical Literature and Art." http://www.theoi.com/greek-mythology/heracles.html

9. In the Euripedes play, Heracles does not slaughter his children until after his return home from his twelve labors (Halleran 285).

10. Colchis or Kolkhis was an ancient kingdom and region in Western Georgia that played an important role in the ethnic and cultural formation of the Georgian nation.

11. Refer to Apollodorus, *The Library*, with an English Translation by Sir James George Frazer, in 2 volumes (Harvard University Press; London, William Heinemann, 1921).

12. Elysium is an afterlife location separate from Hades "...reserved for mortal relatives of the king of the gods." They were transported there "without tasting of death" to enjoy immortality. Later, the idea was extended to include those chosen by the gods, the righteous, and the heroic. The *Elysian Fields* were, according to Homer, located on the western edge of the Earth by the stream of Oceanus (Peck 588, 589).

13. See *The Homeric "Hymn to Demeter": Translation, Commentary, and Interpretive Essays*, translated by Helene P. Foley (Princeton University Press, 1993), p. 14.

14. See footnote 545 in Sophia Papaioannou, *Redesigning Achilles* (Berlin: Walter de Gruyter, 2007), p. 258.

Chapter 4

1. "As we have seen, Descartes defines substance in terms of independence. This, however, is only a very general claim. In order to better understand Descartes' account of substance we need to have a better idea of the way in which substances are independent. On one hand, in his thinking about substance Descartes is working with the traditional conception of independence according to which a substance's existence is independent in a way that a mode's existence is not, since substances are ultimate subjects. Accordingly, let us say that substances are subject-independent. On the other hand, in his account of substance Descartes is also working with a causal sense of independence. After all, the reason that God is the only *Substance* (as opposed to *Created Substance*) is that all other things 'can exist only with the help of God's concurrence' (*Principles* I.51), and Descartes understands this as the causal claim that all other things are God's creation and require his continual conservation. Consequently scholars have seen Descartes as holding that in general (i) God is both causally and subjectively independent (God is not, after all, a mode of anything else), (ii) created substances are causally independent of everything but God and subjectively independent, and (iii) modes are both causally and subjectively dependent in that they both depend on God's continual conservation and on created substances as subjects" ("17th Century Theories"). One may refer to http://www.iep.utm.edu/substanc/

2. Belief in reincarnation was also held in early Christianity throughout the Hermetic literature, which had an impact on the formulation of early Christianity (Ebeling 28). Secondly, the doctrine of reincarnation was discussed by the early Church fathers: St. Augustine, Clement of Alexandriam, and Origen (Gulati 83; Woods 73). Thirdly, reincarnation is prevalent in some of the early Christian Gnostic sects, such as the Valentinian

and Sethians (Logan 303; Givens 102,103). Also, the very earliest discussion of immortality in India was in the *Upanishads* (Thapar, "Sacrifice" 305).

3. The following passage in the *Rig Veda* (9.113. 7–11) is a prayer for apotheosis. "O Pavarnana, place me in that deathless, undecaying world wherein the light of heaven is set, and everlasting lustre shines. Flow, Indu, flow for Indra's sake. Make me immortal in that realm where dwells the King, Vivasvan's Son, Where is the secret shrine of heaven, where are those waters young and fresh. Flow, Indu, flow for Indra's sake. Make me immortal in that realm where they move even as they list, In the third sphere of inmost heaven where lucid worlds are full of light. Flow, Indu, flow for Indra's sake. Make me immortal in that realm of eager wish and strong desire, the region of the radiant Moon, where food and full delight are found. Flow, Indu, flow for Indra's sake: Make me immortal in that realm where happiness and transports, where Joys and felicities combine, and longing wishes are fulfilled. Flow, Indu, flow for Indra's sake."

4. Staal writes that he regards *ephedra* as the least likely among the candidates, and many scholars refute the idea that *soma* was an alcoholic beverage (759).

5. Edwin Quinn writes: "In esoteric Hatha Yoga, it is thought that amrita can be accumulated in the skull above the posterior of the nasal passage. This amrita is understood to be transformed semen that can create bodily immortality. By severing the frenulum, or skin attachment at the bottom of the tongue, a yogi can force his tongue backwards into what is called the Khechara Mudra, in order to drink the amrita" (25).

6. There are many meanings behind the term Asuras. In one sense, they are the "supreme deities," and in another sense Asura was a reference to a "godless" people or a tribe (Bhandarkar 33).

7. The Sanskrit *Asura* is usually translated as "demon" but also sometimes as "Titan" or "antigod." These beings are the principal antagonists of the devas of Hindu religion, especially as it is embodied in the Puranas (Gier 73).

8. According to George M. Williams, the devas ruled the three worlds: heaven, mid-air, and earth. The principal devas of heaven were Dyaus, the sky god and Varuna, Lord of Rita; Mitra, Lord of the day; and Vishnu. The main devas of the mid-air were Indra, Lord of storm and war; Vayu, lord of wind; the Maruts, warrior lords; and Rudras, lords of killing fire. The greatest of earthly devas were Soma, lord of the plant soma; and Agni, lord of the sacrificial fire. These devas or divine beings evolved throughout varied periods in Hindu history to become manifestations of the one supreme Lord of the universe (111). Kamlesh Kapur writes that devas are immortal, birthless, and deathless and are benefactors of humanity; they are countless energies and manifestations of Brahman, the Supreme Being (45).

Chapter 5

1. A mystic religion of ancient Greece, originating in the 7th or 6th century BCE and based on poems (now lost) attributed to Orpheus, emphasizing the necessity for individuals to rid themselves of the evil part of their nature by ritual and moral purification throughout a series of reincarnations.

2. See Thomas F. Glasson, *Greek Influence in Jewish Eschatology* (London: S.P.C.K., 1961), p. 82.

3. The Torah includes: *Genesis, Exodus, Leviticus, Numbers, and Deuteronomy*. The *Hebrew Bible* is not necessarily identical to the Old Testament as it is identified by Christians (although the two closely coincide). The *Hebrew Bible* includes the *Torah*, the books of the prophets, and the writings (or the hagiography). The books of the prophets are *Joshua, Judges, Samuel, Kings, Jeremiah, Ezekiel, Isaiah*, and the Twelve (the Minor Prophets). The books of the writings consist of *Psalms, Proverbs, Job, Ecclesiastes, Song of Solomon, Lamentations, Daniel, Esther, Ezra-Nehemiah*, and *Chronicles*.

4. See *Nicomachean Ethics*, 1097a 30–34. Aristotle. *Nicomachean Ethics*. Ed. and trans. Harris Rackham. Perseaus.tufts.edu, n.d. Web. 21 Jun 2015.

5. See *Nicomachean Ethics*, 1101a10.

6. See also IV Macc. 7:23; 9:8; 17:5, 18.

7. R. Bauckham, "Resurrection as Giving Back the Dead" in *The Pseudepigrapha and Early Biblical Interpretation*, eds. J. H. Charlesworth and C. A. Evans (Sheffield: JSOT Press, 1993). See pages 267–291 and 276–277.

8. The concept of an interim abode for the souls of the dead awaiting resurrection can be found in 1 Enoch 22; 4 Ezra 7: 32; 2 Baruch 30:2.

9. Josephus was a first century CE Jewish historian who wrote *The Jewish War* and *Antiquities of the Jews*.

10. Josephus implies that the Pharisees had some sort of dualistic view; the righteous would experience corporeal resurrection and be rewarded, but the wicked would not be resurrected in bodily form but would face punishment in some form.

11. According to William West, the Pharisees originated during the Maccabean period and died out around 70 CE when the second temple was destroyed. See page 103 in West's *A Resurrection to Immortality*.

12. According to Jacob Neusner, "...the Mishnah [is] the second century philosophical law code that lays the foundation, after scripture, of normative Judaism...." For more on the Mishnah, see pages vii and vii in his Preface to *The Mishnah: Social Perspectives*. Leiden: Brill, 1999.

13. This literal translation of the Greek is from Steve Mason, *Flavius Josephus*.

14. The Talmud is the authoritative body of Jewish law and tradition incorporating the Hebrew *Mishnah* and the Aramaic *Gemara*, and supplementing the scriptural law that was developed in the fourth and fifth centuries CE.

15. The Mishnah was written circa 200 CE and is the product of oral debates by scholars and rabbis of the Hebrew Bible, especially the Torah. The *Gemara* circa 500 CE is further written commentary on the *Mishnah*.

16. Rabbinic Judaism began during the sixth-century CE, after the codification of the Babylonian Talmud. Growing out of Pharisaic Judaism, Rabbinic Judaism is based on the belief that Moses received the Pentateuch at Mount Sinai in addition to the "Oral Torah." The Sadducees, however, did not recognize the oral law as a divine authority and they rejected the Rabbinic procedures used to interpret Jewish scripture (Neusner 1).

17. The *Zohar* is the chief text of the Jewish *Kabbalah*, presented as an allegorical or mystical interpretation of the *Pentateuch*. The *Zohar* was accepted as the work of Rabbi Shim'on, a famous second century CE teacher who reportedly lived as a hermit in a cave for twelve years. By the middle of the 16th century, it ranked with the Bible and the Talmud as a sacred text (Matt 3, 4).

Chapter 6

1. The Tribulation period is thought to be the seven year time frame during which the Antichrist rules the world. It is at the beginning of this time that some denominations profess there will be a rapture of believers who will ascend bodily into heaven, so that these Christians avoid the worst of the tribulation period. The Rapture doctrine, which was the invention of the Plymouth Brethren led by John Nelson Darby (1800–1882), has today been adopted by most Baptists, Pentecostals, Assemblies of God, and a variety of other fundamentalist sects (Mungovan 174–175). For an informative biographical account of Darby, see Ice, Thomas, "John Nelson Darby and the Rapture," *Journal of Ministry & Theology* 17.1 (2013): 99–119.

2. "...and if any one's name was not found written in the book of life, he was thrown into the lake of fire."

3. John H. C. Pippy has written a scholarly linguistic account of the Egyptian origins of the Lake of Fire. See pages 416 and 417 of *Egyptian Origin of the Book of Revelation* (Raleigh: Lulu Enterprises, 2011).

4. This was a common view during the Middle Ages. See pages 49–50 in Justo L. Gonzalez, *The Apostles' Creed for Today* (Louisville: Westminster John Knox Press, 2007).

5. For an attempt to resolve answers to such questions, readers should consult *Christian Theology: An Introduction* (5th edition) by Alister E. McGrath. (Hoboken: Wiley-Blackwell, 2011.)

6. Typhon is Osiris' jealous brother Seth.

7. To read Werner Jaeger's full essay, see his "The Greek Ideas," 135–147.

8. *De Anima* is a discourse on the nature of living things that focuses on the types of souls possessed by different kinds of living things and differentiated by their different functions. For example, plants are able to process nutrients and reproduce, minimum functions for any kind of living organism. Lower animals have powers of sense-perception and movement. Humans have all of the aforementioned, but possess a developed intellect. Aristotle holds that the soul is the *form*, or *essence* of any living thing, but it is not a distinct substance from the body in which it dwells. It is the existence of a specific type of soul that defines an organism; the idea of a body without a soul, or of a soul in the wrong kind of body, is simply incomprehensible. Aristotle argues that some parts of the soul—the intellect—can exist without the body, but most cannot. It is difficult to reconcile these points with the popular picture of a soul as a sort of spiritual substance "inhabiting" a body.

9. From Eusebius' *Evangelical Preparation*, 15.20.6. "Eusebius reports: 'They [the Stoics] say that the soul is subject to generation and destruction. When separated from the body, however, it does not perish at once but survives on its own for certain times, the soul of the virtuous up to the dissolution of everything into fire, that of fools only for certain definite times.'" See Jon Miller, *Spinoza and the Stoics* (Cambridge University Press, 2015), p. 29.

10. Orphism devalued earthly life in favor of the immortal soul as a higher element. This body/soul dualism directly influenced Christianity with its "valley of tears" and its belief that happiness can never be found in materiality, but complete happiness can only be found after one dies (de Jauregui 338).

11. W.C.K. Guthrie writes that Orphism, from which the Orphic mysteries arose, is named for a sixth century BCE religious Greek. "According to legend, Orpheus founded these mysteries and was the author of the sacred poems from which the Orphic doctrines were created. When Zeus proposed to make Zagreus the ruler of the universe, the Titans were so enraged that they dismembered the boy and devoured him. Athena saved Zagreus' heart and gave it to Zeus, who thereupon swallowed the heart (from which was born the second Dionysus Zagreus) and destroyed the Titans with lightning. From the ashes of the Titans sprang the human race, who were part divine (Dionysus) and part evil (Titan). This double aspect of human nature, the Dionysian and the Titanic, is essential to the understanding of Orphism. The Orphics affirmed the divine origin of the soul, but it was through initiation into the Orphic Mysteries and through the process of transmigration that the soul could be liberated from its Titanic inheritance and could achieve eternal blessedness. Orphism stressed a strict standard of ethical and moral conduct. Initiates purified themselves and adopted ascetic practices (e.g., abstinence from eating animal flesh) for the purpose of purging evil and cultivating the Dionysian side of the human character" ("Orphic Mysteries"). See http://www.infoplease.com/encyclopedia/society/orphic-mysteries.html. For the most detailed discussion of the Orphic mysteries, see W. K. C. Guthrie, *Orpheus and Greek Religion* (Princeton University Press, 1993). See also page xiv in Apostolos N. Athanassakis and Benjamin M. Wolkow, *The Orphic Hymns* (Johns Hopkins University Press, 2013).

12. These mysteries celebrated the mystery of death and rebirth; the Lesser Mysteries took place in the spring, and the Greater Mysteries were held in September. Participants engaged in psychotropic drugs in a drink called *kykeon*, participated in secret rituals, bathing in the sea, and fasting. Participants entered the Telesterion, an underground "theatre," where the secret ritual took place, a re-enactment of the "death" and rebirth of Persephone. Virtually every important writer in antiquity was an initiate of the Mysteries. After completing the initiation, the initiates were promised benefits of some kind in the afterlife; Christian writers condemned these acts as pagan abominations.

13. The Pharisees conformed to the laws of the Torah and Moses, were usually from lower social classes, and were not priests in the Jewish temple in any official role.

14. Pelagianism was opposed by Augustine (354–430 CE), Bishop of Hippo; was condemned as heresy at the Council of Carthage in 418 CE, and was confirmed as a heresy by the Catholic Church at the Council of Ephesus in 431 CE. This doctrine remains as a heresy even today; several Protestant sects, such as the Methodists, also consider Pelagianism to be a profane teaching.

15. Irenaeus (120–202 CE), a bishop of Gaul (in what is now Lyon, France) was known as the first great Catholic theologian. For more on Irenaeus, see the following excerpt from: Albert Poncelet, "St. Irenaeus," *The Catholic Encyclopedia*, vol. 8 (New York: Robert Appleton, 1910).

16. The Fifth Lateran Council of 1513 CE condemned conditional immortality (Thiselton 250).

Chapter 7

1. Pure virgin silver for Adam, gold for John the Baptist and Jesus, pearls for Joseph, white gold for Enoch, silver for Aaron, ruby and garnet for Moses and Abraham. This view is in harmony with the seven spheres of Ptolemy (Hughes 170).

2. This "register" resembles the phrase "The Book of Life," used by Jews and Christians.

3. As well as seven heavens, there are also seven earths, as described in detail by Mohammad ibn 'Abd Allah al-Kisa'i: "There are seven earths. The first is called Ramaka, beneath which is the Barren Wind, which can be bridled by no fewer than seventy thousand angels. With this wind God destroyed the people of Ad. The inhabitants of Ramaka are a nation called Muwashshim, upon whom is everlasting torment and divine retribution. The second earth is called Khalada, wherein are the implements of torture for the inhabitants of Hell. There dwells a nation called Tamis, whose food is their own flesh and whose drink is their own blood. The third earth is called Arqa, wherein dwell mule-like eagles with spear-like tails. On each tail are three hundred and sixty poisonous quills. Were even one quill placed on the face of the earth, the entire universe would pass away. The inhabitants thereof are a nation called Qays, who eat dirt and drink mothers' milk. The fourth earth is called Haraba, wherein dwell the snakes of Hell, which are as large as mountains. Each snake has fangs like tall palm trees, and if they were to strike the hugest mountain with their fangs it would be leveled to the ground. The inhabitants of this earth are a nation called Jilla, and they have no eyes, hands or feet but have wings like bats and die only of old age. The fifth earth is called Maltham, wherein stones of sulphur hang around the necks of infidels. When the fire is kindled the fuel is placed on their breasts, and the flames leap up onto their faces, as He hath said: *The fire whose fuel is men and stones* (2:24), and *Fire shall cover their faces* (14:50). The inhabitants are a nation called Hajla, who are numerous and who eat each other. The sixth earth is called Sijjin. Here are the registers of the people of Hell, and their works are vile, as He hath said: *Verily the register of the actions of the wicked is surely Sijjin* (83:7). Herein dwells a nation called Qatat, who are

shaped like birds and worship God truly. The seventh earth is called Ajiba and is the habitation of Iblis. There dwells a nation called Khasum, who are black and short, with claws like lions. It is they who will be given dominion over Gog and Magog, who will be destroyed by them." See *Tales of the Prophets-Qisas al-anbiya*, trans. Wheeler M. Thackston, Jr., *Great Books of the Islamic World* (Chicago: Kazi, 1997), pp. 8, 9.

4. Hadith literature are narratives that recount the Prophet Mohammad's words and actions based upon oral traditions.

5. Christianity makes reference to these layers of heaven. Paul the apostle, in 2 Corinthians 12:2, says: "I know a man in Christ who fourteen years ago was caught up to the third heaven. Whether it was in the body or out of the body I do not know, God knows." Popular Arabic stories of Mohammad's mystical ascent inspired the poet Dante to write his *Divine Comedy* (Bloom 59). While Catholic poets like Dante made this a popular notion, the concept of seven heavens was never confirmed by the Catholic hierarchy.

6. The concept of the Trinity (or Triune God) claims one God existing in three Persons, but this is no way suggests three different Gods: the triune God—three coexistent, co-eternal Persons make up One God: the unknown God, creator and source of all life; Jesus Christ who has revealed the Father, and the Holy Spirit who works to transform the world according to God's purpose. "The word Trinity doesn't appear as a theological term till near the end of the second century. It was first used as 'Trias' by Theophilus, the Bishop of Antioch in AD 180 and later by Tertullian as Trinitas to signify that God exists in three persons" (Ooman 76–77).

7. Many people think Christians, or particularly Roman Catholics, worship statues and icons; nothing could be further from the truth. Christianity has always loved beauty and art; any image that is painted or wrought into a statue is only meant to remind us of God and to incite our minds and imaginations to think on what is divine and lovely.

8. "And he is the head of the body, the church: who is the beginning, the firstborn from the dead; that in all things he might have the preeminence" (Colossians 1:18). "...and from Jesus Christ, who is the faithful witness, the firstborn of the dead, and the ruler of the kings of the earth. Unto him that loveth us, and loosed us from our sins by his blood" (Revelation 1:5).

9. Of special significance for Christians is St. Michael, as he is the "chief of princes" and leader of the army of heaven in their triumph over Satan and his followers. The angel Gabriel first appeared in the Old Testament in the Book of Daniel, when he announced the prophecy of 70 weeks (Daniel 9:21–27). Gabriel appeared to Zechariah to announce the birth of St. John the Baptist (Luke 1:11), and he also proclaimed the Annunciation of Mary to be the mother of our Lord and Savior (Luke 1:26). The angel Raphael first appeared in the Book of Tobit (3:25, 5:5–28, 6–12), where he clearly announces "I am the Angel Raphael, one of the seven who stand before the throne of God" (12:15). It is evident that previous concepts of angelic beings from the Hebrew Bible and from Christian doctrine heavily influenced the revelations of Mohammad.

10. Seraphim are the highest order or choir of angels, as they attend and guard God's throne. They praise God, calling, "Holy Holy Holy is the Lord of Hosts." The one *Bible* reference to them is in Isaiah 6:1–7. One of them touched Isaiah's lips with a live coal from the altar, cleansing him from sin. Seraphim have six wings: two cover their faces, two cover their feet, and two are for flying.

11. Hughes writes that Jinn are said to appear as serpents, dogs, cats, or human beings; they can also suddenly disappear (135).

12. The rational soul, as defined by Muslim thinkers, has no beginning or end—it is eternal. The rational soul is not aware of anything material, including its body, but is aware of its own existence. For Ibn Rushd, the theoretical intellect is the rational soul (Fortney & Onellion 149).

13. "Almost all traditions portray al-Dajjal as a person. In some, he is even said to

resemble a specific person whose name was Abd al-Uzza bin Qatan. Al-Dajjal is known as ugly and dirty and having only one eye (al-Awar). Anas, a companion of the Prophet narrates that the Prophet said, 'No prophet was sent but he warned his community against the one-eyed (al-Awar) liar (al-Dajjal): Beware, he is Awar, and your Lord is not Awar. And there will be written between his eyes the word Kafir (disbeliever).'" See Zeki Saritoprak, "The Legend of Al-Dajjal (Antichrist): The Personification of Evil in the Islamic Tradition" *Muslim World* 93.2 (2003): 291.

14. Zeki Saritoprak writes that "According to al-Ghazzali, within this period of anarchy, Jesus will descend from heaven, acknowledge Mohammad as a prophet, kill the Antichrist, fight with Muslims against the 'red army' (the army of Gog and Magog), and defeat them through belief in God. Although in a general scenario of struggle between Christ and the Antichrist found in Islamic literature, Christians and Muslims are considered supporters of Christ; al-Ghazzali portrays Christians as the supporters of the Antichrist, rather than Christ" (291).

15. Hermas, Shepherd of, Christian apocalyptic work, composed in Rome c. 139–CE. 155. It is a collection of revelations given to Hermas, a devout Christian, by an angel (Shepherd) and is divided into three sections: Visions, Mandates, and Similitudes. The teachings are concerned mostly with matters of penance, morals, and the condition of the church; they were highly regarded by early Christians. The book is extant in fragments of the original Greek and in complete Latin and Ethiopic texts. It has been published in English translation in collections of patristic literature. See "Hermas, Shepherd Of," *Columbia Electronic Encyclopedia*, 6th Edition (2015): 1.

16. In "The Shepherd," there is a story about a shepherd who is inflicting torture on his sheep. Hermas asks the shepherd the reason for this torture, and the shepherd replies: "This shepherd is the angel of vengeance, and he is one of the righteous angels, but is appointed over the punishment of sinners. To him, accordingly, are handed over those who have strayed from God, and served the desires and pleasures of the present world" (Bull 43).

17. See notes 15 and 16.

References

Abboud, Tony. *Al-Kindi: The Father of Arab Philosophy.* New York: Rosen Publishing Group, 2006. Print.

Abel, Ernest L. *Intoxication in Mythology: A Worldwide Dictionary of Gods, Rites, Intoxicants and Places.* Jefferson, NC: McFarland, 2006. Print.

Abu-Nimer, Mohammed, and Ilham Nasser. "Forgiveness in the Arab and Islamic Contexts Between Theology and Practice." *Journal of Religious Ethics* 41.3 (2013): 474–494. *Academic Search Complete.* Web. 8 Sept. 2015.

Abusch, Tzvi. "The Development and Meaning of the Epic of Gilgamesh: An Interpretive Essay." *Journal of the American Oriental Society* 121. 4 (2001): 614–622. Print.

Achuthananda, Swami. *Many Many Many Gods of Hinduism.* North Charleston: CreateSpace, 2013. *Google Book Search.* Web. 15 May 2015.

Adams, Paul V. *Experiencing World History.* New York UP, 2000. Print.

Adiswarananda, Swami. *Meditation and Its Practices.* SkyLight Paths, 2007. *Google Book Search.* Web. 15 May 2015.

Ahmed, Safdar. *Reform and Modernity in Islam: The Philosophical, Cultural and Political Discourses Among Muslim Reformers.* New York. I. B. Tauris, 2013. Print.

Ahrensdorf, Peter J. *The Death of Socrates and the Life of Philosophy.* Albany: State U of New York P, 1995. Print.

Albahari, Miri. "Against No-Atman Theories of Anatta." *Asian Philosophy.* 12.1 (2002) 5–20. Print.

Al-Bukhari. *Sahih Al-Bukhari. Google Book Search.* Web. 25 Aug. 2015.

Al-Ghazali, Imam. *Al-Jami Al-Durrah al Fathirah.* Trans. Jane I. Smith. Cambridge: Harvard University Studies in World Religions, 1979. Web. 27 Aug. 2015.

Al-Kisa'i, Muhammad 'Abd Allah. *Tales of the Prophets-Qisas al-anbiya.* Trans. Wheeler M. Thackston, Jr. Chicago: Great Books of the Islamic World, 1997. Print.

Allen, Diogenes, and Eric O. Springsted. *Philosophy for Understanding Theology,* 2nd ed. Louisville: Westminster John Knox Press, 2007. Print.

Allen, James P. *Middle Egyptian: An Introduction to the Language and Culture of Hieroglyphs.* Cambridge UP, 2000. Print.

"Ambrosia—Food of the Greek Gods." Logia.com, n.d. Web. 22 Sept. 2015.

"Anchises" in *The New Encyclopædia Britannica.* Chicago: Encyclopædia Britannica, 15th ed. 1 (1992): 377.

"The Ancient Egyptian Ba." touregypt.net, 2013. Web. 12 Oct. 2014.

Anderson, Jeff. S. *The Internal Diversification of Second Temple Judaism: An Introduction to the Second Temple Period.* Lanham: UP of America, 2002. Print.

Anderson, Ray S., and John Swinton. *Spiritual Caregiving as Secular Sacrament*. London: Jessica Kingsley, 2003. Print.

Anthes, Rudolf. "The Original Meaning of Maatkheru." *Journal of Near Eastern Studies* 13.1 (1954): 50. Print.

"Anubis Speaks! A Guide to the Afterlife by the Egyptian God of the Dead." *Kirkus Reviews* 81.15 (2013): 180. *Academic Search Complete*. Web. 13 Sept. 2015.

Apollodorus. *The Library of Greek Mythology*. Trans. Robin Hard. Oxford: Oxford UP, 1997. Print.

Appel, Daniel. "5 Ancient Legends About the Secret of Immortality." Ultraculture.org, 5 May 2014. Web. 22 March 2015.

Aristotle in 23 Volumes, Vol. 19. Trans. Harris Rackham. Cambridge: Harvard UP, 1934.

Aristotle. *De Anima*. Trans. R.D. Hicks. New York: Cosimo Classics, 2008. Print.

Arnold, John C. *The Footprints of Michael the Archangel: The Formation and Diffusion of a Saintly Cult*. New York: Palgrave Macmillan, 2013. Print.

Ashton, John, and Tom Whyte. *The Quest for Paradise*. San Francisco: HarperCollins, 2001. Print.

Ashwin-Siejkowski, Piotr. *Clement of Alexandria on Trial: The Evidence of 'Heresy' from Photius' Bibliotheca*. Leiden: Brill, 2010. Print.

el-Aswad, El-Sayed. *Muslim Worldviews and Everyday Lives*. Plymouth: AltaMira Press, 2012. Print.

Augustine. "On Faith in Things Unseen." *The Fathers of the Church*. Trans. Roy J. Deferrari and Mary F. McDonald. Washington: Catholic U of America P, 1947. *Google Book Search*. Web. 15 Oct. 2015.

_____. *The Soliloquies of Augustine*. Trans. Rose E. Cleveland. Boston: Little, Brown, 1910. *Google Book Search*. Web. 11 July 2015.

Averroës. *Ibn Rushd's Metaphysics: A Translation with Introduction of Ibn Rushd's Commentary on Aristotle's Metaphysics*. Ed. Hans Daiber. Trans. Charles Genequand. Leiden: Brill Academic Publishers, 1984. *Google Book Search*. Web. 25 Aug. 2015.

Bahadur, V.S. Rangarao. *Hindu Religion*. New Delhi: Logos Press, 1995. Print.

Balfour, Walter. *Letters on the Immortality of the Soul: The Intermediate State of the Dead and a Future Retribution in Reply to Mr. Charles Hudson*. Charlestown: G. Davidson, 1829. *Google Book Search*. Web. 26 June 2015.

_____, and Otis A. Skinner. *An Inquiry into the Scriptural Import of the Words Sheol, Hades, Tartarus and Gehenna*. Boston: A. Tomkins, 1854. *Google Book Search*. Web. 10 April 2015.

Bansal, Malti. *Now We Set to Settle on Moon: Chandrayaan Discovery Paves the Way*. New Delhi: Mind Melodies, 2010. *Google Book Search*. Web. 29 Sept. 2015.

Bar, Shaul. "Grave Matters: Sheol in the Hebrew Bible." *Jewish Bible Quarterly* 43.3 (2015): 145–153. *Academic Search Complete*. Web. 25 June 2015.

Baring, Anne, and Jules Cashford. *The Myth of the Goddess: Evolution of an Image*. New York: Penguin, 1991. Print.

Barnes, Michael H. *Stages of Thought: The Co-Evolution of Religious Thought and Science*. New York: Oxford UP, 2000. Print.

"Barzakh (Purgatory)—The Stage Between This World and the Hereafter." Al-Islam.org, n.d. Web. 1 Sept. 2015.

Bauckham, Richard. *The Fate of the Dead: Studies on the Jewish and Christian Apocalypses*. Atlanta: Society of Biblical Literature, 1998. Print.

Baur, Ferdinand, and Edward Zeller. "The Myth of Simon Magnus." *The Westminster Review*. Vol. 122. Philadelphia: Leonard Scott, 1884. Print.

Bausch, William J. *Still Preaching After All These Years: 40 More Seasonal Homilies*. Mystic: Twenty-Third Publications, 2005. Print.

Bendann, Effie. *Death Customs: An Analytical Study of Burial Rites*. New York: Routledge, 2007. Print.

Bender, Courtney, and Pamela E. Klassen. *After Pluralism: Reimagining Religious Engagement*. New York: Columbia UP, 2010. Print.

Benjamin, Don C. *Stones and Stories: An Introduction to Archeology and the Bible*. Minneapolis: Fortress Press, 2010. Print.

Bentley, David. *The 99 Beautiful Names for God for All the People of the Book*. Pasadena: William Carey Library, 1999. *Google Book Search*. Web. 3 Sept. 2015.

Bentley, John. *A Historical View of the Hindu Astronomy*. London: Smith, Elder, 1825. *Google Book Search*. Web. 28 May 2015.

Berke, Joseph H., and Stanley Schneider. "The Self and the Soul." *Mental Health, Religion & Culture* 9.4 (2006): 333–354. *Academic Search Complete*. Web. 4 Oct. 2015.

Berlin, Adele. *Poetics and Interpretation of Biblical Narrative*. Warsaw: Eisenbrauns, 1994. Print.

Benardete, Seth. *Herodotean Inquiries*. Netherlands: Springer, 1969. *Google Book Search*. Web. 22 Sept. 2015.

Bernd, Jager. "The Birth of Poetry and the Creation of a Human World: An Exploration of the Epic of Gilgamesh." *Journal of Phenomenological Psychology* 32.2 (2001): 131–154. Print.

Bertman, Stephen. *Handbook to Life in Ancient Mesopotamia*. New York: Oxford UP, 2003. Print.

Bhandarkar, D. R. *Some Aspects of Indian Culture*. New Delhi: Asian Educational Services, 1989. *Google Book Search*. Web. 28 May 2015.

Bial, David. "Gershom Scholem on Jewish Messianism." *Essential Papers on Messianic Movements and Personalities in Jewish History*. New York UP, 1992. Print.

Billmeier, Martin E. Personal Interview. 31 Oct. 2015.

Birth of Athena from the Head of Zeus, from a Vase Painting, c. 19th century CE. German book. minervaclassics.com, n.d. Web. 12 July 2015.

Black, J.A., G. Cunningham, J. Ebeling, E. Flückiger-Hawker, E. Robson, J. Taylor, and G. Zólyomi, *The Electronic Text Corpus of Sumerian Literature*. Oxford UP, 1998–2006. Web. 12 Sept. 2014.

Black, Jeremy, and Anthony Green. *Gods, Demons and Symbols of Ancient Mesopotamia: An Illustrated Dictionary*. U of Texas P, 1992. Print.

Blavatsky, Helena P. *Theosophical Glossary*. London, 1892. *Google Book Search*. Web. 12 Sept. 2014.

Bloom, Jonathan, and Sheila Blair. *Islam: A Thousand Years of Faith and Power*. Yale UP, 2002. Print.

Boccaccini, Gabriele. *Beyond the Essene Hypothesis: The Parting of the Ways Between Qumran and Enochic Judaism*. Grand Rapids: Wm B. Eerdmans, 1998. Print.

Bonazzoli, Giorgio. "Puranic Spirituality." *Hindu Spirituality: Postclassical and Modern*. Eds. K. R. Sundararajan, Bithika Mukerji. Delhi: Crossroad Publishing, 1997. Print.

Bonnefoy, Yves. *Greek and Egyptian Mythologies*. U of Chicago P, 1992. Print.

Borrowman, Shane. "The Islamization of "Rhetoric": Ibn Rushd and the Reintroduction of Aristotle into Medieval Europe." *Rhetoric Review* 27.4 (2008): 341–360. *Academic Search Complete*. Web. 7 Sept. 2015.

Bostock, Andrew. *Greece: The Peloponnese*. Guilford: Globe Pequot Press, 2013. Print.

Boulay, R.A. *Flying Serpents and Dragons*. Escondido: Book Tree, 1999. Print.

Bowra, C. M. *The Greek Experience*. New York: NAL, 1988. Print.

"Brahman." *Encyclopedia Britænnica*. Britannica.com, 4 March 2015. Web. 23 March 2015.

Braunstein, Susan L. "The Meaning of Egyptian-Style Objects in the Late Bronze Cemeteries of Tell El-Far'ah (South)." *Bulletin of the American Schools of Oriental Research* 364 (2011): 1–36. *Academic Search Complete*. Web. 14 Sept. 2015.

Briggman, Anthony. "Irenaeus' Christology Of Mixture." *Journal of Theological Studies* 64.2 (2013): 516–555. *Academic Search Complete*. Web. 8 Oct. 2015.

Brocas, Jock. *The Everything Guide to Past Life Experience: Explore the Scientific, Spiritual, and Philosophical Evidence of Past Life Experiences*. Avon: Adams Media, 2011. Print.

Brodd, Jeffrey. *World Religions: A Voyage of Discovery*. Winona: St. Mary's Press, 2008. Print.

Bromley, Geoffrey W. *The International Standard Bible Encyclopedia, Volume 4*. Grand Rapids: Wm B. Eerdmans, 1995 Print.

Broshi, Magen. *Bread, Wine, Walls and Scrolls*. London: Sheffield Academic Press, 2001. Print.

Brown, David T. *Cannabis: The Genus Cannabis*. Amsterdam: Harwood Academic, 1998. Print.

Brown, Guy. *The Living End: The New Sciences of Death, Ageing and Immortality*. New York: Macmillan Science, 2008. *ebook*. Web. 17 Oct. 2015.

Buck, William. *Mahabharata*. Berkeley: U of California P, 1973.

Budge, Ernest A.W. *The Egyptian Heaven and Hell*. New York: Cosimo Classics, 2011. Print.

_____. *Egyptian Ideas of the Future Life*. London: Kegan Paul, Trench, Trubner, 1908. *Google Book Search*. Web. 12 Oct. 2014.

_____. *Facsimile of Ba Figure from 1300 BCE*, 1890.

_____. *Osiris and the Egyptian Resurrection*. Vol. II. New York: Dover, 1973. Print.

_____. *The Papyrus of Ani, V. 1*. New York: G. P. Putnam, 1913. *Google Book Search*. Web. 18 Oct. 2015. The Papyrus of Ani: A Reproduction in Facsimile edited, with hiero-glyphic transcript, translation, and introduction, by E. A. Walls Budge M.A., Lit. T.D., Keeper of the Egyptian and Assyrian antiquities in the British museum. Published by permission of the trustees of the British museum. In three volumes. Volume one.

Budin, Stephanie L. "A Reconsideration of the Aphrodite-Ashtart Syncretism." *Numen: International Review for the History of Religions* 51.2 (2004): 95–145. *Academic Search Complete*. Web. 26 Sept. 2015.

Buis, Harry. *Historic Protestantism and Predestination*. Eugene: Wipf and Stock Publishers, 2007. Print.

Bull, George. *A Defense of the Nicene Creed Out of the Extant Writings of the Catholick Doctors Who Flourished During the Three First Centuries of the Christian Church*. Vol. 1. Oxford: John Henry Parker, 1851. *Google Book Search*. Web. 25 Aug. 2015.

Burge, S. R. "The Angels in Sūrat Al-Malā ika: Exegeses of Q. 35:1." *Journal of Qur'anic Studies* 10.1 (2008): 50–70. *Academic Search Complete*. Web. 5 Sept. 2015.

Burkert, Walter. *Greek Religion*. 1977. Trans. John Raffan. Cambridge: Harvard UP, 1985. Print.

Bushnell, Rebecca. *A Companion to Tragedy*. Hoboken: Wiley-Blackwell, 2009. Print.

Buxton, Richard. *Myths and Tragedies in Their Ancient Greek Contexts*. Oxford: Oxford UP, 2013. Print.

Byrne, Máire. *The Names of God in Judaism, Christianity, and Islam: A Basis for Interfaith Dialogue*. New York: Bloomsbury Publishing, 2011. Print.

Cahill, Jane. *Her Kind: Stories of Women from Greek Mythology*. Peterborough: Broadview Press, 1995. Print.

Callimachus. *Hymns and Epigrams. Lycophron. Aratus*. Trans. A.W. Mair and G. R. Loeb. Vol. 129. London: William Heinemann, 1921. Print.

Campbell, Joseph. *The Hero with a Thousand Faces*. 3rd ed. Novato: New World Library, 2008. Print.

_____. *The Masks of God: Occidental Mythology*. New York: Viking–Penguin, 1964. Print.

Campo, Juan E. *Encyclopedia of Islam*. New York: Facts on File, 2009. Print.

Canright, Dudley M. *A History of the Doctrine of the Soul: Among All Races and Peoples, Ancient and Modern (1882)*. 2nd Ed. Whitefish: Kessinger, 2009. Print.

Capes, David B., April Deconick, Helen Bond and Troy Miller. *Israel's God and Rebecca's Children: Christology and Community in Early Judaism and Christianity.* Waco: Baylor UP, 2007. Print.

Cartmill, Matt. *A View to a Death in the Morning: Hunting and Nature through History.* Cambridge: Harvard UP, 1993. Print.

"Catechism of the Catholic Church." n.d. vatican.va/archive. Web. 19 May 2014.

Cerveny, Randy. "Power of the Gods." *Weatherwise* 51.1 (1998): 56. *Academic Search Complete.* Web. 19 Sept. 2015.

Chalcraft, David J. *Sectarianism in Early Judaism: Sociological Advances.* London: Routledge, 2007. Print.

Charran, Swami Ram. *Antyesti Puja Handbook.* Heendu Learning Center and lulu.com, 2012.

Chipman, Leigh N. B. "Adam and the Angels: An Examination of Mythic Elements in Islamic Sources." *Arabica* 49.4 (2002): 429. *Academic Search Complete.* Web. 5 Sept. 2015.

Chittick, William. "Love in Islamic Thought." *Religion Compass* 8.7 (2014): 229–238. *Academic Search Complete.* Web. 5 Sept. 2015.

"Choosing Judaism: Concepts of God and Contemporary Judaism." Jewish Outreach Institute. joi.org, n.d. Web. 25 June 2015.

Christman, Jared. "The Gilgamesh Complex: The Quest for Death Transcendence and the Killing of Animals." *Society and Animals* 16.4 (2008): 297–315.

Clare, Israel Smith. *The Unrivaled History of the World Containing a Full and Complete Record of the Human Race from the Earliest Historical Period to the Present Time.* Vol. III. Chicago: Unrivaled, 1899. *Google Book Search.* Web. 16 Aug. 2015.

Clifford, Ross, and Philip Johnson. *The Cross Is Not Enough: Living as Witnesses to the Resurrection.* Grand Rapids: Baker Books, 2012. Print.

Cohen, Shaye. *From the Maccabees to the Mishnah.* Louisville: Westminster John Knox Press, 2014. Print.

Colakis, Marianthe, and Mary Joan Masello. *Classical Mythology & More: A Reader Workbook.* Mundelein: Bolchazy-Carducci Publishers, 2008. Print.

Cooney, Kathlyn M. "Gender Transformations in Death: A Case Study of Coffins from Ramesside Period Egypt." *Near Eastern Archaeology* 73.4 (2010): 224–237. *Academic Search Complete.* Web. 13 Sept. 2015.

Corfield, Penelope J. "'The End Is Nigh.'" *History Today* 57.3 (2007): 37–39. *Academic Search Complete.* Web. 8 Sept. 2015.

Cornell, Vincent J. *Voices of Islam.* Westport: Praeger, 2007. Print.

Coulter-Harris, Deborah. *The Queen of Sheba: Legend, Literature and Lore.* Jefferson: McFarland, 2013. Print.

Court, John. *Reading the New Testament.* New York: Routledge, 1997. Print.

Craig, Edward. *Routledge Encyclopedia of Philosophy.* London: Routledge, 1998. Print.

Crivellato, Enrico, and Domenico Ribatti. "Soul, Mind, Brain: Greek Philosophy and the Birth Of Neuroscience." *Brain Research Bulletin* 71.4 (2007): 327–336. *Academic Search Complete.* Web. 27 Sept. 2015.

Crubellier, Michel, and André Laks. *Aristotle's Metaphysics Beta: Symposium Aristotelicum.* Oxford UP, 2009. Print.

Daderot. *Shamash, the Sun God, Sippar, Early Iron Age, 870 BCE.* Photo of plaster cast of limestone original. Oriental Institute Museum, Chicago.

Dalley, Stephanie. *Myths from Mesopotamia: Creation, the Flood, Gilgamesh, and Others.* New York: Oxford UP, 1998. Print.

Daly, Kathleen N. *Greek and Roman Mythology, A to Z.* 3rd ed. New York: Chelsea House, 2009. Print.

Damrosch, David, *The Buried Book: The Loss and Rediscovery of the Great Epic of Gilgamesh.* New York: Henry Holt, 2006. Print.

Dannaway, Frederick R. "Strange Fires, Weird Smokes and Psychoactive Combustibles:

Entheogens and Incense in Ancient Traditions." *Journal of Psychoactive Drugs* 42.4 (2010): 485–497. *Academic Search Complete*. Web. 26 Apr. 2015.

Dastghaib, Ayatullah Husain. *Barzakh (Purgatory)*. Mumbai: Jafari Propagation Center, 2009. Print.

David, Jacques-Louis. *Apollo and Diana Attacking the Children of Niobe*, 1772. Oil on Canvas. Courtesy Dallas Museum of Art, Foundation for the Arts Collection, Mrs. John B. O'Hara Fund in honor of Dr. Dorothy Kosinski.

David, Rosalie. *Religion and Magic in Ancient Egypt*. New York: Penguin, 2003. Print.

_____. *Voices of Ancient Egypt: Contemporary Accounts of Daily Life*. Westport: Greenwood, 2014. Print.

Davidson, James N. *The Greeks and Greek Love: A Bold New Exploration of the Ancient World*. New York: Random House, 2009. Print.

Davies, Norman. *Europe: A History*. Oxford: Oxford UP, 1996. Print.

Davila, James R. "The Flood Hero as King and Priest." *Journal of Near Eastern Studies* 54.3 (1995): 199–214. Print.

Debroy, Bibek. *Mahabharata Volume 4*. New York: Penguin, 2011. Print.

de Jáuregui, Miguel Herrero. *Orphism and Christianity in Late Antiquity*. Berlin/New York: Walter de Gruyter, 2010. Print.

de Jong, Irene J. F. *A Narratological Commentary on the Odyssey*. Cambridge: Cambridge UP, 2001. Print.

De Motte, Earle. *Egyptian Religion and Mysteries*. Xlibris, 2013. Print.

Dempsey, Liam P. "'A Compound Wholly Mortal': Locke And Newton on the Metaphysics of (Personal) Immortality." *British Journal for the History of Philosophy* 19.2 (2011): 241–264. *Academic Search Complete*. Web. 16 Oct. 2015.

Descartes, Rene. *Descartes: Philosophical Writings*. Trans. and Ed. Gertrude E. Anscombe and Peter T. Geach. Indianapolis: Bobbs-Merrill, 1954. Print.

Desmond, Marilyn. "The Goddess Diana and the Ethics of Reading in the Ovide Moralise." *Metamorphosis: The Changing Face of Ovid in Medieval and Early Modern Europe*. Eds. Alison Dixon-Kennedy, Mike. *Encyclopedia of Greco-Roman Mythology*. Santa Barbara: ABC-CLIO, 1998. Print.

de Vere, Nicholas. *The Dragon Legacy: The Secret History of an Ancient Bloodline*. San Diego: Book Tree, 2004. Print.

Dhavamony, Mariasusai. *Hindu Spirituality*. Rome: Editrice Pontificia Universita Gregoriana, 1999.

Dickin, Alan. *The Pagan Trinity—Holy Trinity: The Legacy of the Sumerians in Western Civilization*. Lanham: Hamilton Books, 2007. Print.

Dickson, Keith. "Enki and Ninhursag: The Trickster in Paradise." *Journal of Near Eastern Studies* 66.1 (2007): 1–32. Print.

_____. "The Wall of Uruk: Iconicities in Gilgamesh." *Journal of Ancient Near Eastern Religions* 9.1 (2009): 25–50. Print.

Donadoni, Sergio, ed. *The Egyptians*. Chicago: U of Chicago P 1997. Print.

Doniger, Wendy. *The Hindus: An Alternative History*. Oxford: Oxford UP, 2010. Print.

_____. *The Rig Veda: An Anthology: One Hundred and Eight Hymns*. New York: Penguin, 1981. Print.

_____. *Splitting the Difference: Gender and Myth in Ancient Greece and India*. U of Chicago P, 1999. Print.

Dowden, Ken. "The Homeric Hymn to Demeter and the Eleusinian Mysteries." *A Companion to Greek Mythology*. Chichester: Wiley-Blackwell, 2011. Print.

_____. *Zeus*. New York: Routledge, 2006. Print.

Drobot, Ana. "Freud on Death." Freudfile.org, n.d. Web. 22 Oct. 2015.

Dunand, Francois, and Roger Lichtenberg. *Mummies and Death in Egypt*. Ithaca: Cornell UP, 2006. Print.

Duncan, George S. "The Sumerian Inscriptions of Sin-Gâsʿid, King of Erech. Transliterated, Translated and Annotated." *The American Journal of Semitic Languages and Literatures* 31. 3 (1915): 215–221. Print.

Dunderberg, Ismo. *Beyond Gnosticism: Myth, Lifestyle, and Society in the School of Valentinus*. New York: Columbia UP, 2008. Print.

Dunn, Geoffrey D. *Tertullian*. London: Routledge, 2004. Print.

Dunning, Stephen N. *Dialectical Readings: Three Types of Interpretations*. University Park: Pennsylvania State UP, 1997. Print.

Durant, Will. *The Story of Civilization: Our Oriental Heritage*. Vol. 1. New York: Simon & Schuster, 2011. Print.

Dylan, John. "Shadows on the Soul: Plotinian Approaches to a Solution of the Mind-Body Problem." *Plato Revived: Essays on Ancient Platonism in Honour of Dominic J. O'Meara*. Ed. Karfik, Filip and Euree Song. Boston: Walter de Gruyter, 2013. Google Book Search. Web. 12 Sept. 2014.

Easwaran, Eknath. *The Upanishads*. Trans. Michael N. Nagler. Petaluma: Nilgiri Press, 1987. Print.

Ebeling, Florian. *The Secret History of Hermes Trismegistus: Hermeticism from Ancient to Modern Times*. Trans. David Lorton. Ithaca: Cornell UP, 2007. Print.

Edmonds, Radcliffe G. *Redefining Ancient Orphism: A Study in Greek Religion*. Cambridge: Cambridge UP, 2013. Print.

The Egyptian Book of the Dead: The Book of Going Forth by Day. Ed. Eva Von Dassow. San Francisco: Chronicle Books, 2008. Print.

The Egyptian World. Ed. Toby Wilkinson. London: Routledge, 2009. Print.

Ehud, Ben Zvi. *Perspectives on Biblical Hebrew: Comprising the Contents of Journal of Hebrew Scriptures*. Piscataway: Gorgias Press, 2006. Print.

Elizarenkova, Tatiana. "About the Status of Sound in the Rgveda." *Elementa: Journal of Slavic Studies & Comparative Cultural Semiotics* 4.3 (2000): 211. *Academic Search Complete*. Web. 29 Sept. 2015.

Ellis, Ralph. *Thoth: Architect of the Universe*. Cheshire: Edfu Books, 2014. Ebook.

El-Zein, Amira. *Islam, Arabs, and the Intelligent World of the Jinn*. Syracuse UP, 2009. Print.

Emerys, Chevalier. *Revelation of the Holy Grail*. Timothy W. Hogan, 2007. Print.

Endjso, Dag Oistein. *Greek Resurrection Beliefs and the Success of Christianity*. New York: Palgrave Macmillan, 2009. Print.

_____. "Immortal Bodies, Before Christ. Bodily Continuity in Ancient Greece and 1 Corinthians." *Journal for the Study of the New Testament* 30 (2008): 417–36. Print.

Engstrom, Stephen, and Jennifer Whiting. *Aristotle, Kant, and the Stoics: Rethinking Happiness and Duty*. Cambridge: Cambridge UP, 1996. Print.

Esposito, John L. *Islam: The Straight Path*. Oxford UP, 1998. Print.

"Essenes." *Jewish Encyclopedia Vol. 5*. Ed. Isidore Singer, Cyrus Adler. New York: Funk & Wagnalls, 1912. Print.

Faguet, Auguste. *Amanita Muscaria*. 1891. Chromolithograph. *Wikimedia Commons*, n.d. Web. 11 Nov. 2015.

Faulkner, Andrew. *The Homeric Hymn to Aphrodite*. Oxford: Oxford UP, 2008. Print.

Faulkner, Raymond, Ogden Goelet, Carol Andrews, James Wasserman. *The Egyptian Book of the Dead: The Book of Going Forth by Day*. San Francisco: Chronicle Books, 2008. Print.

Ferguson, Everett. *Backgrounds of Early Christianity*. 3rd ed. Grand Rapids: Wm B. Eerdmans, 2003. Print.

_____. "The Competition." *Christian History* 17.1 (1998): 34. *Academic Search Premier*. Web. 7 Oct. 2015.

Fiore, John. *Symbolic Mythology: Interpretations of the Myths of Ancient Greece and Rome*. Lincoln: Writers Club Press, 2001. Print.

Fiore, Silvestro, *Voices from the Clay: The Development of Assyro-Babylonian Literature*. Norman: U of Oklahoma P, 1965. Print.

Firth, Shirley. *Dying, Death and Bereavement in a British Hindu Community*. Leuven: Peeters, 1997. Print.

Fishbane, Eitan P. "A Chariot for the Shekhinah: Identity and the Ideal Life In Sixteenth-Century Kabbalah." *Journal of Religious Ethics* 37.3 (2009): 385–418. *Academic Search Complete*. Web. 25 June 2015.

Fitzgerald, Allan, and John C. Cavadini. *Augustine Through the Ages: An Encyclopedia*. Grand Rapids: Wm B. Eerdmans, 1999. Print.

Fleuser, David. *Judaism of the Second Temple Period: Sages and Literature*. Cambridge: Wm B. Eerdmans, 2009. Print.

Flood, Gavin. "Hindu Concepts." Bbc.com, 24 Aug. 2009. Web. 29 Sept. 2015.

Forrect, Kent. *Sumer and Babylonia*. Shelton: Millikin, 1969. Print.

Frankfort, Henri. *Ancient Egyptian Religion: An Interpretation*. New York: Dover, 2011. Print.

Frazer, James G. *The Golden Bough*. London: Macmillan, 1890. *Google Book Search*. Web. 23 July 2015.

Freeman, Phillip. "Lessons from a Demigod." *Humanities* 33.4 (2012): 34–38. Print.

Fudge, William E. *The Fire That Consumes: A Biblical and Historical Study of the Doctrine of the Doctrine of Final Punishment*. Cambridge: Lutterworth, 2012. Print.

Furfaro, Virgil. *A Tormented Soul: Inspirational Poems*. Bloomington: iUniverse, 2010. Print.

Furley, David. J. "The Early History of the Concept of Soul." *Bulletin of the Institute of Classical Studies* 3.1 (1956): 1–18. Print.

Gabriel, Richard A. *Gods of Our Fathers: The Memory of Egypt in Judaism and Christianity*. Westport: Greenwood Press, 2002. Print.

Gahlinger Paul M. *Illegal Drugs: A Complete Guide to Their History, Chemistry, Use and Abuse*. New York: Penguin, 2004. Print.

Galvin, Rachel. "The Imprint of Immortality." *Humanities* 23.5 (2002): 18. Print.

Gandhi, Mahatma. *Hindu Dharma*. New Delhi: Orient Paperbacks, 2005. Print.

Gardiner, Juliet. "Exhibition Journey Through the Afterlife: Ancient Egyptian Book of the Dead." *History Today* 61.1 (2011): 56. *Academic Search Complete*. Web. 13 Sept. 2015.

Gianotti, Timothy J. "Beyond Both Law And Theology: An Introduction To Al-Ghazālī's 'Science of the Way of the Afterlife' in Reviving Religious Knowledge (I yā' 'Ulūm Al-Dīn)." *Muslim World* 101.4 (2011): 597–613. *Academic Search Complete*. Web. 7 Sept. 2015.

Gibson, Lynne. *Hinduism*. Oxford: Heinemann Educational, 2002. Print.

Gier, Nicholas F. "Hindu Titanism." *Philosophy East & West* 45.1 (1995): 73. *Academic Search Complete*. Web. 13 May 2015.

Giller, Pinchas. *Kabbalah: A Guide for the Perplexed*. New York: Continuum, 2011. Print.

Gimbutas, Marija. *The Civilization of the Goddess: The World of Old Europe*. San Francisco: Harper, 1991. Print.

Ginsburg, Christian D. *The Essenes: Their History and Doctrines: An Essay*. London: Longman, Roberts, and Green, 1864. *Google Book Search*. Web. 3 Oct. 2015.

Givens, Terryl. *When Souls Had Wings: Pre-Mortal Existence in Western Thought*. Oxford: Oxford UP, 2010. Print.

"Gods and Men in Greek Religion." faculty.gvsu.edu, n.d. Web. 26 Sept. 2015.

Goldenberg, Robert. "Bound Up in the Bond of Life: Death and Afterlife in the Jewish Tradition." *Death and Afterlife: Perspectives of World Religions*. Ed. Hiroshi Obayashi. Westport: Greenwood Press, 1992. Print.

Gollner, Adam L. *The Book of Immortality*. Quebec: Doubleday Canada, 2013. Print.

González, Justo L. *The Story of Christianity, Volume 1: The Early Church to the Dawn of the Reformation*. New York: HarperCollins, 2010. Print.

Gordon, Brandon L. "The Interconnection between Brahman and Atman: An Explication of Adi Shankara's Writings." *International Journal of Religion & Spirituality in Society.* 2.3 (2013): 145–151. *Academic Search Complete.* Web. 29 Sept. 2015.

Gordon, R. "Death and Creativity: A Jungian Approach." *Journal of Analytical Psychology* 22.2 (1977): 106–124. *Academic Search Complete.* Web. 22 Oct. 2015.

Gordon, Stuart. *The Encyclopedia of Myths and Legends.* London: Headline Books, 1993. Print.

Grant, Mary A. *Folktale and Hero-Tale Motifs in the Odes of Pindar.* U of Kansas P, 1967. Print.

Graves, Robert. *The Greek Myths.* 1955. New York: Penguin, 1960. Print.

Greear, J. D. *Breaking the Islam Code: Understanding the Soul Questions of Every Muslim.* Eugene: Harvest House, 2010. Print.

Greenberg, L. Arik. *"My Share of God's Reward": Exploring the Roles and Formulations of the Afterlife in Early Christian Martyrdom.* New York: Peter Lang, 2009. Print.

Grene, David, and Richmond Lattimore, eds. *Aeschylus I: Oresteia.* Chicago: U of Chicago P, 1953. Print.

Gulati, Mahinder N. *Comparative Religious and Philosophies: Anthropomorphism and Divinity.* New Delhi: Atlantic, 2008. Print.

Gurley, Rosemary. *The Encyclopedia of Magic and Alchemy.* New York: Visionary Living, 2006. Print.

_____. *The Mystical Tarot.* New York: Signet, 1991. Print.

Gyurme, Tenzin. *Thoth: God of the Moon, Magic, and Writing.* House of Goddess, 2010. Ebook.

Haigh, Henry. *Some Leading Ideas of Hinduism: Being the Thirty-second Fernley Lecture.* London: Charles H. Kelly, 1903. *Google Book Search.* Web. 19 Dec. 2014.

Hall, Manly P. *The Secret Teachings of All Ages.* Revised edition. Los Angeles: Philosophical Research Society, 1994. Print.

Halleran, Michael R. *Medea, Hippolytus, Heracles, Bacchae: Four Plays.* Ed. Stephen Esposito. "Appendix Two: The Heracles: An Interpretation." Indianapolis: Hackett Publishing, 2012. Print.

Halligan, Fredrica R. "Atman." *Encyclopedia of Psychology and Religion: L–Z.* Ed. David A. Leeming, Kathryn Fadden, and Stanton Marian. New York: Springer, 2010. Print.

Halverson, Jeffry R. *Theology and Creed in Sunni Islam: The Muslim Brotherhood, Ash'arism, and Political Sunnism.* New York: Palgrave Macmillan, 2010. ebook.

Hard, Robin. *The Routledge Handbook of Greek Mythology.* New York: Routledge, 2004. Print.

Hardford, R.R. "St. Paul, Plato and Immortality." *Hermathena* 65 (1945) 74–79. Print.

Harpur, Tom. *The Pagan Christ: Recovering the Lost Light.* Markham, Ontario: Thomas Allen, 2004. Print.

Hastings, James. *Dictionary of the Apostolic Church.* Vol. I. New York: Scribner's, 1916. *Google Book Search.* Web. 24 July 2015.

_____. *Dictionary of the Apostolic Church.* Vol. II. Honolulu: UP of the Pacific, 2004. *Google Book Search.* Web. 25 July 2015.

Haught, John F. *What Is Religion?* Mahwah: Paulist Press, 1990. Print.

Hayes, Michael. *The Hermetic Code in DNA: The Sacred Principles in the Ordering of the Universe.* Rochester: Inner Traditions, 2008. Print.

Hays, Christopher B. *Death in the Iron Age II and in First Isaiah.* Philadelphia: Coronet Books, 2011. Print.

Hefner, Alan G. "Jinn." *Encyclopedeia Mythica.* 1997. 3 Mar 1997. Pantheon.org, 7 Oct. 2009. Web. 9 Aug. 2011.

Heidel, Alexander. *The Gilgamesh Epic and Old Testament Parallels.* U of Chicago P, 1949. Print.

Helminski, Shaikh Kabir. "Angels in Islam." *The Big Book of Angels*. Emmaus: Rodale Books, 2003. Print.

"Hermas, Shepherd of." *Columbia Electronic Encyclopedia*, 6th Edition (2015): 1. *Academic Search Complete*. Web. 8 Sept. 2015.

Herodotus. *An Account of Egypt*. Trans. George C. Macaulay. Rockville: Arc Manor, 2008, Print.

Hesiod. *Works and Days/Theogony*. Trans. Stanley Lombardo. Indianapolis: Hacket, 1993. Print.

Hetherington, Norriss S. *Encyclopedia of Cosmology: Historical, Philosophical, and Scientific Foundations of Modern Cosmology*. New York: Routledge, 1993. Print.

Higgins, Kathleen M. *Nietzsche's Zarathustra*. Lanham: Lexington Books, 2010. Print.

Hillerbrand, Hans J. *Encyclopedia of Protestantism: Volumes 1–4*. New York: Routledge, 2004. Print.

Hindson, Ed, and Ergun Caner. *The Popular Encyclopedia of Apologetics: Surveying the Evidence for the Truth of Christianity*. Eugene: Harvest House Publishers, 2008. Print.

Hippolytus. *On the End of the World: From Ante-Nicene Fathers*. Trans. J.H. MacMahon. Vol. 5. Ed. Alexander Roberts, James Donaldson, and A. Cleveland Coxe. Buffalo: Christian Literature, 1886.

Hislop, Alexander. *The Two Babylons*. New York: Cosimo, 2007. Print.

Hoekema, Anthony A. *The Bible and the Future*. Grand Rapids: Wm B. Eerdmans, 1999. Print.

Hogeterp, Albert L. *Expectations of the End*. Leiden: Brill, 2009. Print.

Holbein, D. J. Danse Macabre. III. The Expulsion {{de}}Holbein d. J.: Totentanz. III. Die Vertreibung Taken from [http://www.anagkh.net/galerie/thumbnails.php?album=77 Die imposante Galerie], originally uploaded by [http://www.anagkh.net/galerie/pr

Holck, Frederick H. "The Vedic Period." *Death and Eastern Thought: Understanding Death in Eastern Religions and Philosophies*. Ed. Frederick H. Holck. New York: Abingdon, 1974. 25–52.

Holland, Glenn S. *Gods in the Desert: Religions of the Ancient Near East*. Lanham: Rowman & Littlefield, 2009. Print.

The Holy Qur'an. Translation. Sahih International Version: online at http://quran.com/

Homer. *Homeric Hymn to Demeter*. Trans. Gregory Nagy. uh.edu. Web. 12 Jan. 2015.

_____. *Homeric Hymns*. Ed. Sarah Ruden. Cambridge: Hackett, 2005. Print.

_____. *The Homeric Hymns*. Trans. John Edgar. Edinburgh: James Thin, 1891. *Google Book Search*. Web. 11 Nov. 2015.

_____. *The Iliad*. Trans. Samuel Butler. *Internet Classics Archive*. Internet Classics Archive, 2011. Web. 30 Dec. 2011.

_____. *The Odyssey*. Trans. W. H. D. Rouse. New York: NAL, 1937.

_____. *The Odyssey with an English Translation*. Trans A.T. Murray. Cambridge: Harvard UP and London: William Heinemann, 1919.

Hood, Jared C. "The Decalogue and the Egyptian Book of the Dead." *Australian Journal of Jewish Studies* (2009): 53–72. *Academic Search Complete*. Web. 13 Sept. 2015.

Hoogenboom, Lynn. *Juan Ponce de Leon: A Primary Source Biography*. New York: Rosen Pub. Group, 2006. Print.

Hooper, Finley. *Greek Realities*. Detroit: Wayne State UP, 1978. Print.

Hopkins, E.W. "Note on the Development of the Character of Yama." *Journal of the American Oriental Society*.15 (1893): xcv: New Haven: For the American Oriental Society, 1893. *Google Book Search*. Web. 2 Jan. 2015.

Hornung, Erik. *The Ancient Egyptian Books of the Afterlife* (in German). Trans. David Lorton. Ithaca: Cornell UP, 1999. Print.

_____. "Black Holes Viewed from Within: Hell in Ancient Egyptian Thought." *Diogenes* 42.165 (1994): 133. *Academic Search Complete*. Web. 13 Sept. 2015.

Horowitz, Wayne. *Mesopotamian Cosmic Geography.* Warsaw: Eisenbrauns, 1998. Print.

Horton, Robert F. *The Teaching of Jesus: In Eighteen Sections.* New York: Dodd Mead, 1896. *Google Book Search.* Web. 4 July 2014.

Hughes, Bettany. "Helen the Whore and the Curse of Beauty." *History Today* 55.11 (2005): 37–39. *Academic Search Complete.* Web. 26 Sept. 2015.

Hughes, Thomas P. *A Dictionary of Islam: Being a Cyclopædia of the Doctrines, Rites, Ceremonies and Customs, Together with the Technical and Theological Terms, of the Muhammadan Religion.* London: W.H. Allen, 1885. *Google Book Search.* Web. 12 Aug. 2015.

Impelluso, Lucia. *Gods and Heroes in Art.* 1st ed. J. Paul Getty Museum, 2003. Print.

Inman, Thomas. *Ancient Pagan and Modern Christian Symbolism.* Cincinnati: Standard Publications, 2005. Print.

Iqbal, Mohammad. *The Reconstruction of Religious Thought in Islam.* Stanford UP, 2012. Print.

Islam, F., and R. Campbell. "'Satan Has Afflicted Me!' Jinn-Possession and Mental Illness in the Qur'an." *Journal of Religion & Health* 53.1 (2014): 229–243. *Academic Search Complete.* Web. 7 Sept. 2015.

I'Tiqad-Nama. *Belief and Islam.* Trans. Mawlana Diya Ad-din and Khaldid al-Bagdadi. Istanbul: Waqf Ikhlas Publications, 2001. *Google Book Search.* Web. 1 Sept. 2015.

Jacobsen, Knut A. "Three Functions of Hell in the Hindu Traditions." *Numen: International Review for the History of Religions* 56.2/3 (2009): 385–400. *Academic Search Complete.* Web. 13 May 2015.

Jacobsen, Thorkild, *The Sumerian King List.* Chicago: U of Chicago P, 1939. Print.

_____. *The Treasures of Darkness: A History of Mesopotamian Religion.* New Haven: Yale UP, 1976. Print.

Jaeger, Werner. "The Greek Ideas of Immortality." *Harvard Theological Review* 50.3 (1959): 135–47. Print.

Jagannathan, Maithily. *South Indian Hindu Festivals and Traditions.* New Delhi: Abhinav Publications, 2005. *Google Book Search.* Web. 29 Sept. 2015.

Jain, Jasbir, *Narrative of the Village: Centre of the Periphery.* Hyderabad: Rawat Publications, 2006. Print.

James, E. O. *The Ancient Gods.* Edison: Castle Books, 1960. Print.

Janos, Damien. *Method, Structure, and Development in al-Fārābī's Cosmology.* Leiden: Koninklijke Brill, 2012. *Google Book Search.* Web. 25 Aug. 2015.

Jeffrey, David L. *A Dictionary of Biblical Tradition in English Literature.* Grand Rapids: Wm B. Eerdmans, 1992. Print.

Johnston, Philip S. *Shades of Sheol: Death and Afterlife in the Old Testament.* Nottingham: IVP Academic, 2004. Print.

Joines, Karen R. *Serpent Symbolism in the Old Testament.* Haddonfield: Haddonfield House, 1974. Print.

Jones, A.T. "Ancient Sun Worship and Its Impact on Christianity." *The Two Republics.* Review and Herald, 1891. 81–90. Print.

Jones, John P. *The Teaching of Jesus Our Lord.* London: Christian Literature Society, 1908. *Google Book Search.* Web. 14 July 2015.

Jordan, Michael. *Dictionary of Gods and Goddesses.* 2nd ed. New York: Facts on File, 2004. Print.

Josi, Lakshmanasastri. *Critique of Hinduism and Other Religions.* New Delhi: Popular Prakashan, 1996. Print.

Jospe, Eva. "Moses Mendelssohn: Some Reflections on His Thought." *Judaism* 30.2 (1981): 169. *Academic Search Complete.* Web. 4 Oct. 2015.

Jung, Carl G. *Collected Works of C.G. Jung, Volume 13: Alchemical Studies.* Trans. Gerhard Adler. New York: Princeton UP, 1967. Print.

_____. *Memories, Dreams, Reflections.* New York: Fontana (HarperCollins), 1995. Print.

_____. "On Life After Death." *The Nautlis Project.* Elibraryellingtons.org, n.d. Web. 17 Oct. 2015.

Justin Martyr. "Dialogue with Trypho." *The Fathers of the Church.* Trans. Thomas B. Falls. Catholic U of America P, 1948. *Google Book Search.* Web. 15 July 2015.

_____. *The First and Second Apologies.* Mahwah: Paulist, 1997. Print.

Kabbani, Muhammad H. *The Approach of Armageddon: An Islamic Perspective.* Fenton: Islamic Supreme Council of America, 2003. Print.

Kak, Aadil Ami. *The Attitude of Islam Towards Science and Philosophy.* New Delhi: Sarup & Sons, 2003. *Google Book Search.* Web. 20 Aug. 2015.

Kaltner, John. *Introducing the Qur'an: For Today's Reader.* Minneapolis: Fortress Press, 2011. Print.

Kaplan, Zvi Jonathan. "Mendelssohn's Religious Perspective of Non-Jews." *Journal of Ecumenical Studies* 41.3/4 (2004): 355–366. *Academic Search Complete.* Web. 4 Oct. 2015.

Kapur, Kamlesh. *Hindu Dharma-A Teaching Guide.* Amazon Digital Services, 2013. *Google Book Search.* 28 May 2015.

Karamanolis, George E. *The Philosophy of Early Christianity.* New York: Routledge, 2013. Print.

Karasmanis, Vassilis. "Soul And Body In Plato." *International Congress Series* 1286. (2006): 1–6. *Academic Search Complete.* Web. 7 Oct. 2015.

Karkkainen, Veli-Matti. *Trinity and Revelation: A Constructive Christian Theology for the Pluralistic World, volume 2.* Grand Rapids: Wm B. Eerdmans, 2014. Print.

Kassis, Hanna. "Islam." *Life after Death in World Religions.* Ed. Harold Coward. Maryknoll: Orbis Books, 1997 Print.

Katz, Bruce F. *Neuroengineering the Future: Virtual Minds and the Creation of Immortality.* Hingham: Infinity Science, 2008. Print.

Kaufman, Whitley R. P. "Karma, Rebirth, and the Problem of Evil." *Philosophy East & West* 55.1 (2005): 15–32. *Academic Search Complete.* Web. 29 Sept. 2015.

Kee, Howard C. "Defining the First-Century C.E. Synagogue." *Evolution of the Synagogue: Problems and Progress.* Ed. Howard C. Kee and Lynn H. Cohick. Harrisburg: Trinity Press International, 1999. Print.

Khalil, Mohammad H. *Islam and the Fate of Others: The Salvation Question.* Oxford UP, 2012. Print.

Kierkegaard, Soren. *Kierkegaard's Journals and Notebooks: Journals AA–DD. Vol. 1.* Princeton: Princeton UP, 2007. Print.

Kishore, B. R. *Hinduism.* New Delhi: Diamond Pocket Books, 2006. Print.

Knitter, Paul F. "Islam and Christianity Sibling Rivalries And Sibling Possibilities." *Cross Currents* 59.4 (2009): 554–570. *Academic Search Complete.* Web. 5 Sept. 2015.

Koester, Helmut. *History, Culture, and Religion of the Hellenistic Age.* 2nd ed. Berlin: Walter de Gruyer, 1995. Print.

Kohen, Ari. *Untangling Heroism: Classical Philosophy and the Concept of the Hero.* New York: Routledge, 2014. Print.

Kohler, Kaufmann. "Essenes." Jewishencyclopedia.com, 2011. Web. 3 Oct. 2015.

_____. "Immortality of the Soul." Jewishencyclopedia.com, n.d. Web. 20 July 2015.

Knoche, Grace F. *The Mystery Schools.* Pasadena: Theosophical, 1999. Print.

Kohen, Ari. *Untangling Heroism: Classical Philosophy and the Concept of the Hero.* New York: Routledge, 2014. Print.

Kraemer, Joel L. *Maimonides: The Life and World of One of Civilization's Greatest Minds.* New York: Doubleday, 2008. Print.

Kramer, Kenneth. *The Sacred Art of Dying: How World Religions Understand Death.* New York: Paulist Press, 1988.

Kramer, Samuel. N. *History Begins at Sumer.* London: Thames & Hudson, 1958. Print.

_____. *Sumerian Mythology.* Rev. ed. New York: Harper Torchbooks, 1961. Print.

_____. *The Sumerians: Their History, Culture, and Character.* Chicago: U of Chicago P, 1963. Print.

Kristensen, W. Brede. *The Meaning of Religion: Lectures in the Phenomenology of Religion.* Houton: Springer Science and Business Media, 1960. Google Search. Web. 23 Sept. 2015.

Krupp, E. C. "Buttermilk Sky." *Sky & Telescope* 110.6 (2005): 46–47. *Academic Search Complete.* Web. 13 May 2015.

Kuo, Michael and Andy Methven. *100 Cool Mushrooms.* Ann Arbor: U of Michigan P, 2010. Print.

Kyle, Richard G. *Apocalyptic Fever: End-Time Prophecies in Modern America.* Eugene: Cascade Books, 2012. Print.

Land, Nick. *The Thirst for Annihilation: Georges Bataille and Virulent Nihilism.* New York: Routledge, 1992. Print.

Lang, Bernhard. *Hebrew Life and Literature: Selected Essays of Bernhard Lang.* Burlington: Ashgate, 2008. Print.

Langdon, Stephen. "The Chaldean Kings Before the Flood." *Journal of the Royal Asiatic Society* 55. 2 (1923): 251–259. Print.

Laursen, Steffen T. "Early Dilmun and Its Rulers: New Evidence of the Burial Mounds of the Elite and the Development of Social Complexity, c. 2200–1750 B.C." *Arabian Archaeology & Epigraph.* 19. 2 (2008): 156–167. Print.

Lawler, Andrew. "The Everlasting City." *Archaeology* 66. 5 (2013): 26–32. Print.

Leaman, Oliver. *The Qur'an: An Encyclopedia.* New York: Routledge, 2006. Print.

Leeming, David. *Jealous Gods and Chosen People: The Mythology of the Middle East.* New York: Oxford UP, 2004. Print.

Leeming, David, and Jake Page. *Goddesses: Myths of the Female Divine.* New York: Oxford UP, 1994. Print.

Leeming, David A., Kathryn Madden, Stanton Marlan, eds. *Encyclopedia of Psychology and Religion.* New York: Springer, 2010. Print.

Lehtipuu, Outi. *Debates Over the Resurrection of the Dead: Constructing Early Christian Identity.* New York: Oxford UP, 2015.

Leunissen, Mariska. *Explanation and Teleology in Aristotle's Science of Nature.* Cambridge: Cambridge UP, 2010. Print.

Lewis, Eric. "The Stoics on Identity and Individuation." *Phronesis* 40.1 (1995): 89–108. *Academic Search Complete.* Web. 4 Aug. 2015.

"Liberal French Protestantism." *The Westminster Review, Issues 161–162.* 26. 161, 162 (1864): 73. London: Trubner, 1864. *Google Book Search.* Web. 15 July 2015.

Life After Death in World Religions. Ed. Harold Coward. Maryknoll: Orbis Books, 1997. Print.

Lioy, Dan. "Paul's Apocalyptic Interpretation of Reality: A Case Study Analysis of Ephesians 1:15–23." *Conspectus (South African Theological Seminary)* 19 (2015): 27–64. *Academic Search Complete.* Web. 9 Aug. 2015.

Littleton, C. Scott. *God, Goddesses, and Mythology.* New York: Michael Cavendish, 2005. Print.

Litwa, M. David. *We Are Being Transformed: Deification in Paul's Soteriology.* Berlin: Walter de Gruyter, 2012. Print.

Livne-Kafri, Ofer. "Jerusalem in Early Islam: The Eschatological Aspect." *Arabica* 53.3 (2006): 382–403. *Academic Search Complete.* Web. 8 Sept. 2015.

Logan, A.H.B. *Gnostic Truth and Christian Heresy: A Study in the History of Gnosticism.* Edinburgh: T&T Clark, 1996. Print.

López-Ruiz, Carolina. "Greek and Canaanite Mythologies: Zeus, Baal, and Their Rivals." *Religion Compass* 8.1 (2014): 1–10. *Academic Search Complete.* Web. 19 Sept. 2015.

Lorenz, Hendrik. "Ancient Theories of Soul." *The Stanford Encyclopedia of Philosophy.* Ed.

Edward N. Zalta, Center for the Study of Language and Information. Stanford UP, 2009.

Lorey, Frank. "The Flood of Noah and the Flood of Gilgamesh." *Acts & Facts* 26 (1997): 1–3. n.d. Web. 17 May 2014.

Mafouz, Naguib. *Voices from the Other World: Ancient Egyptian Tales.* Raymond Stock, trans. Magnus, Bernd. "Nietzsche and the Project of Bringing Philosophy to an End." *Nietzsche as Affirmative Thinker.* Ed. Yirmiyahu Yovel. Dordrecht: Martinus Nijhoff, 1986. *Google Book Search.* Web. 18 Oct. 2015.

Maimonides. "Introduction to Chapter Ten of Mishna Sanhedrin." *Maimonides' Introduction to Perek Helek.* mhcny.org, n.d. Web. 4 Oct. 2015.

Maitra, Romain. "From Selfhood to Salvation." *UNESCO Courier* 50.4 (1997): 28. *Academic Search Complete.* Web. 29 Sept. 2015.Cairo: American U of Cairo P, 2002. Print.

Majithi, Roopen. "Saṇkara on Action and Liberation." *Asian Philosophy.* 17.3 (2007): 231–249. Print.

Malcolm, Matthew R. *Paul and the Rhetoric of Reversal in 1 Corinthians: The Impact of Paul's Gospel on His Macro-Rhetoric.* Cambridge: Cambridge UP, 2013. Print.

March, Jennifer R. *Dictionary of Classical Mythology.* Oxford: Oxbow Books, 2014. Print.

Martin, Harriet P. *FARA: A Reconstruction of the Ancient Mesopotamian City of Shuruppak.* Birmingham: Chris Martin & Assoc., 1988. Print.

Mason, Steve. *Flavius Josephus: Translation and Commentary, vol. 1b: Judean War.* Leiden: Brill, 2008. Print.

Massey, Gerald. *Ancient Egypt: The Light of the World.*" Vol. 2. London: T. Fisher Unwin, 1907. Print.

_____. *Egyptian Book of the Dead and the Mysteries of Amenta.* New York: Cosimo Classics, 2008. Print.

Ma'súmián, Farnáz. *Life After Death: A Study of the Afterlife in World Religions.* Los Angeles: Kalimat, 2002. Print.

Matt, Daniel Chanan. *Zohar, the Book of Enlightenment.* Mahwah: Paulist Press, 1983. Print.

Matthews, Caitlin, and John Matthews. *Walkers Between the World: The Western Mysteries from Shaman to Magus.* Rochester: Inner Traditions International, 2004. Print.

May, Herbert G., and Metzger, Bruce M (eds.). *The Oxford Annotated Bible with the Apocrypha* (Revised Standard Version). New York: Oxford UP, 1965.

McCall, Henrietta. *Mesopotamian Myths.* Austin: U of Texas P, 1990. Print.

McGinn, Bernard. "Introduction: John's Apocalypse and the Apocalyptic Mentality." *The Apocalypse in the Middle Ages.* Eds. Richard K. Emmerson and Bernard McGinn. Ithaca: Cornell UP, 1993. Print.

Medea: Essays on Medea in Myth, Literature, Philosophy, and Art. Eds. James Joseph Clauss and Sarah Iles Johnston. Princeton: Princeton UP, 1997.

Mehar, Iftikhar Ahmed. *Al-Islam.* 4th ed. North Charleston: BookSurge, 2007. Print.

Mendelssohn, Moses. *Phoedon: Or, the Death of Socrates.* 1789. Bristol: Thoemmes Continuum, 2004. *Google Book Search.* Web. 24 Aug. 2015.

Mendenhall, George E. "From Witchcraft to Justice: Death and Afterlife in the Old Testament." *Death and Afterlife: Perspectives of World Religions.* Ed. Hiroshi Obayashi. Westport: Greenwood Press, 1992. Print.

Meyers, Jody. "Marriage and Sexual Behavior in the Teachings of the Kabbalah Center." *Kabbalah and Modernity: Interpretations, Transformations, Adaptations.* Eds. o az Hus, Marco Pasi, Kocku Von Stuckrad. Leiden: Brill, 2010. Print.

Michaels, Axel. *Hinduism: Past and Present.* Princeton: Princeton UP, 2004. Print.

Mile, Geoffrey. *Classical Mythology in English Literature.* London: Routledge, 1999. Print.

Millen, Rochelle L. *Women, Birth, and Death in Jewish Law and Practice.* Lebanon: Brandeis UP, 2004. Print.

Miller, Barbara. *The Bhagavad-Gita.* New York: Bantam, 2004. Print.

Mills, Nancy. "Something Old, Something New." *Chemistry in Australia* 77.10 (2010): 20–27. *Academic Search Complete.* Web. 13 Sept. 2015.

Miselbrook, Jeremy. *A Portrait of Christ the Hero in the Epistle to the Hebrews.* Dissertation. Paper 422. Chicago: Loyola UP, 2012.

Mishnah Pirkei Avot. Trans. Tsel Harim. Free Torah Library. Shechem.org. Web. 27 July 2015.

Mitchell, Stephen. *Gilgamesh.* Prince Frederick: RB Large Print, 2004. Print.

Moghul, Haroon. "Allah." *Tikkun* 29.3 (2014): 40–42. *Academic Search Complete.* Web. 5 Sept. 2015.

Mohammed, Ovey N. *Averroës' Doctrine of Immortality: A Matter of Controversy.* Waterloo, Ontario: Wilfrid Laurier UP, 1985. Print.

"Moksha, Freedom from Rebirth." *Hinduism Today* 32.1 (2010): 15. *Academic Search Complete.* Web. 29 Sept. 2015.

Moon, Beverly. "Aphrodite, Ancestor of Kings." *Goddesses Who Rule.* New York: Oxford UP, 2000. Print.

Moore, Clifford H. *Ancient Beliefs in the Immortality of the Soul: Our Debt to Greece and Rome.* New York: Cooper Square, 1963. Print.

Moore, George F. *History of Religions: China, Japan, Egypt, Babylonia, Assyria, India, Persia.* New York: Scribner, 1922. Print.

Morenz, Sigfried. trans. Ann E Keep. *Egyptian Religion.* Ithaca: Cornell UP, 1973. Print.

Morford, Mark P. O. *Classical Mythology.* New York: Oxford UP, 1999. Print.

Morris, Ian. *Archaeology as Cultural History.* New York: Wiley, 2008. Print.

Morse, Donald R. "Mithraism and Christianity: How Are They Related?" *Journal of Religion & Psychical Research* 22.1 (1999): 33. *Academic Search Complete.* Web. 7 Oct. 2015.

Mungovan, Timothy R. *The Book of Revelation: A Clear and Precise Understanding.* Bloomington: Trafford Publishing, 2011. *Google Book Search.* Web. 16 July 2015.

Murdock, D.M. *Christ in Egypt: The Horus-Jesus Connection.* Seattle: Stellar House, 2009. Print.

_____, and S. Acharya, "Jesus as the Sun throughout History: Father Tertullian & St. Augustine." Stellarhousepublishing.com, n.d. Web. 11 Oct. 2015.

Murphy, Nancey. "Immortality Versus Resurrection in the Christian Tradition." *Annals of the New York Academy of Sciences* 1234.1 (2011): 76–82. *Academic Search Complete.* Web. 30 July 2015.

Murray, Margaret Alice. "Burial Customs and Beliefs in the Hereafter in Predynastic Egypt." *Journal of Egyptian Archaeology.* 42 (1956): 86–96). Print.

Nadler, Steven. *Spinoza's Heresy: Immortality and the Jewish Mind.* Oxford: Oxford UP, 2001. Print.

Nagy, Gregory. *Greek Mythology and Poetics.* Ithaca: Cornell UP, 1990. Print.

Najovits, Simson. *Egypt, The Trunk of the Tree, Volume II: A Modern Survey of an Ancient Land.* New York: Algora, 2004. Print.

Naseem, Hamid. *Muslim Philosophy: Science and Mysticism.* New Delhi: Sarup & Sons, 2001. *Google Book Search.* Web. 20 Aug. 2015.

Neill, James. *The Origins and Role of Same-Sex Relations in Human Societies.* Jefferson: McFarland, 2009. Print.

Neumann, Eric. *Amor and Psyche: The Psychic Development of the Feminine.* London: Routledge, 1999. Print.

Neusner, Jacob. *Early Rabbinic Judaism: Historical Studies in Religion, Literature and Art.* Leiden: Brill, 1975. Print.

Nigosian, Solomon A. *Islam: Its History, Teaching, and Practices.* Indiana UP, 2004. Print.

Nilsson, Martin P. *The Minoan-Mycenean Religion and Its Survival in Greek Religion.* Lund: C. W. K. Gleerup, 1950. Print.

Norcliffe, David. *Islam: Faith and Practice.* Portland: Sussex Academic, 1999. Print.

Nowell, Irene. *101 Questions and Answers on Angels and Devils.* Mahwah: Paulist, 2010. Print.

Obayashi, Hiroshi. *Death and Afterlife: Perspectives of World Religions.* Westport: Greenwood Press, 1992. Print.

_____. "Death and Eternal Life in Christianity." *Death and Afterlife: Perspectives of World Religions.* Ed. Hiroshi Obayashi. Westport, CT: Greenwood Press, 1992.

O'Keefe, Tim. *Epicureanism.* New York: Routledge, 2010. Print.

Olcott, William Tyler. *Sun Lore of All Ages.* New York: G.P. Putnam's Sons, 1914. Print.

Oliver, Evelyn D., James R. Lewis. *Angels A to Z.* 2nd ed. Canton: Visible Ink, 2008. Print.

Olshansky, Jay S., and Bruce A. Carnes. *The Quest for Immortality: Science at the Frontiers of Aging.* New York: W.W. Norton, 2002. Print.

Ooman, Joseph. "The Concept of Trinity and Its Implication for Christian Communication in Indian Context." *Bangalore Theological Forum.* 34.1 (2002), 75–82.

Orr, James. *The International Standard Bible Encyclopaedia, Volume 4.* Chicago: The Howard Severance Company, 1915. *Google Book Search.* Web. 30 Aug. 2015.

"Other Ancient Civilizations-The Epic of Gilgamesh." ancient literature.com, 2009. Web. 20 May 2014.

Ovid (Publius Ovidius Naso). *The Metamorphoses.* Trans. A. D. Melville. New York: Oxford UP, 1987.

_____. *The Metamorphoses.* Ed. Arthur Golding. Tufts.edu, n.d. Web. 6 Feb. 2015.

Owen, Derwyn R. G., *Body and Soul.* Santa Ana: Westminster Press, 1956. Print.

Owens, Joseph. *Aristotle: The Collected Papers of Joseph Owens.* Ed. John R. Catan. Albany: State U of New York P, 1981. *Google Book Search.* Web. 12 Nov. 2015.

Oxtoby, Willard G. and Alan F. Segal. *A Concise Introduction to World Religions.* 2nd ed., Oxford UP, 2012. Print.

Paliwal, B.B. *Message of the Upanishads.* New Delhi: Diamond Pocket Books, 2006. Print.

Pandit, Bansi. *Explore Hinduism.* Albion Press, 2005. *Google Books Search.* Web. 4 Feb. 2015.

Pankhurst, Juliet Claire. *The Golden Atlantean Book of Healing: Ancient Knowledge Healing Today's World.* AuthorHouse, 2007. ebook.

Papadopoulou, Thalia. *Heracles and Euripidean Tragedy.* Cambridge: Cambridge UP, 2005. Print.

Parker, Robert. *Polytheism and Society at Athens.* Oxford: Oxford UP, 2005. Print.

Partee, Charles. *Calvin and Classical Philosophy.* Louisville: John Knox, 1977. Print.

Pasachoff, Naomi E., and Robert J. Littman. *A Concise History of the Jewish People.* Lanham: Rowman & Littlefield, 1995. Print.

"The Path of Allah." *Canada & the World Backgrounder* 72.1 (2006): 4–8. *Academic Search Complete.* Web. 8 Sept. 2015.

Peck, Harry Thurston. *Harper's Dictionary of Classical Literature and Antiquities,* Vol. 1. New York: Harper, 1897. Print.

Pelikan, Petr. "The Only Source of the Law of Islam Is God's Will." *New Presence: The Prague Journal of Central European Affairs* 10.2 (2008): 15–18. *Academic Search Complete.* Web. 5 Sept. 2015.

Penelhum, Terence. "Christianity." Ed. Harold Coward. *Life after Death in World Religions.* Maryknoll: Orbis Books, 1997. Print.

Percy, William A. *Pederasty and Pedagogy in Archaic Greece.* U of Illinois P, 1996. Print.

Perlmutter, Dawn. "The Politics of Muslim Magic." *Middle East Quarterly* 20.2 (2013): 73–80. *Academic Search Complete.* Web. 5 Sept. 2015.

Pétavel-Olliff, Emmanuel. *The Problem of Immortality.* Trans. Frederick Ash Freer. London: Elliot Stock, 1892. *Google Book Search.* Web. 16 July 2015.

Picken, Gavin. "Tazkiyat Al-Nafs: The Qur'anic Paradigm." *Journal of Qur'anic Studies* 7.2 (2005): 101–127. *Academic Search Complete.* Web. 7 Sept. 2015.

Pinch, Geraldine. *Egyptian Mythology: A Guide to the Gods, Goddesses, and Traditions of Ancient Egypt.* London: Oxford UP, 2004. Print.

Plutarch. *Plutarch's Morals: Theosophical Essays.* Trans. Charles William King. 1908. sacredtexts.com, n.d. Web. 24 July 2015.

"*Pirkei Avot: Ethics of the Fathers Chapter 4.*" myjewishlearning.com, n.d. Web. 24 June 2015.

Plato. *The Phaedo.* Trans. E.M. Cope. Cambridge: Cambridge UP, 1875. *Google Book Search.* Web. 16 July 2015.

Ploeg, Dirk V. *Quest for Middle Earth.* Bloomington: iUniverse-Indigo, 2007. Print.

Polansky, Ronald. *Aristotle's De Anima: A Critical Commentary.* Cambridge: Cambridge UP, 2007. Print.

Poling, Travis. "Salmoneus and the Poets: Poetry in a World of Violence." *Cross Currents* 60.1 (2010): 125–130. *Academic Search Complete.* Web. 26 Sept. 2015.

Poncelet, Albert. "St. Irenaeus." *The Catholic Encyclopedia. Vol. 8.* New York: Robert Appleton, 1910. N.d. Web. 24 Jul. 2015.

Potts, Albert M. *The World's Eye.* Lexington: UP of Kentucky, 1982. Print.

Preuss, Julius. *Biblical and Talmudic Medicine.* Trans. and Ed. Fred Rosner. Lanham: Rowman & Littlefield, 1993. Print.

Raphael, Simcha P. *Jewish Views of the Afterlife.* Lanham: Rowman & Littlefield, 2004. Print.

Rawlinson, George. *History of Herodotus.* Vol. 2. London: John Murray, 1858. Ebook.

_____. *The Seven Great Monarchies of the Ancient Eastern World.* Piscataway: Gorgias Press, 2004. Print.

Reid, Patrick V. ed. *Readings in Western Religious Thought: The Ancient World.* Mahwah: Paulist, 1987. *Google Book Search.* Web. 22 Aug. 2015.

Reisner, George A. *The Egyptian Conception of Immortality.* Ed. Aaron G. Wells. The Ingersoll Lecture, 1911. New York: Houghton Mifflin, 1912 (Forgotten Books, 2012). Print.

Relief with Two Heroes. Relief 10th century BCE Neo-Hittite/Hurritic. Walters Art Museum, Baltimore.

"Religious Comparisons." *Hinduism Today* 37.1 (2015): 42–46. *Academic Search Complete.* Web. 29 Sept. 2015.

Remier, Pat. *Egyptian Mythology A to Z.* 3rd ed. New York: Chelsea House, 2010. Print.

The Resurrection. 1506. Tempera on linden wood. *Wikimedia Commons,* n.d. Web. 2 Nov. 2015.

Richards, William A. "Entheogens in the Study of Religious Experiences: Current Status." *Journal of Religion & Health* 44.4 (2005): 377–389. *Academic Search Complete.* Web. 26 Apr. 2015.

Rinehart, Robin. *Contemporary Hinduism: Ritual, Culture, and Practice.* ABC-CLIO, 2004. Ebook.

Rist, John. *Epicurus: An Introduction.* Cambridge: Cambridge UP, 2010. Print.

Roberts, Alexander, and James Donaldson. *The Ante-Nicene Fathers. Translations of the Writings of the Fathers Down to A.D. 325.* Vol. 5. New York: Scribner's, 1903. *Google Book Search.* Web. 18 July 2015.

Robertson, John M. *A Short History of Christianity.* London: Watts, 1902. *Google Book Search.* 5 Oct. 2015.

Rogers, Mark. *The Esoteric Codex: Magic Objects I.* lulu.com, 2014. *Google Book Search.* Web. 30 Aug. 2015.

Rogers, William. *Persuasion: Messages, Receivers, and Contexts.* Lanham: Rowman & Littlefield, 2007. Print.

Roman, Luke, and Monica Roman. *Encyclopedia of Greek and Roman Mythology.* New York: Facts on File, 2010. Print.

Rose, H.J. (1924). "Anchises and Aphrodite." *The Classical Quarterly* 18.1 (1924), 11–16. Print.

Rosen, Brenda. *The Mythical Creatures Bible: The Definitive Guide to Legendary Beings.* New York: Sterling, 2009. Print.

Ross, David M. *The Teachings of Jesus.* Glasgow: T. and T. Clark, 1904. *Google Book Search.* Web. 17 July 2015.

Roux, Georges. *Ancient Iraq.* 3rd ed. Harmondsworth: Penguin, 1992. Print.

Rubin, Nissan. *Time and Life Cycle in Talmud and Midrash: Socio-anthropological Perspectives.* Brighton: Academic Studios Press, 2008. Print.

Ruggles, D. Fairchild. *Islamic Gardens and Landscapes.* U of Pennsylvania P, 2008. Print.

Rush, John. *Entheogens and the Development of Culture: The Anthropology and Neurobiology of Ecstatic Experience.* Berkeley: North Atlantic Books, 2013. Print.

Rustomji, Nerina. *The Garden and the Fire: Heaven and Hell in Islamic Culture.* New York: Columbia UP, 2013. Print.

Ryan, William, and Walter Pitman. *Noah's Flood.* New York: Simon & Schuster, 1998. Print.

Saggs, Henry, W.F. *The Greatness That Was Babylon.* New York: Mentor, 1962. Print.

Saldarini, Anthony J. *Pharisees, Scribes and Sadducees in Palestinian Society: A Sociological Approach.* Cambridge: Wm B. Eerdmans, 2001. Print.

Samples, Kenneth R. *Without a Doubt: Answering the 20 Toughest Faith Questions.* Grand Rapids: Baker Books, 2004. Print.

Samuel, Gabriella. *The Kabbalah Handbook: A Concise Encyclopedia of Terms and Concepts in Jewish Mysticism.* New York: Penguin, 2007. Print.

Saraswathi, T. S. "Hindu Worldview in the Development of Selfways: The "Atman" as the Real Self." *New Directions for Child & Adolescent Development* 2005.109 (2005): 43–50. *Academic Search Complete.* Web. 29 Sept. 2015.

Sargent, Thelma. *The Homeric Hymns.* New York: Norton, 1973. Print.

Saritoprak, Zeki. "The Legend of Al-Dajjal (Antichrist): The Personification of Evil in the Islamic Tradition." *Muslim World* 93.2 (2003): 291. *Academic Search Complete.* Web. 8 Sept. 2015.

Schafer, Peter. *The History of the Jews in the Greco-Roman World.* London: Routledge, 2003. Print.

Schimmel, Annemarie *Islam: An Introduction.* Albany: State U of New York P, 1992. Print.

Schmidt, Brian B. *Israel's Beneficent Dead: Ancestor Cult and Necromancy in Ancient Israelite Religion and Tradition.* Warsaw: Eisenbrauns, 1996. Print.

Schumann-Antelme, Ruth, and Stephane Rossini. *Becoming Osiris: The Ancient Egyptian Death Experience.* Rochester: Inner Traditions, 1998. Print.

Schwartz, Howard. *Tree of Souls: The Mythology of Judaism.* New York: Oxford UP, 2004. Print.

Scodel, Ruth. *An Introduction to Greek Tragedy.* Cambridge: Cambridge UP, 2010. Print.

Segal, Alan F. *Life After Death: A History of the Afterlife in Western Religion.* New York: Doubleday, 2004. Print.

Segal, Charles. *Tragedy and Civilization: An Interpretation of Sophocles.* U of Oklahoma P, 1999. Print.

Segal, Eliezer. "Judaism." in Coward, Harold (ed.). *Life After Death in World Religions.* Maryknoll: Orbis Books, 1997.

Selin, Helaine. *Encyclopedia of the History of Science, Technology, and Medicine in Non-Western Cultures.* Dordrecht: Kluwer Academic, 1997. Print.

Serrano Delgado, Jose M. "Rhampsinitus, Setne Khamwas and the Descent to the Netherworld: Some Remarks on Herodotus II, 122, 1." *Journal of Ancient Near Eastern Religions* 11.1 (2011): 94–108. *Academic Search Complete.* Web. 14 Sept. 2015.

Setzer, Claudia. "Resurrection of the Dead as Symbol and Strategy." *Journal of the American Academy of Religion* 69.1 (2001): 65. *Academic Search Complete.* Web. 25 June 2015.

"17th Century Theories of Substance." Ed. James Fieser and Bradley Dowden. *Internet Encyclopedia of Philosophy: A Peer-Reviewed Academic Resource.* n.d. Web. 12 May 2015.

Shabti Figure. Harrogate Museums and Arts, Mercer Art Gallery, Harrogate Borough Council.

Shah, Zulfiqar Ali. *Anthropomorphic Depictions of God: The Concept of God in Judaic, Christian and Islamic Traditions: Representing the Unrepresentable.* 1st ed. London: International Institute of Islamic Thought (IIIT), 2012. Print.

Shahi, Brij Lal. "Piercing the Veil of Maya The Creator of All-Pervasive Illusion." *Journal of Religion & Psychical Research* 29.1 (2006): 16–18. *Academic Search Complete.* Web. 13 May 2015.

Sharma, Arvind. *The Philosophy of Religion and Advaita Vedanta: A Comparative Study in Religion and Reason.* University Park: Pennsylvania State UP, 1995. Print.

Shavit, Yaacov. *History in Black: African-Americans in Search of an Ancient Past.* New York: Routledge, 2013. Print.

Sheler, J.L. "Other Faiths, Other Hells. (Cover Story)." *U.S. News & World Report* 110.11 (1991): 64. *Academic Search Complete.* Web. 13 May 2015.

Silverman, Allan. "Plato: Psychology." *The Blackwell Guide to Ancient Philosophy.* Ed. Christopher Shields. Oxford: Blackwell, 2006. Print.

Singer, Isidore, and Cyrus Adler. *The Jewish Encyclopedia: A Descriptive Record of the History, Religion, Literature, and Customs of the Jewish People from the Earliest Times to the Present Day: Volume 5.* New York: Funk & Wagnalls, 1912. Print.

Skirry, Justin. *Descartes and the Metaphysics of Human Nature.* London: Continuum, 2005. Print.

Slater, Thomas. *The Higher Hinduism in Relation to Christianity.* London: Elliot Stock, 1902. *Google Book Search.* Web. 26 Sept. 2015.

Smith, Huston. *World Religions: A Guide to Our Wisdom Traditions.* New York: Harper-Collins, 1994. Print.

Smith, Jane I., and Yvonne Y. Haddad. *The Islamic Understanding of Death and Resurrection.* Oxford UP, 2002. Print.

Smith, William. *Dictionary of the Bible.* Vol. IV. Ed. H.B. Hackett. New York: Hurd & Houghton, 1872. *Google Book Search.* Web. 18 July 2015.

Sneader, Walter. *Drug Discovery: A History.* Chichester: John Wiley & Sons, 2005. Print.

Snell, Bruno. *The Discovery of the Mind in Greek Philosophy and Literature.* Trans. T.G. Rosenmeyer. Cambridge: Harvard UP, 1953. Print.

"Soma, the Rishis' Potion." *Hinduism Today* 34.3 (2012): 14. *Academic Search Complete.* Web. 13 May 2015.

Sonsino, Rifat, and Daniel B. Syme. *What Happens After I Die? Jewish Views of Life After Death.* New York: UAHC Press, 1990. Print.

Spitz, Elie K. *Does the Soul Survive? A Jewish Journey to Belief in Afterlife, Past Lives & Living with a Purpose.* 2nd edition. Woodstock: Jewish Lights, 2015. Print.

Spivey, Nigel. *How Art Made the World: A Journey to the Origins of Human Creativity.* Cambridge: Basic Books, 2005. Print.

Spring, Charles. *On the Essence and Immortality of the Soul: An Inaugural Dissertation (1865).* Whitefish: Kessinger, 2010. Print.

Staal, Frits. "How a Psychoactive Substance Becomes a Ritual: The Case of Soma." *Social Research* 68.3 (2001): 745–778. *Academic Search Complete.* Web. 26 Apr. 2015.

Stehle, Eva. "Sappho's Gaze: Fantasies of a Goddess and Young Man." *Reading Sappho: Contemporary Approaches.* Greene, Ellen, ed. Berkeley: U of California P, 1996. Print.

Steinkraus, Warren E., and Michael H. Mitias. "Claims About the Future: Immortality." *Taking Religious Claims Seriously* (1998): 185–188. *Academic Search Complete.* Web. 13 May 2015.

Stewart, Harry M. *Egyptian Shabtis.* Buckinghamshire: Shire Publications, 1995. Print.

Stone, Tom. *Zeus: A Journey Through Greece in the Footsteps of a God.* New York: Bloomsbury, 2008. Print.

Strauss, Leo, and Martin D. Yaffe. "Strauss on Mendelssohn: An Interpretive Essay." *Leo Strauss on Moses Mendelssohn*. Chicago: U of Chicago P, 2012. Print.

Streeter, B.H., C.W. Emmet and J.A. Hadfield. *Immortality: As Essay in Discovery*. New York: Macmillan, 1917. Print.

Strong, Gordon. *The Way of Magic*. London: Skylight Press, 2012, Print.

Swanson, Mark N. "Resurrection Debates: Qur'Anic Discourse and Arabic Christian Apology." *Dialog: A Journal of Theology* 48.3 (2009): 248–256. *Academic Search Complete*. Web. 8 Sept. 2015.

Taylor, John H. *Death and the Afterlife in Ancient Egypt*. Chicago: U of Chicago P, 2001. Print.

Teeter, Donald E. "Amanita Muscaria; Herb of Immortality." The Ambrosia Society, 2007.

Teeter, Emily. *Religion and Ritual in Ancient Egypt*. New York: Cambridge UP, 2011. Print.

Terry, Michael. *Reader's Guide to Judaism*. New York: Routledge, 2000. Print.

Thapar, Romila. "Sacrifice, Surplus, and the Soul." *History of Religions* 33.4 (1994) 305–324.

Thiselton, Anthony C. *The Thiselton Companion to Christian Theology*. Grand Rapids: Wm B. Eerdmans, 2015. Print.

Thomas, Susanna. *Ahmose: Liberator of Egypt*. New York: Rosen Publishing Group, 2003. Print.

Thompson, William I. "The Evolution of the Afterlife." *Journal of Consciousness Studies*. 9.8 (2002): 61–71. Print.

Tigay, Jeffrey H. *The Evolution of the Gilgamesh Epic*. Philadelphia: U of Pennsylvania P, 1982. Print.

Tomasino, Anthony J. *Judaism Before Jesus: The Events and Ideas That Shaped the New Testament World*. Leicester: InterVarsity Press, 2003. Print.

Tonelli, Robert D. *Science of Spirit: Lost Keys to the Kingdom ... on Earth*. Xlibris, 2011. ebook.

Trobe, Kala. *Invoke the Gods: Exploring the Power of Male Archetypes*. Woodbury: Llewellyn, 2001. Print.

Tyagananda, Swami. "The Heart Beyond Hearts." *Religion & the Arts*. 12.1–3 (2008) 186–189. Print.

Uttal, William R. *Dualism: The Original Sin of Cognitivism*. New York: Routledge, 1899. Print.

Vance, Donald R. "Heaven and Hell, Angels and Demons: The Other Side in the Second Temple Period." *Heaven, Hell, and the Afterlife: Eternity in Judaism, Christianity, and Islam*. Ed. J. Harold Ellens. Santa Barbara: Praeger, 2013. Print.

Virgil. *The Aeniad*. Trans. John Conington. New York: Macmillan, 1917. Google Book Search. Web. 11 Sept. 2015.

Vernant, Jean-Pierre. *Mortals and Immortals: Collected Essays*. Princeton: Princeton UP, 1991.

Viviano, Benedict. *Study as Worship: Aboth and the New Testament*. Leiden: Brill Academic, 1978. Print.

Walker, Williston. *A History of the Christian Church*. New York: Scribner's, 1918. Print.

Wall, Terance. *The Symmetry of Gnosis: The Universe Explained?* Bloomington: Trafford, 2014. Print.

Walton, John H. *Ancient Near Eastern Thought and the Old Testament*. Grand Rapids: Baker Academic, 2006. Print.

Ward, J.S.M. *Freemasonry and the Ancient Gods*. Whitefish: Kessinger, 1919. Print.

Warren, James. "Removing Fear." *The Cambridge Companion to Epicureanism*. Ed. James Warren. Cambridge: Cambridge UP, 2009. Print.

Wasilewska, Ewa. *Creation Stories of the Middle East*. London: Jessica Kingsley Publishers, 2000. Print.

Wasson, Gordon, and Stella Kramrisch, Jonathan Ott, Carl A. P. Ruck. *Persephone's Quest: Entheogens and the Origins of Religion.* New Haven: Yale UP, 1992. Print.

Webster, Richard. *Encyclopedia of Angels.* Woodbury: Llewellyn, 2009. Print.

Wegner, Mary-Ann P. "Gateway to the Netherworld." *Archaeology* 66.1 (2013): 50–53. *Academic Search Complete.* Web. 5 Oct. 2015.

West, William. *A Resurrection to Immortality: The Resurrection, Our Only Hope of Life After Death.* Bloomington: WestBow Press, 2011. Print.

Wherry, E.M. *A Comprehensive Commentary on the Quran.* Vol. 1. London: Routledge, 2001. Print.

White, David A. *Myth and Metaphysics in Plato's Phaedo.* London: Associated University Presses, 1989. Print.

_____. *Rhetoric and Reality in Plato's "Phaedrus."* Albany: State U of New York P, 1993. Print.

White, Dominic. *The Lost Knowledge of Christ: Contemporary Spiritualities, Christian Cosmologies, and the Arts.* Collegeville: Michael Glazier, the Liturgical Press, 2015. Print.

White, Edward. *Life in Christ. Four Discourses upon the Scripture Doctrine That Immortality Is the Peculiar Privilege of the Regenerate.* London: Jackson & Walford, 1846. *Google Book Search.* Web. 19 July 2015.

Wilde, Lyn Webster. *On the Trail of Women Warriors.* New York: St. Martin's Press, 2000. Print.

Wilde, Richard E. *The Immortal Self.* 2nd ed. Tucson: Wheatmark, 2010. Print.

Wilkins, W.J. *Hindu Mythology: Vedic and Puranic.* London: W. Thacker, 1900.

Wilkinson, John G. *A Second Series of the Manners and Customs of the Ancient Egyptians.* Vol. London: John Murray, 1841. *Google Book Search.* Web. 22 Oct. 2015.

Wilkinson, Richard H. *The Complete Gods and Goddesses of Ancient Egypt.* London: Thames & Hudson, 2003. Print.

_____. *Reading Egyptian Art, A Hieroglyphic Guide to Ancient Painting and Sculpture.* London: Thames & Hudson, 1992. Print.

Willems, Harco. *Historical and Archaeological Aspects of Egyptian Funerary Culture.* Leiden: Brill, 2014. *Google Book Search.* Web. 19 Sept. 2014.

Williams, George M. *Handbook of Hindu Mythology.* Oxford: Oxford UP, 2003. Print.

Willis, Roy G. *World Mythology.* New York: Henry Holt, 1993. Print.

Wilson, H.H. trans. *A Collection of Ancient Hindu Hymns: The First Ashtaka, or Book of the Rig Veda.* London: N. Trubner, 1866. *Google Book Search.* Web. 22 July 2015.

Wilson, John A. *The Culture of Ancient Egypt.* Chicago: U of Chicago P, 1951. Print.

Witt, Charlotte. "Dialectic, Motion, and Perception: *De Anima* Book I." *Essays on Aristotle's De Anima.* Eds. Martha C. Nussbaum and Amélie O. Rorty. Oxford: Oxford UP, 2003. Print.

Woods, J. Craig. *How the Churches Got It Wrong: Christianity Revealed.* Bloomington: iUniverse, 2012. Print.

Wright, Edward J. *The Early History of Heaven.* New York: Oxford UP, 1999. Print.

Wun, Chok Bong. *The Gods' Machines: From Stonehenge to Crop Circles.* Berkeley: Frog Books, 2008. Print.

Zabkar, Louis V. *Study of the Ba Concept in Ancient Egyptian Texts.* SAOC 34. Oriental Institute of the University of Chicago, U of Chicago P, 1968. Print.

Index

Numbers in **bold italics** refer to pages with photographs

203